THE **WHARNCLIFFE COMPANION** TO

PRESTON

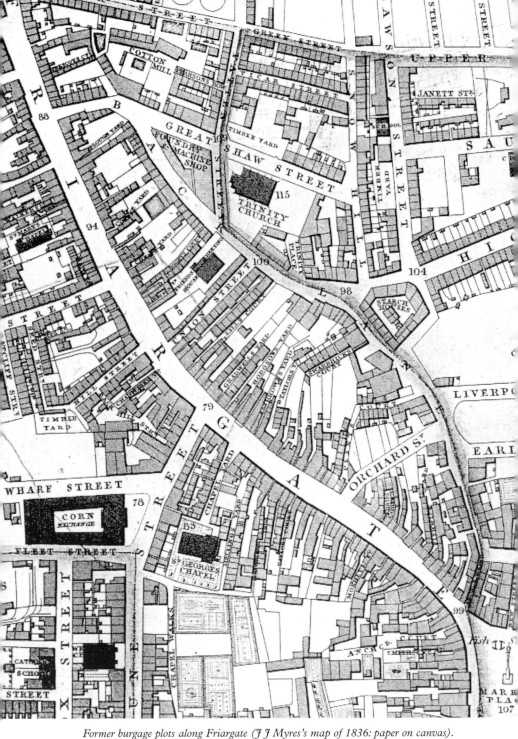

Former burgage plots along Friargate (J J Myres's map of 1836: paper on canvas).

THE **WHARNCLIFFE COMPANION** TO

PRESTON

AN **A** TO **Z** OF LOCAL HISTORY

DAVID HUNT

Wharncliffe Books

For Terry

First published in Great Britain in 2005 by
Wharncliffe Books
an imprint of
Pen & Sword Books Ltd
47 Church Street
Barnsley
South Yorkshire
S70 2AS

ISBN 1-903425-79-4

A CIP catalogue record for this book is
available from the British Library

Typeset in 10/11.5pt Plantin by Wharncliffe Books
Printed and bound in England by CPI UK

Pen & Sword Books Ltd incorporates the Imprints of Pen & Sword Aviation,
Pen & Sword Maritime, Pen & Sword Military, Wharncliffe Local History,
Pen & Sword Select, Pen and Sword Military Classics and Leo Cooper.

For a complete list of Wharncliffe titles, please contact
Wharncliffe Books Limited
47 Church Street, Barnsley, South Yorkshire, S70 2AS, England
E-mail: enquiries@pen-and-sword.co.uk
Website: www.wharncliffebooks.co.uk

Contents

Preface and Acknowledgements

Preston is a fine town, and tolerably full of people . . . The people are very gay here, though not perhaps the richer for that, but it has by that obtained the name of Proud Preston.

(DANIEL DEFOE, 1725)

Our town's colourful past has always been a subject of great interest to its inhabitants. On occasion it has played a leading role in British history, dashing the hopes of kings (real or pretended), or advancing the cause of parliamentary democracy as circumstances dictated. Prestonians have proved themselves to be a most industrious and enterprising lot, whether inventing the Industrial Revolution, smashing pub windows for Women's Suffrage, building railways across the Americas or christening the highest mountain in the world. Preston products are no less distinguished, from the Horrockses long cloths used as currency in the more distant parts of the Empire, to the trams beloved of Joseph Stalin and the revolutionary aircraft 'Made in Preston' - the Vampire, Canberra and TSR-2. The scales of success weigh heavily in the old town's favour, even without recourse to Preston's sporting and cultural achievements. Local historians and fellow travellers have been tracing these developments since the 1680s, and this volume merely seeks to be a friendly companion with whom to explore them.

Thanking folk

In such endeavours the writer despite his best efforts clearly cannot win: all the faults and omissions are his, whilst a great many people have enthusiastically contributed towards the completion of the project. In this respect I have always been extremely fortunate, and have great pleasure in acknowledging my real debt to a considerable number of people. Pride of place must go to the librarians and archivists: Robert Rushton and the staff of Leyland Library, Anne Dennison of the Harris Reference Library, John Convey of the LCC Local History collection, Aidan Turner-Bishop of the University Library (of whom more later), and Bruce Jackson and the staff of the Lancashire Record Office. Along the way I was ably assisted in various ways by Jack Rice, Stephen Sartin, Chris Aspin, Heather Halton, Sylvia Birtles, Brian Rhodes, Joe Hodgson, Jim Rawcliffe, Colin Dickinson, Zakir Patel, Margaret Burscough, Marian Roberts, Bryan Gray, Emma Hesslewood, Ishwer Tailor, and Howard Hammersley. In the final production of the book I am most grateful to David Ashmore, Pam Harvey, Ian Barrow, Brian Tomlinson and Keith Launchbury. Anne Dennison assisted with obtaining line drawings and engravings, and Stephanie Murray kindly gave me access to her fine photograph collection. Members of the Leyland Historical Society, the Friends of South Ribble Museum & Exhibition Centre, the BAE Systems Heritage Group (Warton) and the Preston Branch of the Lancashire Family History and Heraldry Society all assisted in various ways.

The past historians (Kuerden, Hardwick, Hewitson, Clemesha and James Barron) would rightly wish to be remembered, and I have been considerably assisted in my task by the really splendid work of their successors at the start of the new century - Nigel Morgan, Frank Harrison, David Hindle and of course Alan Crosby. As ever I owe an enormous debt to George Bolton, Elizabeth Shorrock and W E Waring - indeed the latter shepherded me along on a daily basis! Rupert Harding of Wharncliffe Books and Anne my wife (despite distractions occasioned by indifferent spells at Deepdale) have at all times been both helpful and encouraging. Finally I must acknowledge my great debt to Aidan Turner-Bishop, who has freely shared his ideas, and whose understanding and love of the history of Preston has few equals.

Getting the most out of your book

Linking and related entries are indicated in the text thus: THEATRE ROYAL. A number of the important themes interlink: for example the sequence AGITATION - LUDDISM - ANDREW RYDING - CHARTISM - RICHARD MARSDEN - SPINNERS STRIKE - LOCK OUT - LANCASHIRE COTTON FAMINE uncovers the fraught story of the town's early labour history. Given the introductory nature of the publication only a brief bibliography has been provided: more detailed trails into Preston's past can be picked up from A Crosby, *The History of Preston Guild* (1992), and D Hunt, *A History of Preston* (1992), updated in *Preston: Centuries of Change* (2003).

But as Leo Warren used to say, we must get on: ABC strikes the path through Preston's remarkable THEATRE LAND, and so 'a very good place to start'. Happy wandering!

David Hunt
Longton, January 2005

Abbreviations

GHS	The Gujarat-Hindu Society
LRO	Lancashire Record Office, Bow Lane, Preston
ODNB	*Oxford Dictionary of National Biography* (2004)
PRI	Preston Royal Infirmary
THSLC	*Transactions of the Historical Society of Lancashire and Cheshire*
WSPU	Women's Social and Political Union

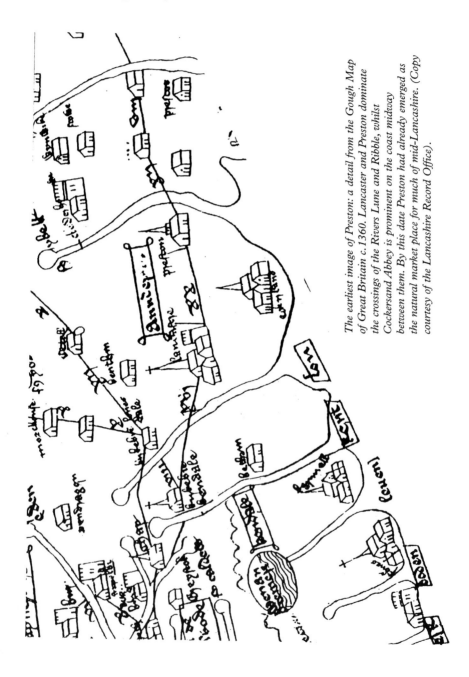

The earliest image of Preston: a detail from the Gough Map of Great Britain c.1360. Lancaster and Preston dominate the crossings of the Rivers Lune and Ribble, whilst Cockersand Abbey is prominent on the coast midway between them. By this date Preston had already emerged as the natural market place for much of mid-Lancashire. (Copy courtesy of the Lancashire Record Office).

The Wharncliffe Companion to Preston

A

ABC
Cinema, Fishergate. See THEATRE ROYAL.

ADDISON, THOMAS BATTY (1787-1874)
Recorder of Preston and arch-opponent of JOSEPH LIVESEY. A member of a well-to-do Preston family, Addison was educated at Clitheroe Grammar School and Charterhouse School, before being called to the Bar in 1808. In 1818 he became Bailiff to the Corporation, and in 1832 he was appointed Recorder of Preston. He was originally a Whig in politics, but after the Great Reform Bill meeting (which he chaired at the CORN EXCHANGE on 28 March 1831) his views lurched to the right. Yet he was strongly committed to progress; he had been one of the founders of the Literary and Philosophical Society, and was a shareholder in the Preston Waterworks Company and the Longridge Railway - indeed one of the latter's engines was actually named 'Addison'.

Looking east along Fishergate from the corner of Corporation Street c.1910.

Fishergate, Preston

In most matters he clashed with the Radical-turned-Liberal Livesey, but the two served together on many public bodies, and when the Institution for the Diffusion of Knowledge was formed in 1828, for example, Addison was chairman, ROBERT ASCROFT secretary and Livesey the treasurer. Their lifelong dispute came to centre on the workhouse question (1834-67), and here Addison at last prevailed. As chairman of the Board of Guardians the unemployed could expect short shrift from him. He himself got into trouble when denouncing the jury in a case he had tried as 'Blockheads' when they had come to a decision not to his liking. As his obituary concluded, 'Kind and generous ... his line of conduct in public affairs was characterised by fortitude, firmness and stoic inflexibility'. He lived in style at 23 Winckley Square and would not have approved of the current use of his former home as a popular restaurant!

Obituary: *Preston Chronicle* (6 June 1874).

AGITATION

The term given to labour organization in pursuit of higher wages in the period before 1824-5 when it was illegal to organize a 'strike'. As a result of the 'agitation' of 1808 'considerable destitution prevailed', and a further demand for an increase in the wages in HANDLOOM WEAVING caused 'much excitement and uneasiness'. Events came to a climax on 2 June when a meeting of 'great numbers' of weavers on Preston Moor 'to consult and induce their employers to raise their wages' was dispersed by the military. On the following day the magistrates handed out weapons 'to all the recruiting parties in the town' who then joined the 84th Regiment in readiness. The weavers paraded to the traditional meeting places on the Moor and along the pebble shore of the river at Walton ('common ground' where assembly was permitted), and it seems dispersed without serious incident. Such events were not uncommon and similarly 'formidable demonstrations' followed in 1818. The organization of a relatively small number of key factory workers gave a much greater chance of success. In 1821 the Preston spinners struck for three weeks against a 10 per cent reduction in their wages, setting the pattern for wage disputes in the local cotton industry for the next century.

H I Dutton and J E King, *Ten Per Cent and No Surrender: The Preston Strike of 1853-4* (1981).

See LUDDISM; ANDREW RYDING; CHARTISM.

ALBERT EDWARD, OR PRESTON DOCK

The controversy which for twenty years had surrounded the various schemes to construct a wet dock close by the centre of Preston and 16 miles up a tidal creek from the open sea faded into insignificance in comparison to that which accompanied the dock's actual construction (1884-92). On a tide of enthusiasm its supporters decided that the dock would not be large enough, and increased its size to 40 acres, making it the largest in the country and as far as anyone knew the largest freshwater dock in the world! Work began in 1884, the money ran out in 1887; the 'Party of Caution' now seemed to be in the ascendant and work was halted for two years. Money for the scheme was borrowed on long mortgages, optimistically arranged to 'come in' at a very distant 1945 and 1952, and repayments and other expenses would be met by a separately levied 'Ribble Rate'. The potential size of this rate ('Ten pence a year for fifty years!') now caused panic as the cost of the scheme swelled. By the time that the first sod was cut by Alderman Gilbertson on 11 October 1884 the estimated cost had grown to well over a million pounds, and Prestonians remembered how old SAMUEL HORROCKS replied to a request for funds earlier in the century - that if he wanted to 'put money into the Ribble' he would go onto Penwortham bridge and throw it in!

The local elections of 1888 became a popular plebiscite on the scheme. All the 'Cautioneers' were defeated, but not all the voters were ratepayers so a special poll of this group was organized. When the enthusiasts carried the day (12,569 to 4,834) a Bill to borrow a further half million pounds was obtained and the workings were reopened. In a sense the controversy would never subside. In the 1890s the hard-pressed Corporation led by Gilbertson even tried to force North End to pay a 'realistic rent' for DEEPDALE, and in 1901 all council candidates agreed to prohibit any further spending on the scheme. Albert Edward, Prince of Wales, had laid the foundation stone on 17 July 1885, and on Monday 2 May 1892 the protecting wall was breached and water trickled into the enormous hole named after him. The dock took a month to fill, and was ready to be opened by the Duke of Edinburgh on 25 June. Across Watery Lane a large banner proclaimed 'Success to the Preston Dock'.

The Albert Edward was indeed a wonder. Edward Garlick and his partner and successor Benjamin Sykes were the engineers, and Thomas Walker was the project's main contractor. They had excavated four million cubic yards of earth, sand and gravel, and another million of rock. Over 770,000 cubic yards of rock ballast had been used to reclaim almost 200 acres of storage grounds. The pairs of lock gates weighed 260 tons, and the chimney of the dock's powerhouse was 156 feet high. Some 1600 men had been employed on the scheme, along with 214 trucks, 277 wagons and 15 miles of temporary railway.

The wet dock is 40 acres in extent and the entrance sill is 38 feet below road level, allowing a depth of 29 feet of water over it at high spring tides. The immense walls enclosing a space 3020 by 600 feet are of concrete with a granite coping; they are 40 feet high, 17 feet 6 inches thick at the bottom and 10 feet thick at the top. Entrance is by way of a tidal basin and locks. The entrance to the tidal basin is 90 feet wide at the Bullnose, narrowing to 60

The then Prince of Wales (Edward VII) laying the foundation stone of Preston Dock, 1885.

feet at the gates, and the basin measures 850 by 300 feet (4.75 acres), and connects with the dock proper through a lock 550 feet long. The diversion of the RIBBLE 400 yards to the south of the original course, through an artificial channel 2,800 yards long and 300 feet wide, enabled the construction of a new riverside quay (the 1500 feet long 'Diversion Quay') which became the base of the shipbreaking trade. In all there are one and a half miles of quays! The depth of water at high tide (29 feet), the width of the entrance gates (60 feet), and the length of the entrance lock (550 feet) thus dictated the maximum size of shipping able to use the PORT OF PRESTON. But to do so shipping had first to pass 16 miles up a shallow river, and here the problems were far from over!

J Barron, *The History of the Ribble Navigation* (1937). J Dakres, *The Last Tide: The Port of Preston 1806-1986* (1986), LRO, DDX1242, Cochrane collection.

See RIBBLE NAVIGATION COMPANY.

APPRENTICESHIP

Many tradesman made their way onto the Guild Rolls as a BURGESS having served their term of apprenticeship. This procedure was carefully regulated from the earliest times, and is described in the town's code (the CUSTOMAL). Just before Christmas 1393 the Preston mercer 'John of Walton' agreed to employ another John from Walton-le-Dale as his apprentice. This would almost certainly provide the lad with a profession for life, and he was to 'faithfully serve' his master for six years

. . . doing such requirements for his master as a master apprentice ought to do. His master will instruct him in his art and will keep him in food, clothing, shoes and all other necessaries...The apprentice shall not take holidays without leave of his master unless he can show reasonable excuse. His master's doors and windows he shall not leave open by his negligence. During his term he shall not marry without his master's assent. He shall see no damage done to his master without doing his best to amend it or letting his master know and any money lost or wasted by him he shall repay doubly.

In his sixth and final year he was to be paid 10 shillings. Fully instructed in the mystery of his art, and duly established among the brethren of Preston as a burgess, the time-served apprentice would now only be in want of a wife.

J H Lumby, *The De Hoghton Deeds and Papers* (1936), document 310.

ARCHAEOLOGY
See PRESTON DOCK FINDS; POULTON-LE-FYLDE ELK; BOG BURIAL; ROMAN ARCHAELOGY; POTTER LANE.

ARKWRIGHT, SIR RICHARD (1732-1792)
Barber and pioneer of the Industrial Revolution. Born in Preston in 1732, Arkwright was a Prestonian through and through. His family had originated in the Fylde, were enrolled at the 1562 Guild, and in the seventeenth century lived in Back Lane off Friargate (now Back Market St). After his apprenticeship with a Kirkham barber he moved to Bolton in 1750 where he married and became a prosperous wig maker. Clearly a man with a shrewd eye for business, Arkwright is said to have become obsessed with the possibilities of mechanical yarn spinning whilst buying up tresses of hair for wig making from the many spinsters in the country districts around the town. Working with Thomas Hayes and John Kay, he perfected a system of spinning and twisting the fibres at speed as they passed through successively faster pairs of rollers. The early machines were turned by a horse gin, but the availability of water power meant that the number of sets of rollers could be increased almost indefinitely, and the water frame was born.

Such machines were rightly perceived by the hand spinners as a threat to their livelihood, and Arkwright and Kay left Bolton for Preston in 1768 to develop their prototype amidst much secrecy at the Reverend Ellis Henry's house at the bottom of Stoneygate. When voting at the GREAT ELECTION OF 1768 Arkwright was variously described as working on a machine to find out the longitude, and as a barber working on clockwork. When Kay was asked his business directly he was particularly unforthcoming, saying only that 'he was about a machine'. Of course he had no idea what it was for! The house on Stoneygate, happily restored after years of neglect and known as Arkwright House, must thus be regarded as one of the birthplaces of the Industrial Revolution. Unfortunately the popular restaurant at the house is misnamed the Spinning Jenny Cafe: Arkwright would most definitely not have been amused!

Although others claimed with some justification to have 'invented' most of the elements of the machine, it was Arkwright who patented it in 1769, and thereafter enjoyed a virtual monopoly of mass-produced yarn until his general patent was overthrown in 1785. Yarn spun on the Arkwright frame was much stronger than that produced by the 'Jenny', enabling cotton to be used as the warp in the weaving process. Arkwright's genius lay in the financing of his enterprises and the integration of his machine into a factory system of production which he pioneered at his mill at Cromford. As far as possible all the stages of manufacture were mechanized and carefully protected through patents. Rivals such as JOHN WATSON at Roach Bridge mill thus had to pay him to be allowed to operate his system. So far as possible, all functions were to be performed by young children, and ideally by orphans - the cheapest source of labour.

The hatred of his rivals - who justly argued that his patents held back the progress of the textile industry - does not seem to have concerned Arkwright unduly. When his patent was overturned he is said to have overheard one of them gloat 'Well that's the end of the old barber', to which he darkly retorted 'I have a razor that will shave you all!' By this he meant his own factories whose massive profits poured into government stocks, allowing him in turn to crow that he could afford to pay the National Debt. Cantankerous and

Sir Richard Arkwright (1732-92). Prestonian barber-cum-publican and Father of the Industrial Revolution.

argumentative, he fell out with John Dale of New Lanark over the location of the mill bell, and made peace with his son only after discovering that he was the owner of a 'well-run' mill he had recently visited: he had been impressed at the work rate of the children. Arkwright died 'immensely rich', and the Cromford mills would spin on for 200 years.

R S Fitton, *The Arkwrights: Spinners of Fortune* (1989). C Aspin, *The Water-Spinners: A New Look at the Early Cotton Trade* (2003).

ASCROFT, ROBERT (1805-1876)

Solicitor and town clerk (1852-75), Ascroft was a leading Liberal and frequently found himself in the middle of the Addison-Livesey disputes. He served on many public bodies, and as the much respected chairman of the Board of Guardians (1859-66) played a central role in the measures to combat the worse effects of the LANCASHIRE COTTON FAMINE. Anthony Hewitson wrote of him, 'Not a cuter, not a more far seeing, not a more strategical man is there in Preston'.

A Hewitson *Preston Town Council, or Portraits of Local Legislators* (1870).

ATLANTIC SPEED RECORD

In April 1951 a Preston-built CANBERRA BOMBER set a new record for the Atlantic crossing of 4 hours 40 minutes. Other long-haul records held by the plane included those for the UK to Darwin (1-4 April 1951, 21 hours 41 minutes), London to Capetown (17 December 1953, 12 hours 21 minutes), and Tokyo-London (17 hours 4 minutes). In all the aircraft held 26 world records, including that for altitude (28 August 1957, 70,310 feet).

BAE Systems, North West Heritage Group.

AUGUST 1914

Following the assassination of the Archduke Franz Ferdinand on 28 June 1914, events moved at first slowly and then very rapidly to war. Austria declared war on Serbia on 28 July, Russia mobilized two days later, and Germany followed suit and declared war on Russia on 1 August. Like Hitler in 1940 German planning visualized a quick 'knock-out blow' to France before attacking in the east. War was declared on France on 3 August and during 3-4 August German forces swarmed into Belgium, in whose defence Britain declared war on Germany on 4 August. Events had been driven by the combatants' mobilization timetables, so that rather amazingly the 1st Battalion of the Loyal North Lancashire Regiment (see QUEEN'S LANCASHIRE REGIMENT), stationed at FULWOOD BARRACKS, was able to parade on the Market Square and lay up its colours with the Mayor at the TOWN HALL on Wednesday 5 August, before marching to the railway station through huge cheering crowds the next day en route to France.

Sir Harry Cartmell – Mayor of Preston throughout the war – later described the scenes:

The crowd became literally wild in their display of enthusiasm

Ann and John Jenkinson's houses (1629) fronting the south side of the Market Square: a drawing of 1839 (from T C Smith, Records of the Parish Church of Preston, 1892).

...During the whole of that first day, and indeed for some time afterwards, great crowds of people thronged the principal streets, everyone evincing a conviction that we were on the eve of great things. For many of these men their war would be a short one; as part of the British Expeditionary Force they suffered enormous casualties at the Battle of Mons, but by November the great German attack had been contained along the Aisne River. The Germans had failed to win the war in the west quickly, Paris was saved and the resulting deadlock would not be broken by the battles at Verdun and on the SOMME, or by the enormous German onslaught in early 1918. The war would claim around eight and a half million military and thirteen million civilian casualties. A huge number of Prestonians served in the forces, and Lord Derby's recruitment campaign of August 1915 alone was claimed to have secured 9,418 Preston men. By contrast W E Waring estimates the losses of the 1st/4th Battalion of the LNLR (in which many locals served) to have been in excess of 3,000 men: 873 dead, 2,093 wounded, 83 returned POWs and 44 missing. Even a small town like Preston would be changed for ever.

H Cartmell, *For Remembrance: An Account of Some Fateful Years* (1919). W E Waring, pers. comm.

See PALS COMPANY; SOMME; WAR PRODUCTION (1914-1918); VICTORY 1981.

AVENHAM PARK, AVENHAM WALK
See PUBLIC PARKS.

B

BAE SYSTEMS
See DICK, KERR.

BANGLADESHI COMMUNITY
Though numbering just 273 people in 1994 the community has played a central role in the evolution of Preston's extensive restaurant and take-away food trade. In 1959 Abdul Mozid Choudhury opened an 'Indian' restaurant in Friargate, and in 1961 Syed Abdul Hannan opened a second in Derby St.
Bangladeshis in Preston and their Socio-Cultural Activities (1995).

BARBIROLLI, SIR JOHN
In November 1961 the corporation tried to prevent large numbers of music lovers standing at the Public Hall (see CORN EXCHANGE) during concerts, and issued a 'no-standing ban'. Accordingly 200-300 concert-goers had to be turned away from the regular crowd of around 1,800 people. Sir John sided with them, and threatened to refuse to visit Preston again if the ban was not removed, which it duly was in January 1962.
Lancashire Evening Post (12 Nov. 1961, 24 Jan. 1962).

BATTLES OF PRESTON
1315 see BATTLE OF DEEPDALE; 1648 see CIVIL WAR; 1715 see OLD PRETENDER.

BAYNARD, ANN (1672/3-1697)
Mystic, 'coveter of knowledge' and strong candidate for the title of 'Brain of Preston'. Born in Preston, she was educated by her father, the 'physician and poet' Edward Baynard (1641?-1717) - an ardent advocate of cold baths and the author of a paper entitled 'Case of a Small Boy Who Swallowed Two Copper Farthings'. The family moved to London where she proved to be a prodigy, mastering all the subjects that then comprised an advanced education. By her early twenties she had 'a vast and comprehensive knowledge, a large and exalted mind, a strong and capacious memory, still covetting more and more knowledge'. All this she felt was useless however unless it led the student to God. After two years meditating in Barnes churchyard she died aged 25, urging young people and especially her fellow women to spend more time in study and learning 'By which they would be better enabled to serve God, and help their neighbours'.
G Ballard, *Memoirs of Several Ladies of Great Britain* (1752). *ODNB*

BEATLES, THE

A Merseyside pop group, strongly influential in the popular music of the 1960s and 1970s. In 1962 local impresario Vin Miller risked £18 to book the obscure group to play at the Preston Grasshoppers RFC annual supper and dance, with an option for a return visit the following year if a success. The rest is the stuff of legend, but the return saw the Public Hall (see CORN EXCHANGE) packed with 2,000 people paying 6s each to scream at the sensational band. The Beatles drove around the overflowing town in the back of an old van, trying to effect their entrance and escape through a variety of disguises. Those lucky enough to have had a ticket can recall hearing none of the music!

D Hindle, *Twice Nightly: An Illustrated History of Entertainment in Preston* (1999).

A Beattie sketch of Joseph Livesey's birthplace, Victoria Road, Walton-le-Dale, 1892 (from J Pearce, The Life and Teachings of Joseph Livesey, *1887).*

BEATTIE, EDWIN ROBERT (1845-1917)

Popular landscape artist. The son of a Preston portrait painter and the brother of the landscape artist Frederick Beattie, Edwin Robert was born in Liverpool and grew up in Southport. After a varied career which included a spell in Canada, he settled in Lancashire 'and achieved considerable success with his pen and ink and water-colour sketches of old historic buildings, manor houses, churches etc'. His sketches reached a wide public through their publication in the *Preston Guardian* and his work has won a renewed popularity through the reproduction of his water-colour views of Preston's long vanished townscape.

Obituary: *Lancashire Daily Post* (13 Feb. 1917).

BENNETT'S ELECTRIC THEATRE

A typical inter-war local cinema of the 'laugh and scratch' variety. In time it became the 'Dominion' and later the 'Rex'. Located close to the old shot-mill in Craggs Row (off Moor Lane), it was operated by Mr Ike Bennett. According to David Hindle, his patrons were fond of the following refrain which they sang with gusto:

Oh, ring down the curtain I can't sing tonight,
Those little creatures they scratch and they bite,
No more to the pictures will I ever go,
To Fleckie Bennett's in dirty Craggs Row!

D Hindle, *Twice Nightly: An Illustrated History of Entertainment in Preston* (1999).

BLACK DEATH (1347-1351)
A pandemic of bubonic and probably pneumonic plague, and the greatest single destroyer of human beings up to that time. It is an infectious fever caused by the bacillus Yersinia Pestis which cannot pass between people but is transmitted to them from infected rats by the 'rat flea'. Bubonic plague is characterized by large swellings ('buboes') in the groin and armpits, whereas pneumonic affects the lungs. The first symptoms are usually shivering and sickness followed by a high temperature (40°C). Originating in China the pandemic passed to Western Europe via the Mediterranean ports, reaching England in the autumn of 1349. Records are very imprecise, but in Preston and North Lancashire half of the parish priests and perhaps 13,000 people were dead by the end of the winter. The towns - Preston, Kirkham and Lancaster - were particularly badly affected, and Preston's LEPER HOSPITAL was overwhelmed: further outbreaks occurred in 1361 and 1369. By 1400 the population of England was perhaps half what it had been a century before, and did not really recover until the 1500s. Massive manpower shortages produced a 'seller's market' for labourers, serfdom declined, paid wages became the norm - and rose significantly. These processes were particularly marked in Preston, where 'trouble with the labourers' was reported and the old subservient medieval order was coming to an end.

D Hunt, *A History of Preston* (1992). For a radical reappraisal see C Duncan and S Scott, *Biology of Plagues* (20040.

BLACK FEET
The name given to the advocates of HENRY HUNT at the elections of 1830. Many were mill men or mechanics, and their oily footwear attracted the sobriquet. They promoted the cause of a freedom-loving democracy in general and the interests of their 'Orator' in particular. The *Preston Pilot* described what happened to one elector whose choice was not to their liking:

> In one instant several hundreds were upon him, the ejection from the Booth . . . became the work of a minute, and in as short a space of time the fragments of his apparel were to be seen flying about in all directions amidst the shouts and exultations of the delighted multitude.

W Proctor, 'Orator Hunt: MP for Preston', *THSLC* 114 (1962).

BLEASDALE CIRCLE
Located on the edge of the Bleasdale upland this prehistoric site has been excavated twice, in 1899-1900 and 1933-5. It comprised a ditched timber 'enclosure' 150 feet in diameter within which a cairn of orthodox 'Bronze Age' type overlay a smaller circle of posts. The cairn covered a pit containing two cremation burials of a type prevalent around 1500 BC. The site is well preserved and is easily accessible, though care must be taken to stay on the

path. Many questions remain unanswered: the ditched enclosure could be related to the henge circle tradition of around 2800 BC or it may be the remains of an enclosed building or large house, whilst the burial might be a later or quite separate development. Recent re-analysis of the finds has identified fragments of linen cloth associated with the burial, and one of the timber posts (several of which were intact at the time of excavation) produced a Carbon-14 date of around 2200 BC.

W J Varley, 'Excavations at Bleasdale', *Antiquities Journal* 18 (1938)

BLITZ IN PRESTON, THE (1940-1941)

Strict press censorship means that many details of wartime life remain obscure. The fall of France brought the North-West within the Luftwaffe's bombing range, and over 100 incidents were reported in the Preston district during late 1940. Occasional damage was followed in October 1940 by a more serious attempt to knock out the Leyland Motors factories. On 21 October three workers were killed and nine injured at the Farington works, and six days later Ward St at nearby Lostock Hall was hit, killing 25 people. Germany's attack on Russia brought this interlude to an end, but a raid in September 1941 killed two people at Kirkham. Many wartime incidents went unreported, and an appeal in 2001, for example, produced no eyewitnesses to the defusing of the enormous one and a quarter ton 'Hermann Goering' bomb dropped on Bamber Bridge during the night of 29 November 1940. This, the largest device recorded in Lancashire, had to be dug from a crater 39 feet deep in the garden of Darwen Bank. Had it gone off . . .

For the best contemporary account see *Lancashire Daily Post* (7 Oct. 1944).

BLOODY SATURDAY, 13 AUGUST 1842

See CHARTISM.

BLOSSOM

The Preston slaver: her voyage to the West Indies via the Windward and Gold coasts of West Africa carried 131 people in 1756. On her return she was offered for sale:

25 June 1756

FOR SALE AT PRESTON.

The good snow or vessel called the *Blossom*, Samuel Gawith commander, burthen 100 tons more or less, built at Preston, and has been one voyage only (on the coast of Africa), a very strong and tight vessel of proper dimensions and every way compleat for the Slave Trade.

The vessel was lying in the river off Lytham, nothing is known of her subsequent career, and her sale marked the end of the Preston-based SLAVE TRADE. The career of Samuel Gawith (or Touchet) was far from over, he went

on to be the master of three Liverpool ships and made eight further voyages.
M M Schoffield, 'The Slave Trade from Lancashire and Cheshire Ports outside Liverpool 1750-1790', *THSLC* 126 (1976).

BOB'S BONES

During the election of 1820 HENRY HUNT's horse died following his return from the assizes at Lancaster. The Huntites and BLACK FEET naturally suspected that he had been poisoned by their political opponents and duly organized a splendid funeral for Bob, followed by his interment in a garden along Ormskirk Road. After a decent time the horse's remains were exhumed and made into souvenirs of all kinds. In 1883 Hewitson had recently seen one of poor Bob's shin bones used for 'rubbing up' leather.
A Hewitson, *History of Preston* (1883).

BOG BURIAL

Before their reclamation the extensive mosses to the north and south of Preston must have preserved considerable pollen and related evidence of the district's prehistoric past. The best example comes from Pilling, where a 'bog burial' of the type identified on Lindow Moss seems to have been discovered by workmen in 1825:

At a depth of six feet from the surface a piece of coarse woollen cloth, of a yellow colour was discovered, in which were contained the remains of a human skull, with a great abundance of hair of a beautiful auburn.

Associated jet and amber beads indicated a prehistoric date for the find which was subsequently interred in Pilling churchyard.
B J N Edwards, 'Archaeological Notes', *THSLC* 123 (1969). I M Stead, J B Bourke and Don Brothwell, *Lindow Man: The Body in the Bog* (1986). For recent research on the local mosses see R Middleton, C E Wells and E Huckerby, *The Wetlands of North Lancashire* (1995); R Middleton, M J Tooley and J Innes, *The Wetlands of South-West Lancashire* (forthcoming).

BOND MINI-CARS

Pioneering three-wheeled motor vehicle, and many people's 'first car'. Lawrence Bond was born in Preston in 1907 and established the Bond Aircraft and Engineering Company in 1948, though his succession of designs (for mini-cars, scooters and jet water-skis) was manufactured by a number of companies. Keenly aware of the restricted market for motor vehicles in post-war Britain, Bond hit on the idea of a three-wheeler to avoid the prohibitive level of purchase tax on four-wheel cars, qualify for the lower level of road tax, and be energy efficient to run on the six-monthly petrol ration of 18 gallons! Built at Longridge the 'One-eighth litre Shopping Car' was taken over by Sharp's Commercials and manufactured in Ribbleton. Early in 1949 Bond and a passenger drove a prototype the 228 miles to London on two gallons of petrol. Around 26,500 increasingly sophisticated vehicles were produced at Preston until 1966, but rising levels of domestic income and the reduction in car purchase tax in 1962 made the three-wheeler a less attractive option. Three years later the company was taken over by Reliant, and what was perhaps 'Lawrie' Bond's most memorable car - the futuristic fibreglass 'Bond Bug' - began production in 1970 (in any colour so long as it was tangerine!).

Nick Wotherspoon, *Lawrie Bond. The Man and the Marque: The Illustrated History of Bond Cars* (1993).

BONNIE PRINCE CHARLIE

Charles Edward Louis Philip Casimir Stuart (1720-1788), AKA the Young Pretender. When the French Armada of 1744 was dispersed by a great storm Charles decided to try win the throne for his father - The Old Pretender - alone. His colourful force beloved of song and ballad entered Edinburgh on 17 September 1745, and after the victory at Prestonpans four days later, set off for London by the ill-fated west coast route. The force reached Preston on 27 November, entering the town to the tune 'The King Shall Have His Own Again'. The Prince apparently stayed at 'Lawyer Starkies' in Mitre Court at the entrance to Gin Bow Entry, where as an eyewitness later reported, 'He

Central Fishergate looking west c. 1962. Much of this scene was soon to be swept away in the redevelopment of the mid-1960s. The ancient Mitre Inn (where Jacobite prisoners were held after their defeat in 1715) can still be seen, wedged between later buildings (by the third car from the left).

was dressed in a Scotch plaid, a blue silk waistcoat with silver lace, and a scotch bonnet with JR on it'. The Highlanders had a superstitious dread of the town after their party's earlier failures there (in 1648 and 1715), and thought that they were 'doomed' never to proceed beyond it. Charles took time to have his miniature portrait painted (it can be seen in the Harris Museum), and to tour key sites of the battle of 1715 with veterans. Scots quartered south of the river - to counter their strategic error of 1715 - helped themselves to the stores at Walton Hall farm. Having reached Derby the force turned homewards, passing through Preston again on 13 December, this time to the tune of 'Hie Thee Home Again'. The Victorians did their best to add a distinctly Prestonian tinge to the Jacobite myth - with full parts for wine, women and song - but critically little practical support had been forthcoming from the town: once again their eighteenth-century predecessors had enjoyed the fun but had stayed at home.

C Hardwick, *History of the Borough of Preston* (1857). H W Clemesha, *A History of Preston in Amounderness* (1912). D Hunt, *A History of Preston* (1992). R C Jarvis, *The Jacobite Risings of 1715 and 1745* (1954).

See Mock Corporation of Walton-le-Dale; Old Pretender.

BOROUGH

An urban community with legal rights. Preston was the first Lancashire town to be officially recognized, with the grant of Henry II's charter in 1179; Lancaster followed in 1193, Liverpool in 1201 and Manchester in 1301. An earlier Preston Charter from 1100 may have existed, certainly in 1631 Judge Walmesley swore that he had seen it. Alternatively it is possible that Roger of Poitou established a borough here in the years immediately after the Conquest.

See Burgess; Charters.

BOUNDARY RIDING

An annual ride or walk around the boundaries of the Borough undertaken by the Mayor and Corporation, usually accompanied by the town colours and a 'Band of music'. This was a widespread tradition to facilitate the detection of any encroachment into the 'home' territory from the neighbours, and in Preston became a central part of the Shrove Tuesday celebrations. Participants were free to stop for refreshments, and the triumphal progress which had started amidst much pomp and ceremony would of course quickly degenerate. The route led the party to a pond at the bottom of Marsh Lane, as Hewitson described:

> On reaching the 'Colt Hole' . . . some of those in the procession crossed the hole, a few managing to jump over it, but more floundering in the water, and making ludicrous spectacles of themselves.

The local government reforms of 1835 put an end to this event and to the initiation of the newly elected council officials which accompanied it. These hapless individuals could be left in no doubt as to whose servants they were; they were 'severely whipped' around the town water pumps before Preston's strong-armed blacksmiths moved in to belabour them with iron rods!

A Hewitson, *Preston Court Leet Records* (1905).

BOUNDS OF PRESTON

DR KUERDEN described the bounds - or boundaries - of the ancient Borough of Preston in the 1680s:

> The bondary confining the franchises and libertyes of this Burrough of Preston, beginneth upon the south side, at the much famed river of Ribell, at a place cal'd the washing stood, and from thence ascend up, easterly, by a little rill or rivulet called the Swill-brooke, crossing the London road and passing upward to the head thereof, till you come over against the town of Fishwick, from which the brooke parteth this burrough aforesaid; and from thence the bonds pass to the norward, to the entrance upon Ribbleton more, nere if not close by, the crosse upon the highway a little above Ribchester, toward the citty of Yorke; and from this crosse, passing by the west side of that more, still northward, through some few closes unto Eavs brook, and thus it is separated from the village of Ribbleton; upon the east from thence, passing down the Eavs brook untill it fallith into the water of Savock, and thus it is parted from the forest of Fullwood and Cadily more; so descending the water of Savock to a certain old ditch which is the bondary betwixt Preston and Tulketh; soe following that old ditch southward, by Lancaster-lane, untill you arrive to Preston Marsh, a little west from the water Milne; and so following the milne stream westward, after the north side of the marsh, untill it crosse up southward towards Rible, but following that stream to Rible water; and so following Rible eastward, by the midst of that water, until it come past the boat over against Preston, to the afore mentioned washing steads, into the Swill-brook.

R Kuerden, *A Brief Description of the Burrough and Town of Preston* (?1682, published by J Taylor, 1818).

BRAZIL, ANGELA (1868-1947)

Girls' story writer. Though born at 1 West Cliff, Preston, her father's work in the cotton trade soon took the family home around the neighbouring mill towns. Angela Brazil attended an exclusive girls' school and later studied art in London. Comparatively well-to-do, she travelled widely and lived variously in the Conwy Valley and Cornwall before settling with her brother and sister

in Coventry (1911). Not until her thirties did she embark on the series of girl's school stories that made her famous, but by the 1920s she was the accepted master of the genre. Her most 'ripping' books abound with such girl's names as Ulyth, Ingred, Merle and Lesbia, and include *A Fourth Form Friendship* (1911), *A Pair of Schoolgirls* (1912) and *For the Sake of the School* (1915). Her output of almost fifty books was maintained in print for half a century.
ODNB.

BRIDLING
An inhuman punishment usually reserved for overly talkative or foul-mouthed women ('Scolds'), and discontinued at Preston's House of Correction after a public outcry in 1838. The 'bridle' was an iron frame which closed over the victim's head and prevented utterances by inserting a 'bit' into her mouth to prevent movement of the tongue. The 'brank' fastened at the back and could not be removed by the wearer, whilst a conveniently attached chain allowed the 'scold' to be paraded about. In 1659 Roger Haworth's wife Ellen was ordered to pay a fine of 2/6d, 'otherwise Mr.Maior is desired to cause the said Ellen punished by bridleinge her through the Towne'. Following certain 'Informacon' she had been accused of 'scowleinge and abuseing Mary, the wife of John Higham, with very uncivell Language, to the bad example of others (if unpunished)'.
A Hewitson, *History of Preston* (1883); *Preston Court Leet Records* (1905).

BRUCE, ALEXANDER ROBERT (1952-)
Free-scoring and remarkably consistent PRESTON NORTH END forward during the 'Big Hair' days of the 1970s. Born in Dundee, Bruce joined Preston in 1968, making his league debut at the age of 19 in 1972. He quickly made his mark as a goal-machine in the Tommy Roberts and Tommy Thompson mould and was transferred (£120,000) to Newcastle United in January 1974. His return 18 months later as a part of the John Bird transfer resulted in the departure of manager Bobby Charlton, but heralded a spectacularly successful period for goal-poacher Bruce. As in 1970 his departure in August 1983 (for Wigan Athletic) led to North End's relegation. In his ten years at Deepdale he was leading scorer eight times, and only TOM FINNEY has scored more goals for his adopted club - up to the present time.
D Hunt, *A History of Preston North End Football Club: The Power, the Politics and the People* (2000).

BRUCE, ROBERT THE

A number of incursions into the North-West in the decade after 1314 are popularly associated with Robert the Bruce, though his personal participation seems rather unlikely. For over 600 years up to 1745, Preston played an important role in all the lamentable disputes with the Scots. Indeed a case can be made that, for a short spell in the twelfth century, Preston was actually a part of Scotland! In 1303 the wife-killer Aveyse de Preston was spared if he would fight in Scotland, and Edward I was briefly based in the town in 1306. Though Preston seems to have been looted in retaliation on a number of occasions, the locals proved very creative when estimating their losses in claiming compensation. In 1317 they succeeded in having their town's taxation cut by two-thirds, and were still blaming the 'ravages of the Scots' for their difficulties thirty years later.

The major raid of the summer of 1322 is particularly associated with Robert the Bruce and the burning of Preston. Samlesbury church was looted and the goods apparently taken from it were worth an enormous £18 6s 8d. The following year a number of local people were prosecuted for stealing goods and animals from refugees who had fled south across the River Lostock. The early fourteenth century was thus the worst of times for the Prestonians, marked by a short-term deterioration in the weather and failed harvests, famine in 1315, the ravages of the Scots and the demands of the king. Yet worse was to come: in the early 1340s something in distant China caused the behaviour of the fleas which inhabit the fur of rats to change, and in 1349 the BLACK DEATH reached Lancashire...

D Hunt, *A History of Preston* (1992).

BUFFET AT PRESTON STATION (1915-1919, 1939-1945)

A buffet for travelling servicemen was established under the auspices of the Mayoress in August 1915. Working 12-hour shifts the 700 women volunteers had served 3,148,593 men by its closure in May 1919. Their record spell was the Christmas of 1916 when 12,449 men were served in 36 hours. A second shift established at the start of the Second World War had served up 12,342,000 cups of tea by mid-December 1945!

H Cartmell, *For Remembrance: An Account of Some Fateful Years* (1919). *Lancashire Daily Post* (21 Dec. 1945).

BURGAGE

A parcel of land suitable for a house, usually granted to a BURGESS on admission to the GUILD MERCHANT. In Preston these plots were carefully laid out in the period 1150-1350 along CHURCHGATE, FISHERGATE and FRIARGATE, giving the old town the distinct herring-bone pattern which is such a feature of the early maps. The street frontage had to be at least 12 feet wide, and the plot would form a narrow strip extending back to a lane or

Preston Town Centre c.1925. A very clear view of the town's plan extending north from the line of the Syke to Starchhouse Square, and west from Tithebarn St (Preston's Theatreland) to St George's church. Indeed up to 1800 this virtually was 'Preston'. The medieval burgage strips show up very well because 19th-century housing was simply shoehorned into them.

some sort of natural feature. Strips along the north side of Friargate reached back to the line of Back Lane (now Market St), and those to the south of Churchgate to the Syke. Beyond these 'backsides' lay the open townfields. If no house existed on the site a burgess had 40 days to build one or face a fine of a shilling. Many burgesses built barns and animal stics on their 'backsides'; others developed tasteful gardens and the result can clearly be seen in Buck's engraving 'A Prospect of Preston'. During the town's period of very rapid growth in the early nineteenth century, whole rows of houses could be thrust onto individual strips, producing some of the very worst housing. Vestiges of this ancient pattern may still be seen on the south side of Fishergate-Church St between Stoneygate and Cannon St.

H W Clemesha, *A History of Preston in Amounderness* (1912).
　　See LEASES.

BURGESS

An urban resident with legal rights. In pre-industrial Preston membership of the GUILD MERCHANT conferred burgess rights. Lists of the burgesses - the Guild Rolls - were updated at the regular intervals marked by the Preston Guild. The names of dead members were struck out, and their sons were added along with those of time-served apprentices and acceptable newcomers. Residents were known as In-Burgesses, whilst out-of-town residents with an interest there were known as Out-Burgesses. With the steady influx of outsiders the system came under strain and in 1562 a third class was recognized. These were the Stallingers, traders who were allowed to

have stalls in the town but were not admitted to full burgess rights. The central tenet of this restrictive system was that wealth was not a commodity to be endlessly increased by the mutual exchange of goods and services, but rather that it was essentially restricted. It followed that any profits which were to be made in Preston should go to the right people. Better value saddles or ironmongery from Euxton or Leyland, for example, were thus to be kept out of the market. Alternatively, in 1653 Roger Woodroffe was punished for illegally exporting 1000 bricks! Burgesses also had valuable rights to the TOWNFIELDS, and had the first pick of the goods for sale in the various produce markets. They also had 'a voice' (of sorts) in the selection of their self-appointing Corporation, but had direct control over the behaviour of their fellow townspeople through the COURT LEET. Today all Preston residents possessing the right to vote in local elections might consider themselves burgesses.

A burgess: the Bushell Brasses preserved in the Minster. Rediscovered when the parish church was rebuilt in the 1850s the brasses commemorate the life of Seth Bushell, 'Woollen Draper, Bayliffe and a Brother of Preston'. This is perhaps the earliest surviving portrait of a Prestonian (1623), and his open hands show that he comes in peace! (from H Fishwick, History of the Parish of Preston, 1900).

A Hewitson, *Preston Court Leet Records* (1905).
H W Clemesha, *A History of Preston in Amounderness* (1912). A Crosby, *A History of Preston Guild* (1992).

C

CANAL TRANSPORT

Canals provided an ideal means of transporting bulky goods and raw materials during the early phase of the Industrial Revolution. Preston's greatest need was for Wigan coal, and this was catered for by the improvement of the Douglas Navigation in the middle of the eighteenth century. The transport situation of Lancaster and Kendal to the north was much more pressing, and an engineer was appointed in 1771 to survey a canal route. Nothing else was done for twenty years, but by the end of the century Preston alone was consuming 20,000 tons of coal a year and renewed plans from Lancaster met with widespread support. A company with drawing rights of over £400,000 was formed, and John Rennie (1761-1821) was appointed engineer. Remarkably, a level line was found through the Fylde, but expensive works were needed to carry the waterway over the Rivers Lune and Ribble, and to tunnel it through the Whittle Hills on its way to Wigan.

The 'North End' between Preston and Lancaster was opened on 22 November 1797, but the expense of the superb 600 foot Lune Viaduct led the directors to opt for a simple tram road to transport cargo from Preston across the Ribble to link with the 'South End' at Whittle. This was opened on 1 June 1803. The first horse-drawn 'train' of six coal wagons was accompanied by a band of music, and 'Old and young left their habitations to witness a site so novel'. Critically, the Lancaster company had won the race to get to Wigan with the Leeds & Liverpool (Act of Parliament 1770), and when the latter moved to cross the Pennines it grafted the descent at Johnson's Hillock onto the Lancaster's line. Preston's rapid growth after 1790 suggests that it was the canal's greatest beneficiary. The path of the canal through the west end of the town acted as a great stimulus to mill building in the vicinity, a process led by John Horrocks whose Spittals Moss and Canal St factories were served by their own canal wharf.

The company enjoyed a virtual monopoly for thrity-five years, carrying coal north and limestone south. It also operated a successful passenger service in 'fast fly boats' which gave the early railway a run for its money on the run up to Kendal. Indeed, when the Lancaster Railway hit financial problems the canal company took over the running of its trains!

C Biddle and C Hadfield, *Canals of North-West England* (1970). S Baritt, *The Old Tram Road* (2000).

CANARY ISLANDS

Late nineteenth-century terraced-housing development off Deepdale Road in which the streets are named after birds. See HOUSING (1790-1914).

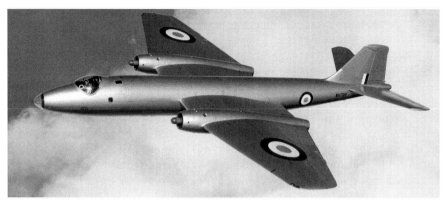

A Canberra PR MK 7. This photograph highlights the large wing and clean lines of this superb aeroplance, c.1955 (photo: BAE Systems Heritage Group, Warton).

CANBERRA BOMBER

The world's first jet bomber, designed and built at Preston. The Canberra replaced the Lincoln bomber, flying twice as fast and twice as high. By 1947 English Electric (see DICK, KERR) had become convinced that a large future market for jet aircraft existed, and established a design team under W E W Petter in Barton Motors' former car showroom in Corporation St. Wing assembly was undertaken at Samlesbury and fuselage construction at Strand Road. The prototype flew from Warton in May 1949 and only two years later chief test pilot Roland Beamont delivered the first Canberra to the RAF. It was one of the most successful British aircraft, and even the Americans were forced to acquire it, manufacturing the Canberra under licence as the B-57.

R Fairclough and S Ransom (1987) *English Electric Aircraft and their Predecessors* (1987). G Green (1988) *British Aerospace: A Proud Heritage* (1988).

See ATLANTIC SPEED RECORD.

CARRYING FIRE

The lighting of household fires by 'carrying the fire' in tongs from a neighbour's hearth was a sight which terrified Prestonians, fearful of the firing of their thatch and timber town. It was regarded as a very serious crime against the community: William Blackledge's wife was heavily fined in 1696 for 'carrying fire in the open street'.

A Hewitson, *Preston Court Leet Records* (1905).

CARYON

The disposal of those parts of dead animals which the Prestonians could no longer make any use of posed a constant problem. Like motorcar parts today the general response was to leave them in the street. In April 1654 the COURT

LEET considered the problem:
A great abuse in this Towne by reason of carryon, dead Swyne, Doggs, and other noysome, filthie carryon beinge throwne in St. John's Weind and other weends and backe lanes belonginge to this Towne, to the great annoyance both of men and Cattell, passengers and others, And for redresse thereof wee give in verdict That if anie man or their servants shall throw anie carryon in anie weend or backe lane or suffer anie to lye uncovered upon theire middings or before theire barnes to forfeite for everie offence 6s 8d.

A Hewitson, *Preston Court Leet Records* (1905).

CATHOLIC COLLEGE
See WINCKLEY SQUARE.

CENTRAL LANCASHIRE NEW TOWN
See HOUSING (1945-2005).

CHARTERS
Preston grew up in response to the need to exchange goods locally. As the settlement developed, it began to offer its own goods and services to outsiders and to act as a centre for trade over an ever wider area. This process must already have been well advanced by the time of the Norman Conquest, and with it came a steady presumption on the part of the townspeople to manage their own affairs. In a society in which authority cascaded down from the monarch, towns could acquire legal recognition of their market function and a measure of protection for their citizens' individual rights through the acquisition of a royal charter. The town's earliest proven charter is that of Henry II (1179). For a hundred marks the king granted all the usual rights of a royal borough; the town's market status was recognized, local merchants could trade (largely) toll-free throughout the realm and, critically, they could enjoy what for the time was considerable freedom to regulate their own affairs. An institution called the GUILD MERCHANT gave access to, and regulated these rights.

Between 1179 and 1828 Preston obtained fourteen royal charters which confirmed and extended these freedoms. King John's charter (1199) was particularly important; it recognized among other things the burgesses' right to hold fairs and to take timber from the Royal Forest of the Fulle-woode. A century later the town's emerging civil rights were codified in a document called the CUSTOMAL. It became the practice to obtain a confirmatory charter from most successive monarchs, and since these bore the Royal Seal and are usually ornamental they are extremely interesting objects in themselves. With the rest of the town's papers they can now be inspected at the Lancashire

Record Office. The grant of city status under Elizabeth II (14 March 2001), which brought the 800-year old royal borough to an end, was not made by the grant of a charter but by the issue of 'letters patent'.

H W Clemesha, *A History of Preston in Amounderness* (1912).

See MARKETS.

CHARTISM (1838-1846)

A predominantly working-class movement which sought the enshrinement in law of the six points of the 'People's Charter' for parliamentary reform drafted by William Lovett in May 1838. It was hoped to influence the government through the presentation of 'Charters' (petitions) signed by enormous numbers of supporters, but opinion was less united on the question of what was to be done when Parliament inevitably rejected the Chartists' invitation to reform itself.

In 1837 the Preston Radical Operative Association was formed and set about collecting signatures. On 5 November 1838 Fergus O'Connor - the national leader - addressed a mass meeting on Preston Moor. A grand procession included no less than eight bands of music and some forty banners. The mottoes on the banners tell us a lot about the basis of the movement in Preston; one bore the words 'Better to die by the sword than perish of hunger', another 'Universal Suffrage, Equal Laws and Equal Rights'; but the erstwhile workpeople at William Bashall's Cuerden Mill were more direct and knew what was to be done 'Sell thy garment and buy a sword'! RICHARD MARSDEN of Bamber Bridge was elected to represent the town at the great National Convention but when first charter was rejected in 1839 the town's participation in the ensuing general strike lasted only three days.

The rejection of the enormous second petition in May 1842 led to the 'Plug Riots', and the serious confrontation on 13 August - Preston's Bloody Saturday. Amidst much confusion and a fairly general strike, rioters and onlookers confronted the authorities in Lune St. Events quickly ran out of control and, amidst much stone throwing, the Mayor Samuel Horrocks junior, having tried to reason with the militant elements in the crowd, read the Riot Act. At this point it seemed that the rioters were about to get behind the police and troops who were standing higher up the street (in the vicinity of what is today an entrance to St George's shopping centre), and the order was given for the troops to fire on the crowd. The Prestonians who had gathered to watch events from a safe distance had expected to see blanks fired, but live ammunition was used, killing four people and injuring others, three of them seriously.

Shocked local Chartists went to great pains to distance themselves from these events, but it is hard to believe that they had no complicity in the 'Relief

Column' that set out from Chorley on the following Wednesday. With troops guarding the Ribble bridges and the curious festooning the tower of the Parish Church tower to spy its approach, a hostile mob forced the plugs from the boilers at the Farington and Bamber Bridge mills. Having smashed 1,300 panes of glass at Withy Trees Mill and stormed the adjacent workhouse, the mob reached Walton and 'stopped' William Calvert's Flatts Mill. As they approached the bridge rural constables under the orders of THOMAS BATTY ADDISON dispersed them, with the military standing by. Richard Marsden was arrested but released without charge. 'And so terminated', rejoiced the *Preston Chronicle*, 'the apprehended sacking of Preston by the Battle of Walton Bridge'.

A trade revival subdued the movement, but a return of hard times in 1846 stimulated it to a last revival. Buoyed by the success of the revolution in France early in 1848 an enthusiastic meeting again elected Marsden to represent the town at the National Convention. The third and final petition was rejected and support for the Chartist movement slipped away. Yet, in time all but one of the six proposals became law, and their Chartist experiences were to prove to be the making of the generation of responsible trade union and labour leaders who emerged and achieved so much after 1860.

J E King (1981) *Richard Marsden and the Preston Chartists: 1837-48* (1981).

CHARTULARY OF COCKERSAND ABBEY

A chartulary was a bound register of land deeds. A number of abbeys owned parcels of land in medieval Preston, among them the small abbey by the mouth of the River Lune at Cockersand. Once the abode of 'Hugh the Hermit' the abbey was established by papal bull in 1190. Large numbers of people gave it money 'for the health of their souls', and in 1267 one of the brothers - Brother Robert - began work on the chartulary, completing it the following year. The donations usually took the form of individual field strips in the large open fields around the town (such as Platford Dales or the Avenham), but Alice of Ashton left a larger plot in Tulketh. The location of these plots is often difficult to work out today. For example, her land boundary started at six ash trees then passed north along to an old oak tree, then south-west to old William of Tulketh's old hedge, to a stream eastward 'to a pit digged there', then south to the RIBBLE, then east, then north back to her six trees!

W Farrer, *The Cockersand Chartulary* (1898).

CHURCHGATE (PRE-17TH CENTURY) OR CHURCH STREET

Saxon in origin and site of the parish church (the MINSTER) and perhaps the first market, the track followed the prominent ridge which rises above the

Former burgage plots to the south of Church St (J J Myres's map of 1836: paper on canvas)

Property along Avenham St (right) and Old Cock Yard (left) to the south of Church St, 2004. Demolition of a building reveals the precise dimensions of one of the ancient field strips on the rise between the Churchgate ridge and the Syke (photo: author).

Avenham fields to the south: the later medieval town was carefully laid out off and around it. This was Preston's oldest and most important 'street' and originally the main way through the town to the market, to the river (FISHERGATE), and northwards onto PRESTON MOOR (via the FRIARGATE). The length east of Manchester Road was known as Fenkel St, though DR KUERDEN noted that the name was passing out of use as early as the 1680s.

D Hunt, *A History of Preston* (1992).

See BURGAGE STRIP; WELLS.

CINEMAS

Motion pictures were probably introduced to Preston by Hugh Rain (alias 'WILL ONDA') after 1903. At first the short reels were simply shown as features at circus tents or on the bill of the music halls. Purposely designed buildings in which to show them only emerged some years later. The first specifically designated picture-house was Joseph Livesey's old Temperance Hall on North Road taken over by Rain in 1908. Such conversions were quite common, and even in the mid-1930s the warehouse at Calvert's India Mill on New Hall Lane was reborn as the Plaza (and has gone on to become a petrol station). By 1913 the town had thirteen converted halls, but a purpose-built cinema was not constructed until the PALLADIUM opened on Church St in 1915. The number of cinemas quickly grew to over twenty, and the 1930s saw the construction of an entirely new class of super-cinema - led by the NEW VICTORIA (1928) and the RITZ (1937). Preston's final central cinema to be built was the ABC, opened amidst much glitz in 1959.

The cinemas greatly reinforced and expanded the town centre's important leisure function, especially in the 'West End' area, and their decline had an equally serious impact on the pattern of use in the central area. Changing leisure habits saw theatres convert to cinemas in the 1920s, and with the advent of television cinemas converted to bingo halls in the 1960s. Few could have anticipated the phenomenal revival of cinema-going in the 1990s. This was based at motorcar-served out-of-town sites at Riversway (UCI) and the Capitol Centre at Walton-le-Dale (Warner Brothers), opened in 1990 and 1991 and with ten and eight screens respectively. By 1993 the Riversway site alone was attracting over 20,000 customers per week.

J Cotterall (1988) *Preston's Palaces of Pleasure* (1988). D Hindle (1999) *Twice Nightly: An Illustrated History of Entertainment in Preston* (1999).

CIVIL WAR (1642-1648)

The open conflict between the supporters of the Crown and Parliament arising out of the disputes of the 1630s. Preston was ostensibly 'For the King' and under the control of the Earl of Derby, but proved itself to be as flexible in this regard as the changing circumstances required. Both parties recruited support at a mass meeting held on Preston Moor in June 1642, but practical support for either side was disappointing. The town celebrated the Preston Guild of 1642 as normal, but divisions quickly emerged and by October Preston had in effect two mayors, the Royalist Adam Morte and the Parliamentary Edmund Worden. Having failed in an attack on Parliamentary Blackburn Sir Gilbert Hoghton retreated to Preston and chained up WALTON BRIDGE. During the evening of 7 February 1643 Sir John Seaton stormed up into the town, probably by way of Swillbrook. Adam Morte was killed in the fighting and windows along Church St were smashed by the jubilant Parliamentary soldiers.

Having burned Lancaster but failed to capture the castle, Lord Derby evaded a Parliamentary force at Ellel which had been sent from Preston to confront him, and barely a month later was able to recapture the town. Entering at night along Friargate he quickly took Preston. It was now the turn of Edmund Worden's house to be looted. In April a large Royalist force again set out to attack Parliamentary forces around Blackburn by way of Whalley. It was ambushed near Read Hall and thrown back in panic; it was said that Lord Derby did not rein in his horse until he reached Penwortham! Shortly after this he left for exile in the Isle of Man. Once again the Parliamentarians had control of Preston. By June 1643, after six months' fighting, the first civil war was effectively over in Lancashire. Yet there was one final interlude.

In 1644 Prince Rupert's large Royalist army passed through Lancashire en route to York and the Battle of Marston Moor. Lavishly but nervously entertained by the Corporation of Preston, the Prince was not impressed, famously remarking that 'Banquets are not fit for soldiers'. The Mayor and bailiffs were arrested and incarcerated in Skipton Castle from whence they were later extricated with great difficulty. Defeated by Cromwell in Yorkshire, fleeing parties of Royalists briefly regrouped in Preston before being driven out into the Fylde. Here the troops accompanied by their many 'strumpetts' went on a spree of looting, before finally escaping south by way of the ford at Freckleton.

In July 1648 the Duke of Hamilton marched a large if badly organized Scottish army south through Lancashire in support of the King. Cromwell had anticipated his approach down the east coast and was in Yorkshire, but quickly deployed his forces west to intercept the Scots on the Ribble crossing at Preston. On the evening of 16 August he camped at Stonyhurst, but his opponent's army was stretched out between Wigan (cavalry) and Garstang (rearguard). During the wettest summer in living memory the river was in flood, and the capture of the Ribble bridge would be central to the outcome of the following day's battle. Fighting began just before noon along Ribbleton Lane close by Gamull Lane. Hamilton could not be convinced that this was in fact Cromwell's main force, and failed to reinforce his well-positioned troops. After four hours the New Model Army was able to push through to Preston and drive across the Ribble and Darwen bridges, cutting the Royalist force into two. Cromwell himself was said to have narrowly escaped death during fighting at the foot of Swillbrook. On the evening of the 17th his men occupied the houses at Walton Green, then they moved south to Wigan where the Royalist remnants were finally destroyed. Six months later, as a direct consequence of the 'Battle of Ribbleton and Walton Bridge', Charles I was executed.

The orderly march south of future Charles II via Preston to defeat at Worcester (1651) provides an interesting footnote to these events, and reveals a good a deal about their impact on local opinion:

The young king road through every streete to be seen of the people. yet it was observed that he received small intertainement there, only one woman who seemed to show more respect to him than all the towne besides which it was said was some greef to him.

E Broxap, *The Great Civil War in Lancashire* (1910). D Hunt, *A History of Preston* (1992). R Holmes, *Preston 1648* (1985). See especially Stephen Bull's *The Battle of Preston 1648* (1998).

CLAY, JOHN (1796-1858)

Prison chaplain and social reformer. Born in Liverpool and apprenticed to a commercial firm, Clay was encouraged to join the church by John Swainson, a member of the great cotton dynasty of Cooper Hill, Walton-le-Dale, and a fellow archery enthusiast. Whilst curate at Walton, Clay was appointed first assistant, and subsequently chaplain, to Preston prison (1823). His progressive, positive and reformist attitude to the treatment of prisoners was in marked contrast to the treadmill and other punitive notions prevailing at Preston, and Clay found himself in fairly constant conflict with the authorities there. He was however supported in his views by THOMAS BATTY ADDISON (chairman of the local magistrates), and played a full part in the progressive forces and movements of all kinds which became such a powerful force for change in the Preston of the 1830s and 1840s.

Clay took a direct interest in the lives and life histories of his confined flock, spending many hours each day in conversation with them in their cells. His mission was to convert and educate them, but also to train them for their lives beyond confinement and find employment for them. One of the great Victorian social researchers, he sought to identify the factors (poor parenting, lack of religious and general education, bad company, drunkenness, etc.) which had brought about their demise. He became a recognized authority on his subject and his views carried weight at the highest level. Though amateur, his reports are models of Victorian statistical analysis, and his oft-quoted *Report on the Sanitary Condition of Preston* (1842) famously established the life expectancy at birth of the poorest Prestonians ('surrounded by the miasmata generated in filth and putridity . . . with minds sunk in ignorance') as 18 years, whilst even the richest could 'look forward' to just 47 years. His son, Alfred Borron Clay (1831-68), was a noted historical genre painter.

Rev John Clay (1795-1858). Social reformer and archery enthusiast (from W L Clay, The Prison Chaplain: A Memoir of John Clay, 1861).

W L Clay, *The Prison Chaplain: A Memoir of the Rev John Clay* (1861). M DeLacy, *Prison Reform in Lancashire* (1986). *ODNB*

See HOUSING.

COBBETT, WILLIAM (1763-1835)

Journalist and champion of traditional rights; unsuccessful candidate at the 1826 Preston election. By a roundabout route this most conservative of thinkers came to see political radicalism as a means of challenging the new industrial order. His attempts to win a parliamentary seat at Coventry in 1820 and Preston in 1826 finally met with success at Oldham in 1832, and he was an important contributor to the Reform Bill campaign. Facing E G Stanley (subsequently thrice Premier of Britain) for the family seat at Preston he could only manage to trail in fourth. Enormous sums had been spent by the Stanleys - 'The town presented a complete Saturnalia' - and Cobbett could boast to the crowd that 'I have done much good to you by coming. I have sweated your tyrants ... I have made the silly Honourable throw £15,000 among you!' A colourful picture of local politics was duly recorded in his *Political Register*, with 'old SAM HORROCKS' in particular earning his invective from the hustings.

W Dobson (1868) *Parliamentary Representation of Preston* (1868). S M Hunt, 'The Radical Party in Preston 1815-32' (unpublished thesis, 1950, copy in LRO). W Urbanski, 'Parliamentary Politics in an Industrial Borough: Preston' (unpublished Ph.D. thesis, Atlanta, Ga., copy in LRO).

COLD WAR (1947-1991)

The pre-eminent international concern of the second half of the twentieth century. See CUBAN MISSILE CRISIS; TOP SECRET PRESTON.

COMPLAINTS ABOUT THE ROADS

Historically it was the Preston-Wigan road (A49) that was singled out for criticism. In 1648, having left Preston by the Ribble and Darwen bridges in pursuit of the broken Royalist army, Oliver Cromwell wrote:

> We lay that night in a field close by the enemy (near Wigan) being very dirty and weary, having marched twelve miles of such ground as I never rode in all my life, the day being very wet.

The route was even worse a century later as the great traveller Arthur Young recorded in 1770:

> I know not, in the whole range of language, terms sufficiently expressive to describe this infernal highway. Let me most seriously caution all travellers ... to avoid it as they would the devil, for a thousand to one but they break their necks or their limbs by overthrows of breakings down. They will here meet with ruts which I actually measured four feet deep, and floating with mud only from a wet summer. What must it therefore be in winter?

C Hardwick, *History of the Borough of Preston* (1857).

CONVALESCENT HOSPITAL, MOOR PARK
At the outbreak of the First World War Preston had a shortage of military beds, so the Royal Lancashire Agricultural Show's pavilion was brought from Blackpool, re-erected on Moor Park and run by the Voluntary Aid Detachment. It held 35 beds but was extended to house a complement of 174 beds and 17 nurses, catering for 1,150 patients per year. After the war the wooden buildings were dismantled but a section still serves in Strand Road as home to the Preston Sea Scouts.
H Cartmell, *For Remembrance: An Account of Some Fateful Years* (1919).

CORBISHLEY, THOMAS (1903-1976)
Jesuit, theologian and pioneer of the Ecumenical Movement. Born in Preston, he was educated at Preston Catholic College, Stonyhurst and Oxford University before joining the teaching staff at Stonyhurst in 1930. By the time of his ordination (1936) he had established himself as a classical scholar, but by 1939 had become active in the early moves towards greater church unity promoted by Archbishop Temple and Cardinal Hinsley. A popular theologian and academic, his books included *Roman Catholicism* (1950), and *The Spirituality of Teilhard de Chardin* (1971), but this unassuming man is best remembered for his ecumenical work.
ODNB.

CORN EXCHANGE OR PUBLIC HALL, LUNE ST
The site of the town's corn and other markets, later developed as Preston's largest meeting room - the Public Hall. Building work on the splendidly Georgian Corn Exchange began in 1821, the rooms were used at the 1822 Guild, and the building was completed in 1824. Located at the canal terminus and overlooked by the wharfside warehouses, this was a convenient site for the agricultural produce markets, notably butter and eggs. The open space at the back of the exchange was developed as a public meeting place and photographs of the Golden Jubilee of the Temperance Movement celebrations show the galleries and stage thronged with people, but in the open air. In 1881-2 the area was roofed over to form what Hewitson thought was the largest hall in Lancashire. This served as the town's principal public meeting place for events of all kinds until its closure in 1973, and demolition in 1990 ahead of the completion of the inner ring-road. Lit by no less than 230 gas jets, it had a gallery on three sides and capacity for 3,564 people: 1,957 downstairs, 807 in the gallery and 800 standing. The room had a sprung ballroom floor and was dominated by the enormous organ built by Wilkinsons of Kendal (3,673 pipes, 66 draw stops) with a water-powered hydraulic engine. It must have been the most remarkable cargo ever moved on the canal as it was shipped down from Kendal to the adjacent wharf!

Many leading artists and politicians performed here; a joyous crowd of 5,000 welcomed the FA Cup's first visit to Preston in 1889, cinema was first demonstrated here in 1903, and during the first days of the First World War men from all over the country were billeted here. Among the world's greatest artistes to appear at the hall were Ignaly Paderewski, Anna Pavlova, Anton Rubinstein, Myra Hess, Fritz Kreisler, Clara Butt, Nellie Melba and Paul Robeson. The packed arena could generate tremendous atmosphere, and both SIR JOHN BARBIROLLI (Halle) and Sir Charles Groves (Liverpool Philharmonic) performed here with great aplomb in the 1950s and 1960s, and on occasion Sir Thomas Beecham (an ardent Blackburn Rovers supporter) would address the concert-goers directly above the noise of the encircling traffic.

The pop stars also came, among them the Inkspots, Fats Domino, Cliff Richard, Adam Faith and the BEATLES. Most of Britain's leading politicians appeared here; Churchill's men-only meeting in 1913 was stormed by suffragettes who fastened themselves to the seats, Oswald Mosley addressed a mass meeting more suited to contemporary Munich than Lune St, and during the 1945 general election Aneurin Bevan promised 'to bring the Temple down on the Tories heads!' With closure and demolition the centre of these activities shifted to the Guild Hall, but the great success of the old Public Hall emphasizes the remarkable vitality of Preston's musical and cultural life throughout the cotton trade's depression years.

D Hindle (1999) *Twice Nightly: An Illustrated History of Entertainment in Preston* (1999).

COTTON INDUSTRY

The town's industrial staple for 150 years, from *c*.1790-*c*.1940. Initially the industry in Preston progressed rather slowly. The town itself was not blessed with swiftly flowing streams and a variety of power sources had to be utilised - a windmill (at Collinson & Watson's factory), a donkey at John Horrocks's - but in most cases the early spinning devices were turned by hand. Steam held the key to Preston's rapid growth, and after 1803 all new mills were steam-powered. Yet though JOHN HORROCKS was the largest spinning firm in the world, growth in the next two decades remained sluggish, with just nine new mills built by 1820. The boom of 1825 saw intensive investment, and production increased accordingly. Preston's geographical advantages asserted themselves, and the town's mills became a magnet for labour migrants from the surrounding agricultural districts - particularly of the Fylde. Preston wages were significantly lower than those of the manufacturing district to the south, giving the local mill owners a significant advantage. Indeed, the town's labour costs were among the lowest in the county, and labour disputes here (particularly the SPINNERS STRIKE OF 1836 and the LOCK-OUT OF 1853-4) set the pattern regionally and were usually the most desperate.

1830-1865: boom town

The most marked period of expansion now followed, and Preston was the boom town of the early 1830s. Houses were thrown up 'to shelter the workers', and the resulting housing problems would dog the town for the next century. The nature of the industry began to change: the family-run firm passed to the ownership of shareholders and directors, whilst the wholesale mechanisation of weaving in the 1830s led to the emergence of combined spinning and weaving firms. These dominated the industry until the 1880s when a trend to the separation of the two processes became apparent. Mills erected in this period include Fishwick (1823), Brunswick Mill (1826) and Greenbank (1835). Leonard Horner, the factory inspector, listed 42 mills in 1842, employing about a fifth of the town. These comprised 15 spinning mills (2,527 operatives) and a further 5 mills doubling yarn, 3 weaving mills and 15 combined firms (6,639 operatives with 1,422 at Horrockses); 4 mills were not running. The rise of the power loom is more apparent in the employment figures, with 2,432 people on the spinning side and three times that number weaving. The bulk of the workforce was under 30 years of age and over half were women.

The 1850s and early 1860s saw a further spurt of mill building, including Higher Walton (1850, 1860), New Preston (1851), New Hall Lane (1856), Shelley Road and Queens Mill (1861). By 1850 Preston had 64 firms employing 20,000-25,000 people or a third of the population. Their 1,100,000 spindles spun 800,000lb of No. 32 yarn and 2,000 power looms wove 90,000 'Indian shirtings' - every week. But long-term changes were already becoming apparent, and Horrockses apart, the export market for finer fabrics (the 'fine end' of the trade) was already slipping away to American and European rivals, and the Preston mills were forced to specialize in supplying heavy cloths to the Indian and Chinese markets (the 'coarse end'). Clearly any upset in these markets could have disastrous consequences in what had dangerously become a 'one-industry town'. In the early 1860s over-expansion, speculation and the failure of the monsoon brought about the 'Cotton Panic' or, as it has become better known, the LANCASHIRE COTTON FAMINE. In a stark warning for the 1930s, much of the town's industry closed or at best ran half-time.

1865-1913: hurrah for a life in the factory!

Recovery came in the late 1860s but Preston's era of rapid growth had passed, and Oldham and Bolton were the new boom towns. The timing of these phases of growth had important consequences for the balance of a town's industrial base. Preston's development had preceded the booms in weaving (1850s) and spinning (1890s) and was relatively diverse, so that the town ranked as both the fourth spinning town and the third weaver after

Burnley and Blackburn. It also followed that much of the town's mill architecture dated from before the 1850s. Curiously, this was a period when square mill chimneys (rather than round ones after 1860) were the norm, and Preston was famous for them. A craze to build the tallest chimney developed; the surviving New Preston lumb reached 63yds, Greenbank 80yds, and Higher Walton 90yds. As Colin Dickinson has demonstrated, ever more powerful steam engines and the use of modern steel-framed construction techniques enabled the emergence of super mills in the years before the First World War. It marked a shift back to separate spinning and weaving operations and though particularly associated with Oldham and Bolton it had architecturally spectacular consequences in Preston.

Behind its conservative italianate façade, Horrockses' £125,000 Centenary Mill (opened in 1895) was a radical departure from all that had gone before; it was a modern steel and concrete building and the enormous £7,000 engine also drove electricity generators. Cliff Mill in Dundonald St followed in 1904, Tulketh two years later and the 'New Factory' at Bamber Bridge in 1907. All were specialized spinning mills. Tulketh was immense, it had among the largest spinning rooms in Lancashire, and required over 400 feet of rope belting to turn the 140,000 spindles. The mill lodges held one and three-quarter million gallons of water and 1,750 gallons of hot water left the engine condenser each minute. By contrast to these gracefully high steel and glass structures, the new generation of weaving mills were single-storey, and seven new sites were established in the decade before 1914. These included Stocks Bridge (1904), Emerson Road Mill (1907) and Bute Mill (1910).

1913-1945: boom and bust

1913 was the 'annus mirabilis' of the Lancashire cotton trade; over two billion pounds of cotton were consumed and seven billion yards of cloth exported. The Japanese spinning industry was still only about seven times the size of Horrockses, Crewdsons & Co., and although India's domestic industry had trebled in size since 1900 the Subcontinent was still a crucial market, taking two-thirds of Lancashire's output. The war brought perhaps the industry's most profitable boom, as early as 1917 Horrockses had won war orders worth £800,000, and in the years to 1919 declared profits of half a million each year! Peace brought enormous demand to restock war-starved markets and even greater profits followed. A craze for cotton mill shares developed in 1919, take-overs at inflated prices were common and saddled the new owners with enormous mortgage payments. When bust followed boom many were ruined and the trade never recovered. By 1928 it was also clear that the great export trade had been lost for ever, and even Horrockses was probably technically bankrupt.

The war had masked an intensification of the long-term shift of the trading advantage away from 'Lancashire'. By 1928 Britain's share of world textile production had fallen by a third, largely due to the rise of the Indian industry which enjoyed tariff protection after 1930. Chinese domestic manufacture was also increasing. For towns depending on these markets the result was not long delayed: 'We all know how this affected Preston', J H Spencer wrote in 1941, 'all the mills serving the Indian and Chinese markets have closed down, and especially our local trade, is confined to the finer counts and specialised fabrics'. By 1940 around twenty mills had closed, wage reductions led to bitter strikes and parents urged their children to find alternative careers. In these circumstances it is perhaps surprising that the industry survived as long as it did: in 1929 textiles accounted for half of the jobs (25,000) in the Preston Employment Area (a district which included Garstang and Fulwood, but not South Ribble), by 1939 it had fallen to a quarter, and by 1946 to 16 per cent. Alternatively the development of the great COURTAULD FACTORY at Red Scar marked the emergence of an important man-made fibres sector which would prosper until the late 1970s.

1945-1979: weaving out

The Second World War brought some respite, and production was 'concentrated' into efficient mills. Once again demand for war goods soared, and cloth prices advanced by a third at the outbreak of war. It was reported in December 1939 that every mill that was capable of doing so was running at full capacity, and a labour shortage had developed. With foreign rivals

Employees leaving the Yard Works, 1905.

destroyed, the end of the war brought increased exports, and it was hoped that a streamlined industry would be able to keep the high-quality home market in which Preston had a number of 'household names'. The post-war boom lasted until 1951 and from the mid-1950s mill closures resumed with Queens Mill. During 1958 alone six mills had closed by August and Preston was now fast weaving out: nationally 344 had gone since 1955. Horrockses was taken over in 1960 and the celebrated Yard Works closed in 1962. Expensive plans to modernize Tulketh failed in the late 1960s, though a number of firms survived a little longer. King Cotton had left Lancashire and returned home to the sunnier climes from where the endeavours of Arkwright & Co. had tempted him two hundred years before.

D Hunt, *A History of Preston* (1992). F Harrison, 'Industrial Preston through Slump and War' (1994, unpublished but available in the LRO and the Central Reference Library). C Dickinson, *Cotton Mills of Preston: The Power behind the Thread* (2002). M Rose (ed.), *The Lancashire Cotton Industry: A History since 1700* (1996). G. Timmins, *Four Centuries of Lancashire Cotton* (1996)

See Sir Richard Arkwright; Handloom Weaving; Samuel Horrocks; Cyril Lord; Thomas Miller Senior; Thomas Miller Junior; Mosney; John Watson & Sons.

COURT LEET

An institution of Saxon origin. It was essentially a meeting of 'angry ratepayers' who assembled to punish wrongdoers - from interlopers into the town's trade ('Forrainers'), to idle council employees and the owners of annoying dogs ('Insufferable dogges'). The accused had no proper right of defence, they were simply wrongdoers who were to be punished. The Court comprised a jury presided over by the Mayor, and appointed its own officers to supervise the operation of the rights enshrined by royal charter and common usage: they checked the strength of the local ale (the Preston Yard), the weight of the Preston loaf, organized the cleaning of streets, upheld public morals, supervised the operation of the townlands and regulated the movement of animals around the common fields. They were always very eager to get their work done as cheaply as possible and George Werden (Worden) found himself their multifunctionary in the 1650s, with predictable reward:

> George Werden is continued beidle and scavenger, is very negligent therein, and the Towne is full every day of Country poor, and the said office altogether neglected, to ye discredit of our towne and hindrance of our owne poore. Also . . . ye said George Werden is swyneard, also receivinge wages for Both and performing neither.

In a town in which every inhabitant was a potential informer, the records of the Court Leet provide a fascinating insight into the life of pre-industrial Preston.

A Hewitson, *Preston Court Leet Records* (1905).

COURTAULD FACTORY

The Red Scar Works was the largest rayon factory in the world. Although the cotton trade declined steadily in the inter-war years, the period saw considerable progress in the development of man-made fibres. At the height of the depression an enormous effort was made to secure for Preston the gigantic rayon plant that Courtaulds were known to be planning. Land at Red Scar was secured in 1929, but in 1933 the firm decided not to proceed, only to reverse their decision and opt for 'a full size mill' at Preston two years later. By April 1938 £2 million had been spent, and 4.3 million lb of viscose yarn was produced in the first year (1939), rising to over 10 million lb in the next. During the post-war period the factory became an important employer of immigrant labour, and at its peak employed 3,800 people. Closure with loss of the remaining 2,600 jobs in 1979 (a terrible year for Preston manufacturing) was thus a serious blow to the town.

Lancashire Evening Post (1 Jan., 21 Nov. 1938).

CUBAN MISSILE CRISIS (14-28 OCTOBER 1962)

The major danger point during the Cold War (1947-91). On 13 October North End disposed of Scunthorpe United 3-1 (Dawson 2, Alston) in front of a crowd of 10,107 at Deepdale. The following day U-2 spyplanes proved the existence of Russian missile sites on Cuba, Kennedy was advised to launch strikes against them and world affairs had suddenly entered their most deadly phase of the second half of the twentieth century. Hostilities would have inevitably involved Britain, and key targets in the North-West (such as the US airbase at Burtonwood, Liverpool Docks, and the urban-industrial conurbation at Manchester) would have been attacked with disastrous consequences for Prestonians. It was estimated that a 25-megaton bomb dropped on Manchester would devastate much of the region; woodwork would spontaneously ignite at Blackburn 20 miles away, and clothing burst into flames 30 miles away in Preston. The town has a very exposed position and clearly an attack on the potential targets at the Warton and Samlesbury airfields would have ended this history somewhat prematurely. In the event Kennedy warned Kruschchev of the potential consequences, war seemed imminent over the 22nd and 23rd but on the 24th Russian ships carrying missiles to Cuba suddenly turned back. Russian missile sites in Cuba and American sites in Turkey were eventually dismantled. The day after Kruschchev's agreement to remove the installations (28 October) North End won their cup replay against Northampton Town 2-1 (Alston, Dawson) - a game that might never have taken place. People in the crowd of 7,040 at Deepdale were largely unaware of just how close their town and country had been to total destruction.

CUCKSTOOL (OR DUCKING STOOL)

A punishment usually - but not universally - reserved for female gossips and petty criminals. It comprised a secure seat fastened at the end of long timbers, which could be swung out over deep water and raised and lowered to 'duck' the victim. In Preston the ancient CUSTOMAL prescribed that a burgess who persistently sold 'underweight' bread or ale should be sent to the cuckstool for his fourth offence. The seemingly much used mechanism caused the authorities no end of trouble, and the bailiffs were frequently fined for not having it in good repair. In 1704, for example, they were accused of not providing 'a Sufficient Ladder at the ducking stool'. A number of separate pits seem to have been used; in March 1654 the Court Leet ordered the bailiffs to 'erect and cause a cukstoole sett upon the wall of the washinge pool, else to pay 3/4d'. The 'Cuckstool' field-name occurs on a number of

maps in the vicinity of Schleswig and Holstein Sts, where a fragment of this machine seems to have survived up to 1826. The pits here may have originated in the excavations left by earlier 'brick-getters'. One was known as the 'Washing Pool', though another example - the 'Washing Stead' - was located where the Swillbrook enters the Ribble; the 'Old Cuckstool Pitt' near the Swillbrook is mentioned in a document of 1701. Clearly the cuckstool was moved from place to place over time in search of likely deep waters. There seems to have been a steady demand for its services.

A Hewitson, *History of Preston* (1883); *Preston Court Leet Records* (1905).

Coins of the Cuerdale Hoard. At the time of its discovery in 1840 (and for some time after) the Norse silver trove was the largest treasure found in England (from Numismatic Chronicle *(1842), 'Cuerdale Coins')*

CUERDALE HOARD

One of the largest treasures ever found in Britain came to light in 1840 during flood repair work along the Ribble at Cuerdale. A lead-lined chest had contained money bags holding 7,000 silver coins, cut-up jewellery, and small bars of silver bullion - in all around 1,300 ounces. The latest coins suggest a date of around AD 905, indicating that the hoard may be related to the expulsion of the Norse from Dublin and their brief interlude in Lancashire (the hoard contained over 40 Irish brooches). The truth of how this remarkable treasure came to rest in the banks of the Ribble and why it was never recovered may never be known, but it provides an intriguing glimpse into the wider Norse world. Indeed, some of the coins may have circulated among the market traders of Constantinople and Araby.

Preston Chronicle (22 Aug. 1840). F A Philpott (1990) *A Silver Saga: Viking Treasure from the North-West* (1990). J Graham-Campbell (ed.), *Viking Treasure from the North-West: The Cuerdale Hoard in its Context* (1992).

CUSTOMAL

The Customal, or 'Ordnances of the Preston Gild', is one of the town's most interesting documents. In forty-seven clauses listed in a crabbed hand on a single page it codifies the townspeople's rights as they had evolved by around 1300: 'These are the Liberties of Preston in Aumundernesse...' The burgesses regulated their monopoly of the town's trade through an institution called the GUILD MERCHANT ('Gilda Mercatoria'), for 'no one who is not of that Gild shall make and merchandise in the said town'. To become a member of this clique an outsider had to make formal application to the existing members or burgesses. Membership brought with it the grant of a BURGAGE on which to build a house, and gave him the right to graze his animals on the TOWNFIELDS. In practice most applicants were the sons of existing burgesses.

The Customal extends into all areas of life, from the price of the Prestonian's beloved ale, to just how serious a wound on a fellow burgess had to be to attract a large fine: 'For every hidden cut of a thumb's breadth 4d: for every open or visible wound 8d'. A burgess could marry his daughter or granddaughter to whoever he liked, and if he should die suddenly his family could have his possessions 'unless he has been publicly excommunicated'. The wives of burgesses also had some measure of legal rights; on their husband's death they could marry who they liked, and should their good reputation be questioned ('If anyone call a woman a whore...') and this be found unsubstantiated, the slanderer should be fined 3 shillings, unless 'he shall take himself by the nose and say that he hath spoken a lie'.

H W Clemesha, *History of Preston in Amounderness* (1912). A Crosby, *History of Preston Guild* (1992).

D

DEEPDALE

Probably the oldest professional football ground in the world, the Theatre of FINNEY. The development of Moor Park in the 1860s led the North End cricket club to rent the Corporation's 'Old Hey Field' for use as a private ground. They built a 'pavilion' of sorts, and did their best to even out the

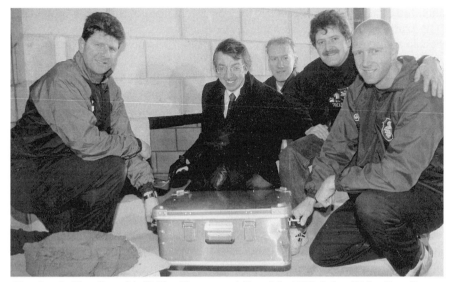

'Burying the Time Capsule', Sir Tom Finney stand, Deepdale, 1997. Left to Right: Gary Peters, Bryan Gray, David Robinson, a representative of the supporters, Andy Saville.

medieval undulations in the former oat-field. They diversified into winter sports to help to pay the rent and a banking about 12 feet high was heaped around the sports surface and two narrow timber 'grandstands' were erected along the west side adjacent to 'Mr.Sudell's dressing tent' at the NW corner. This fearful firehazard and deathtrap hosted crowds of around 4,000 during the 'Invincible' era, rising to 10,000 for derby games. The early years of the twentieth century saw a steady improvement with the construction of the Town End (1904), West Stand (1906), Spion Kop (1921) and the east Pavilions (1935-9). After the Second World War the club's sporting success was not matched by rebuilding; and successive financial crises postponed the wholesale reconstruction of the arena until the 1990s when Ben Casey designed the essentially Italian stadium which today graces the Old Hey Field.

D Hunt, *A History of Preston North End Football Club: The Power, the Politics and the People* (2000).

See PUBLIC PARKS; PRESTON NORTH END; WILLIAM SUDELL.

DEEPDALE, BATTLE OF (4 NOVEMBER 1315)
A serious uprising, with strong support from the west of the county, against Edmund Earl of Lancaster resulted in a pitched battle on the eastern edge of Preston Moor in the environs of Deepdale. In barely more than ninety

minutes the locals were trounced, and a week later their leaders (Thomas and Adam Banaster, and Henry de Lea) were beheaded on Leyland Moor at a point close by the junction of Heald House Lane and the A49. The supporters of the uprising were severely punished.

W Farrer and J Brownhill, *Victoria County History of Lancashire*, vol. 2 (1906).

DELTIC

'The King of Diesel Locomotives', built at the English Electric West Works, Strand Road, Preston. Work began on the prototype in November 1951, and 'Deltic' (so-called from 'delta' - the Greek letter 'D' - a triangle similar to the engine's configuration) entered service in March 1961. After 200,000 miles of service the futuristic engine was retired to the Science Museum in April 1963, before moving to York in 2004. By this time the production series of twenty-two Class 55 locomotives had 'revolutionised East Coast main line services' out of Kings Cross. The 100-ton twin-engined units could produce 3,300bhp, with the 18-cylinder Napier Delta engines idling at 700rpm (faster than most diesels at maximum), and could run up to 1,500rpm. Indeed their withdrawal from service (1980-2) was partly due to the fact that British Rail could envisage no service that would require such powerful engines! The

The prototype 'Deltic' locomotive nears completion in the West Works of the English Electric Company, Strand Road (photo: BAE Systems Heritage Group, Warton).

Deltic was the first train to be maintained by component replacement, and an engine could be changed in a single day, enabling one of the locomotives to clock up two million miles in just twelve years. A thriving Delta Preservation Society based at Westhoughton exists to care for and promote the surviving engines.

www.thedps.co.uk

DERBY INTEREST

The Stanley family acquired lands in Preston on the creation of Thomas Stanley as the first Earl of Derby in 1489. The subsequent relationship of earls and town was to be a fruitful one for each, and was to endure until 1830. Preston's value to the family lay in its rising significance as the de facto county town, and the two members it could send to Parliament. The Stanleys provided civic prestige and patronage. During the CIVIL WAR Preston was very much Lord Derby's town, and though frequently at odds with the 'Tory' town council successive earls seem to have been genuinely popular among the townspeople. In 1688 Sir Thomas Stanley (a junior member of the family) married Elizabeth Patten. She brought with her extensive landholdings in Preston and PATTEN HOUSE, which duly became the centre of the Derby Interest in the town. Their son ultimately succeeded as the 11th Earl in 1736.

Subsequent years saw the golden age of the Derby Interest; Preston Guild became a major regional event, and the prosperous country town developed attractions capable of supporting its own social season. The Stanleys sponsored the local horse races, cock fighting and charities of all kinds. They could well afford to, for as the Industrial Revolution gathered momentum in the 1780s the value of the family estate rose steadily to reach around £100,000 per year in 1800. Throughout these years the town's political support was maintained, so when JOHN HORROCKS emerged as a strong Tory threat to their position the Stanleys provided a mill (the Lords Mill on Church St) for his Whig rival JOHN WATSON. At the height of the contest the two parties even had their own party sedan chairs.

In 1830, however, E G Stanley was defeated by the radical HENRY HUNT. Local Tories, disgusted by Stanley's support for even a very moderate Reform Act, had voted for their arch-enemy Hunt! The response was immediate; Patten House was sold and the family withdrew from Preston. The future 14th Earl and thrice Premier of Britain wrote:

> Gentlemen, a Parliamentary connection has, for many years subsisted between your borough and the family to which I belong, which I had hoped had not been unproductive of advantage to the town of Preston. The rupture of that connection has been your act. I acquiesce in your decision, and shall make no attempt in future to renew it.

J J Bagley, *The Earls of Derby* (1985). W Dobson (1868) *Parliamentary Representation of Preston*

(1868). H W Clemesha, *History of Preston in Amounderness* (1912). For details of the important Stanley Estate within Preston, see D Hunt, *A History of Preston* (1992).

DEVIS FAMILY OF PAINTERS (1712-1822)

The family comprised Arthur Devis (1712-87) portrait painter; his half-brother Anthony Devis (1729-1816/17) who painted landscapes; and Arthur's sons Thomas Anthony Devis (1751-1810) and Arthur William Devis (1762-1822). Their most famous work is the latter's celebrated *Death of Nelson*. They quickly fell out of fashion following their deaths but appreciation of the family's work has grown steadily since the 1930s, and their paintings are at the heart of the Harris Museum's fine art collection.

S H Paviere, *The Devis Family of Painters* (1950). S Sartin, *Polite Society by Arthur Devis, 1712-1787: Portraits of the English Country Gentleman and his Family* (Harris Museum exhibition catalogue, 1983). S.Whittle, *Arthur William Devis* (Harris Museum exhibition catalogue, 2000).

Anthony Devis (1729-1816/17)

Landscape painter. Born in Preston, he was described at the 1742 Guild as 'of London, Painter'. He exhibited at the Royal Academy in 1772 and 1781.
ODNB: 'Arthur Devis'.

Arthur Devis (1712-1787)

Portrait painter specializing in gentry groups. Born in Preston the son of a town councillor, Arthur is described in the 1742 Guild Roll as 'of London, portrait painter'. His earliest surviving painting is *Hoghton Tower* painted in 1735. A student of the seventeenth-century Dutch artists he specialized in painting carefully planned groups or 'Conversation Pieces' (detailed figures accompanied by their family and possessions, set within their home or estate). He produced a large number of such works (over 300), and is today regarded as a master of painting the eighteenth-century English gentry.
ODNB: 'Arthur Devis'.

Arthur William Devis (1762-1822)

Portrait painter. He was trained by his father and at the Royal Academy Schools. He is particularly important for his Indian paintings, a country he reached following his remarkable voyage as map-maker for the East India Company on the *Antelope*. The trip through the South China Sea included an attack by natives (in which Devis was injured), shipwreck and eventual escape on a boat fashioned from the wreck: all duly recorded by the voyage's painter. Devis decided to stay in India (1784), where he produced an important series of landscapes and found himself in great demand among the British elite as a portrait painter. In 1792 he was paid £2,500 for his *Lord Cornwallis receiving the sons of Tipu Sultan as hostages*. Returning to London he tried to establish his career in England, but was dogged by financial problems, and was eventually imprisoned for bankruptcy in 1804. On his release he painted his greatest work, the oft-reproduced *Death of Nelson* and his career revived. For this work he sailed on the *Victory*, examined Nelson's body and watched the removal of the bullet from it, met and painted the witnesses at the melancholic event, and carefully worked out where each had been positioned! Though he went on to achieve modest success as a painter of child portraits, enjoyed a degree of royal patronage and produced a number of large-scale works he was denied the Associateship of the Royal Academy on the grounds of his 'irregular living'.

ODNB: 'Arthur William Devis'.

DICK, KERR

One of the town's major twentieth-century employers and the forerunner of BAE Systems (via English Electric, the British Aircraft Corporation and British Aerospace). Works along the east side of Strand Road were developed by the North of England Carriage & Iron Co. (1867-78) on land facing the open river. The enterprise was a natural development of the west end's heavy engineering industry, based on iron founding and ship building and repairing. The partnership of W B Dick and John Kerr was formed in Kilmarnock in 1875, and though the former soon disappeared from the scene, a subsidiary of the firm took over the Strand Road site in 1898. This duly became the Electric Railway and Tramway Carriage Works Ltd, or more popularly 'Dick, Kerr's'. The Preston plant with its capacity of 800 vehicles a year and workforce of 600-800 men developed rapidly in the fast-growing urban transport market. When the firm decided to produce their own drive units (rather than import them from America) a second Preston firm was formed - the English Electric Manufacturing Co. - based across Strand Road at the West Works (1903).

Enormously expanded WAR PRODUCTION (1914-1918) saw employment soar to 8,000. In addition to wartime munitions the firm had begun its long association with aircraft production with manufacture of the Felixstowe F3 flying boat. Progress was rapid, and a site at Lytham provided land for new hangers and direct access to the estuary. Consolidation in 1918 saw the amalgamation of the various Dick, Kerr interests into English Electric and the firm returned to its more prosaic activities - supplying Blackpool's famous trams in 1933-9. The depression had seen the closure of the West Works, but rearmament began a second cycle of spectacular growth after 1937. Employment which had stood at 1,000 in 1938 soared to over 13,000 by 1942, and the civil aerodrome at Samlesbury was taken over for the production of Hampden and Halifax bombers. After the war the East Works, Samlesbury and the former American base at Warton naturally progressed to

English Electric's (Dick, Kerr) Works from the air c.1950. Strand Road runs from bottom left to top right. The Chimney on the right is Spa Mill, part of the company's site, and Preston Dock is off to the left. (photo: BAE Systems Heritage Group, Warton).

the manufacture of advanced jet aircraft; the VAMPIRE was followed by the CANBERRA, the Lightning, the TSR-2, the Jaguar and Tornado, and latterly the multinational Eurofighter or Typhoon. After the war the West Works specialized in the manufacture of heavy locomotives - famously producing the advanced DELTIC engine - and became a part of GEC in 1969.

W G S Hyde and F K Pearson, *The Dick, Kerr Album* (1973). R Fairclough and S Ransom, *English Electric Aircraft and their Predecessors* (1987). G Green, *British Aerospace: A Proud Heritage* (1988). The BAE Systems NW Heritage Group are based at Warton Aerodrome.

See YANKS.

DICK, KERR'S LADIES FOOTBALL TEAM (1917-1965)

In October 1917 Grace Sibbert, frustrated at the failings of the firm's male side, organized a match against fellow munitions workers at Coulthards to raise money for the Moor Park Hospital. On Christmas Day 1917 a 10,000 strong crowd saw the team play at DEEPDALE; in their black and white striped costumes - with 'natty close-fitting hats to match' - they were a novel sight in very difficult times. Under Alfred Frankland's management interest in their game grew, and in Lily Parr (1905-78) the Preston side had found a goal-scorer whose fierce shot was capable - when the honour of their side and sex demanded it - of smashing the arm of an antagonistic male goalkeeper! But others were noting the women's success...

In the post-war leisure boom enormous crowds began to follow this new development of the beautiful game, and in 1921 Dick, Kerr's Ladies swept aside the Rest Of The World 9-1 at Anfield in front of an enormous crowd, and over 40,000 saw them play at Goodison Park. Alert to the rise of a potential rival the Football Association took action to thwart future progress, ruling that 'The game of football is quite unsuitable for females'. But Dick, Kerr's continued unabashed, they toured the continent and North America, and in 1937 (playing as Preston Ladies) defeated their Edinburgh counterparts to secure the 'Championship of Great Britain and the World'. At this time their record was one that Messrs Wenger and Ferguson would envy: played 437, won 424, drawn 6, lost 7, goals for 2863, goals against just 207.

G J Newsham, *In a League of their own: Dick, Kerr's Ladies Football Team 1917-65* (1994).

The Dick, Kerr Ladies Football team.

DOMESDAY SURVEY (1086)

The Domesday scribes sought to describe and compare the ownership of land before and after the Norman Conquest. In short William I wanted to know precisely what he had won, and although the account of North-West England is patchy it is no less interesting for that. Preston had long been the 'capital manor' of Amounderness – in effect the ecclesiastical and administrative centre of the Fylde – and was quite distinct from the royal manors to the south of the Ribble. Here the Wessex kings had gradually extended their control, and in the early tenth century had succeeded in closing the river to Norse shipping. Preston was probably among the lands along the RIBBLE given to the monastery of ST WILFRID at Ripon in 670, and in 930 King Athelstan granted Amounderness to the cathedral church at York. By the time of the Conquest, however, the district had been seized by Tostig, Earl of Northumberland. In contrast to the manors to the south, Preston thus found itself in the kingdom of Northumberland and the diocese of York. Domesday Book thus includes Preston and Amounderness in the separate folio describing Yorkshire.

Though 'Prestone' was a Saxon town, the Norse presence in the Fylde was very strong. Accordingly the area of taxable land is given in 'carucates' (an area of around 120 acres) rather than the Saxon 'hide'. At Preston Tostig had 6 carucates, representing perhaps 700 acres, and in Domesday Book there follows a list of 62 settlements in the Fylde; 'All these villages and 3 churches belong to Preston'. These survive to the present day, apart from the lost village of 'Aschebi' which may have been in the vicinity of Myerscough. The land holdings at Ribby, Marton, Layton, Staining, Thornton, Singleton, Garstang and Preesall were as large as that at Preston, and Ribby was larger. With over 20,000 acres of agricultural land, this had been a relatively prosperous district in Edward the Confessor's time, but it has been suggested that subsequent fighting (probably caused by Tostig and his enemies at York rather than by the Normans) impoverished the district, which was now among the confiscated lands granted to William's henchman Roger of Poitou. Accordingly, where there had been 62 villages, '16 of them have a few inhabitants, but how many is not known. The rest are waste.' Alternatively some scholars have argued that 'waste' merely indicates that the land was worked as pasture, and the locals may have deliberately underestimated the productivity of their district to avoid taxation.

Thus although great caution must be exercised whilst examining the wording of the Domesday Book, it reveals a geography of the Fylde which is very familiar to us. By plotting the sequence of places it lists on a modern map it is possible to reconstruct the actual 'round' followed by the Saxon tax gatherers. The route out from Preston, for example, runs west: Ashton - Lea - Salwick - Clifton - Newton - Freckleton. Thus Preston emerges from Domesday Book fully formed into our written history, as a place already long established as an important administrative centre for Saxon and Norse speakers alike, and as one of the leading places on the distant fringe of 'England'.

P Morgan, *Domesday Book: Cheshire Including Lancashire, Cumbria and North Wales* (1978). C P Lewis, *The Lancashire Domesday* (1991).

'DOWN YOUR WAY'

The popular radio series visited Preston in October 1949. Local historian J H Spencer was given two minutes to summarize the town's history and presenter Richard Dimbleby ate a bag of apples. At the end of the recording he swept out with the time-honoured 'Right then, off to Deepdale'.

Preston Herald (7 Oct. 1949).

DUNN, DADDY (?1745-1827)

Fr Joseph Dunn served Preston as Catholic priest for fifty-one years from 1776, an era which saw the full revival of Catholicism in the town following the Reformation. A colourful and larger-than-life character - in powdered wig, breeches and silk stockings - he also helped to establish the Fox Street School (1814), the Preston Trustee Savings Bank, the Preston Gas Light Co. (1815), the Literary and Philosophical Society and the House of Recovery (1813).

L Warren, *Through Twenty Preston Guilds: The Catholic Congregation of St. Wilfrid's, Preston* (1993).

E

EAVEDROPPERS

A Preston speciality; persons standing beneath the overhanging eaves of their neighbours' houses in order to overhear the conversations within. Regarded as a most heinous crime tending to promote strife between neighbours, the 'common Eve dropp' could expect no mercy from the COURT LEET, which of course was composed of his or her victims. On 20 October 1654 Margaret Berchall was fined for 'herking' (or 'lisoning') at William Dobson's window, but he was also fined for carefully emptying a chamber pot onto her from upstairs as a prelude to throwing it at her. In the closely packed and overcrowded houses, where all had a healthy interest in everyone else's business, a no less serious crime was the 'carrieing' of stories between neighbours. For this and other crimes Thomas Silcocke was fined a mark (6s 8d) in 1661.

A Hewitson, *Preston Court Leet Records* (1905).

EGBERT THE TANK

Of the many fund-raising efforts during the First World War Egbert's visit was the most spectacular (21 January 1918). The Victory War Loan of 1917 raised over a million pounds in Preston alone, but the second issue fell flat. There was great interest in the new tanks, so war-weary veterans were sent clanking around the provinces to great success – Glasgow raised £14,500,000 – and Egbert 'A Giant Toad' duly arrived in Preston. His driver and crew of three had been killed in action and an enthusiastic crowd 20,000-strong gathered to watch his royal progress down Fishergate and onto the Market Place. Here they heard an appeal for a million pounds by the Mayor, standing on the turret in full civic rig, while the Mayoress stared out serenely from inside Egbert. £422,235 was raised that day, and the target was met. A third appeal in July 1918 raised £384,000, and by 1919 Prestonians held £2,509,079 in War Bonds.

H Cartmell, *For Remembrance: An Account of Some Fateful Years* (1919).

ELECTORAL SENSATION

Parliamentary election of December 1832. Result: Hunt 3,730, Stanley 3,392. See HENRY HUNT.

ELECTRICITY

Electricity would change the world in the twentieth century, but lectures on 'Galvanism' were held at the Institution for the Diffusion of Knowledge as early as the 1840s, and a regular course of lectures on the subject was established in 1849. The photographer ROBERT PATERSON was an early enthusiast, demonstrating the 'Electric Flashlight' at the Preston Arts and Sciences Exhibition of 1865. A spectacular demonstration of its future importance was sponsored by that beacon of human progress, PRESTON NORTH END. In October 1878 they experimented with the round-ball game ('score Eagley one goal, North End nil') and also pioneered electrical lighting in a rugby match against Preston Rovers. Though Messrs Park and Bibby's apparatus produced 'a wonderful electric light in the darkness of the night' at Deepdale, the two lights facing in opposite directions on the half-way line made rugby extremely dangerous as the screams of speeding players colliding on the distant parts of the pitch attested. Though the experiment 'fell short of complete failure', it had been witnessed by two crowds (paying customers inside the ground, and a second host suspended from trees on Moor Park to watch the illuminations for free), was widely reported and anyway North End had won.

In April 1922 Preston Corporation (which had operated the electrical tramway system since 1904) took over the National Electricity Supply Company (founded in the 1890s) as a prelude to the construction of a modern turbine station at Penwortham. In 1927 the four-turbine steam plant at Penwortham 'A' replaced the smaller stations at Crown St and the tramways generator. The electrification of Preston really began at this point. Electricity use rose from 32 million units that year, to over a 100 million in 1931, and 185 million at the outbreak of war. The pit of the world economic depression was thus marked by the progressive modernization of the region's infrastructure. As Frank Harrison has demonstrated, this was carried over into the domestic context; in 1926 the Electricity 'Show Room' sold an impressive 900 cookers and 50 washers, but in 1939 the figures were 2,200 and 800 respectively. During the same period the number of 'consumers' (a new word in the 1930s) rose from 4,646 in 1925 to 44,160.

With a supply monopoly the council was in a strong position to develop electricity use on its new housing estates, Ribbleton in 1925 and Holme Slack in 1929. In the critical late 1920s and early 1930s the numbers of consumers quintupled, a statistic which clearly demonstrates that economic depression and progress went hand in hand in the Preston of the 1930s. A National Grid in which nearby towns pooled resources was generally operative by 1934 and in November 1939 the Electricity Board ordered the construction of the Penwortham 'B' station. Built at a cost of almost £4 million the plant was secretly opened during the war in 1941, ran at full power during the winter of 1947 and was 'opened' officially by Manny Shinwell in September 1947. The works was intimately connected to the progress of the dock site from which it drew coal on the spectacular overhead conveyor and circulating water through tunnels under the river. With the development of the nuclear station at Heysham the works closed and, having powered the town's post-war development, was demolished in 1982-3.

F Harrison, 'Industrial Preston through Slump and War' (1994, unpublished). D Hunt, *A History of Preston North End Football Club: The Power, the Politics and the People* (2000).

EMPIRE THEATRE

Located opposite the Parish Church on Church St, it was a theatre 1911-30, a cinema 1930-64, and a bingo hall 1964-74. This wonderful 2,500-seater music hall, built at a cost of £65,000 and decorated in the high Louis XIV style, was opened on 22 May 1911. The *Lancashire Daily Post* reported that 'The inaugural performance was witnessed by a crowded house and the environs were thronged for a long while by people unable to gain admission'; but significantly a 'Bioscope' film was featured on the opening night. The Empire formed a part of what was perhaps Preston's first 'leisure complex', which included shops and a hotel. Understandably, given its location, the management sought to ensure 'Clean, wholesome amusement'. The years up to 1918 were most successful, and as late as 1929 GEORGE FORMBY was playing here twice nightly in his 'Formby Night Out', but the following year saw the Empire's conversion to cinema. During the Second World War 'the Gods' were closed for safety reasons (reducing capacity to just over 1,000 people), and in the 1950s the cinema claimed to have the town's first Cinemascope screen - 'our mammoth wonder screen'. The Empire became a bingo hall in 1964 and was demolished in 1976.

J Cotterall, *Preston's Palaces of Pleasure* (1988). D Hindle, *Twice Nightly: An Illustrated History of Entertainment in Preston* (1999).

ENGLISH ELECTRIC COMPANY
See DICK KERR.

ETHNIC HISTORY
Throughout history the Preston region has absorbed a steady flow of newcomers. This process may have reached its proportionate peak in Roman times, and the surviving 'British' population was subsequently submerged by 'Dark Age' migrants: Anglo-Saxon settlers who came through the Ribble Valley and large numbers of Scandinavians who settled to the west. This process was barely complete when the Conquest of 1066 added a strong Norman-French element to the ruling class. The successful Tudor town attracted merchants and traders, and increasing numbers of people from the surrounding district. Nineteenth-century textile mills required a constant stream of hands to operate them, and the Port of Preston provided a natural gateway into industrial Lancashire for large numbers of Irish people. Indeed, as early as 1870 perhaps one in six Prestonians had either been born in Ireland or had Irish parents, and today few white Prestonians can have no Irish ancestry at all.

The Second World War displaced massive numbers of Central Europeans, and the post-war boom led large numbers of Poles, Ukrainians and White Russians to settle in Preston. They naturally found work in the textile and engineering sectors and by the census of 1951 accounted for 1 per cent of the population. Continuing labour shortages in most sectors of the economy were partly met in the period 1955-65 by workers from the New Commonwealth countries, particularly India, with the majority of people coming from the Punjab and Gujarat. In Preston many found work in the town's textile mills, and the community was particularly badly hit by the closure of the enormous COURTAULD plant in 1979. By 1984 half of the Asian community had been born in Preston, and the expansion of cultural and religious facilities for the Muslim and Hindu communities brought new interest to the town's skyline, whilst the first 'Indian' restaurant (1957) marked a new dietary departure for their fellow Prestonians.

The census of 2001 identified 85.5 per cent of the 129,633 Prestonians as of 'White' extraction, 11.6 per cent as 'Asian or Asian British' (Indian 8.8 per cent; Pakistani 2.1 per cent; Bangladeshi 0.2 per cent), and 0.9 per cent as 'Black' or Black British': figures which had scarcely altered since 1982. In addition the town has an important Chinese community.

D Shepherd and S Harrison, *Islam in Preston* (1979). L Connell, *Moving Stories: A History of Settlement in Preston* (1998). D Hunt, *Preston: Centuries of Change* (2003). HMSO, *2001 Census* (2002).

Preston Market place c.1900. The market place has been the stage for much of Preston's history: the ailing inhabitants were boarded up in their houses during the pestilence of 1631, the Scots laid down their arms here in 1715, and the ill-fated 'Preston Pals' marched away in 1914.

F

FAIRS

Fairs provided a timely boost to the local economy, and like the holding of markets, their legal recognition (and therefore protection) was an important feature of town CHARTERS. Along with other valuable privileges King John's charter, for example, gave the Prestonians the right to have a fair lasting eight days from the Feast of the Assumption (15 August). Hewitson listed the fairs surviving in the late nineteenth century; these comprised four horse fairs (January, March, August, November), six cattle fairs (February, March, August and November), three cheese fairs (March, June and September) and three pot fairs. The latter were held on 27 March for three days, on 25 August for seven days and on 7 November for five days. The August event survives as the celebrated 'Preston Pot fair' - a very rare use today of the town's ancient market place.

A Hewitson, *History of Preston* (1883).

FELLOWES, CHRISTINA

The last woman to be publicly flogged in Preston. In 1786 she was fastened to a cart, taken to the principal street corners and publicly whipped across her bare back.

A Hewitson, *Preston Court Leet Records* (1905).

FERRIER, KATHLEEN (1912-1953)

Contralto: recipient of the gold medal of the Royal Philharmonic Society, and the finest singer that England has produced. She was born at Bank Terrace, Higher Walton, the daughter of the local headmaster. Kathleen's career developed slowly at first, but after her debut in Handel's *Messiah* at Westminster Abbey (1943) her remarkable voice and warm personality were quickly and widely appreciated in war-torn Britain. Her recordings date from 1944, and two years later her triumph in Benjamin Britten's *The Rape of Lucretia* brought her a world-wide acclaim which soared to even greater heights during her partnership with conductor and Mahler specialist Bruno Walter. Yet Kathleen Ferrier had been no less at home singing to parties of troops, and her early death in 1953 was mourned as a major national loss. She was one of the leading artists in the remarkable post-war British renaissance, and on the fiftieth anniversary of her death her voice was as popular - and as much loved - as ever.

W Ferrier, *The Life of Kathleen Ferrier* (1955). P Campion, *Ferrier: A Career Recorded* (1992).

FIENNES, CELIA (1662-1741)

Celia Fiennes made a series of journeys around the country in the years 1685-1712, ostensibly 'to improve her health'. Her journals provide an interesting account of the England of her day. She came to Preston during her 'Great Journey' of 1689:

> Preston stands on a hill is a very good market town. Satterday is their market which day I was there and saw it was provided with all sorts of things leather, corn, coales, butter, cheese and fruite and garden things: there is a very spacious Market place and pretty church, and severall good houses: at the entrance of the town was a very good house which was a Lawyers, all stone work 5 windows in the front and high built: the generality of the buildings especially in 2 or 3 of the greete streetes were very handsome, better than is most country towns, and the street spacious and well pitch'd.

The Illustrated Journeys of Celia Fiennes, ed. C. Morris (1982).

FINNEY, SIR TOM (1922-)

The finest footballer that the English game has produced, and accordingly a PRESTON NORTH END player. Finney's childhood in the Preston of the 1920s and 1930s was little different from that of many of his fellow townspeople, and perhaps harder than most. During visits to DEEPDALE with his father the 'quiet, thoughtful boy' saw his childhood hero ALEC JAMES whom he sought to emulate in his street play. The 'Holmslack Wonder' was something of a prodigy, and at the age of 13 was reported to James Taylor's 'watchers'. Care was taken not to arouse undue expectations in the child and he was only

Tommy Finney creates a Splash, Deepdale, 2005 (photo: Preston City Council).

signed (and then in great haste!) on New Year's Day 1940 - for the princely fee of 10 shillings a game.

Much has been written of Finney's playing style: Allman and Berry put the case very succinctly: 'If all the brains in the game sat in committee and designed the perfect player, they would come up with a reincarnation of Finney'. The club's Scottish passing game suited him perfectly, and perhaps only at Deepdale could he have emerged as the complete player that he became. He was a member of North End's 1940-1 'War Double' winning side, the Second Division Championship team of 1950-1, and the two League runners-up sides of the 1950s (1952-3, 1957-8). In the League he scored 187 goals in 433 games - a remarkable feat for a player who was essentially a goal provider rather than a goal-scorer. In the FA Cup he played 40 games (23 goals) and captained the 1954 Cup Final side. In all he scored 210 goals in 473 games in a career interrupted by the war, illness and frequent injury.

His claim to world eminence is strongly supported by his career as an England player, playing 76 times and scoring 30 goals. Remarkably he filled all the forward positions to devastating effect and in 1958 became England's leading goal-scorer. He was a leading figure in England's three great triumphs of the post-war era: the 4-0 defeat of Italy in Turin (1949), the 3-2 defeat of Austria in the Russian Zone of Vienna (1952) and the 3-1 defeat of West Germany at Wembley (1954). After his retirement in 1960 Tom Finney continued to be a leading figure in Preston affairs, lending his support to all manner of good causes: indeed when the National Football Museum was established (1997-2000) Robert Pratten found that over the years he had parted with virtually all of his international caps for fund-raising efforts. As the club's elder statesman he leant his support to the management, particularly during the severe difficulties encountered during the chairmanship of Keith Leeming, and his award of a long overdue knighthood was acclaimed by all of the footballing world.

T Finney, *My Autobiography* (2003).

FISHERGATE

The path from the market square along the western end of the CHURCH STREET ridge to the ferry and the extensive salmon fisheries along the RIBBLE. It was a prestigious early nineteenth-century address, and the Preston mill owners were known in song as 'The Swells of Fishergate'

See BURGAGE; FRIARGATE.

Fishergate from the air c.1925. A superb view of old Preston before the 'developments' of the 1960s. The Victorian streets and weinds clearly reveal the town's underlying medieval street plan. The scene is dominated by the spires of the Town Hall, the Sessions House and the Parish Church, whilst in the distance the enormous industrial massif of the Yard Works can be seen: eight centuries of history are revealed on a single photograph. Note the large shopkeepers' window blinds open against the early morning sun along Fishergate.

FOOTBALL SPECIAL

On Friday 30 March 1889 the front axle of the West Lancashire Railway's FA Cup Final excursion train suddenly failed at Penistone near Sheffield, derailing most of the nineteen carriages and killing one passenger. Men from a nearby steelworks pulled the battered and dazed survivors out of the smash, and undeterred these stalwart Longton and Penwortham Northenders duly waited for a later train to London. Railway passengers were clearly a tough lot in those days, though this party did manage to see North End win the cup!
Preston Herald, Preston Chronicle (31 Mar. 1889).

FOREST OF FULWOOD

This was a Crown hunting preserve extending eastwards from Ingol to Grimsargh, and northwards from Deepdale almost to Broughton. The royal forests had their own code of laws to protect the deer, and both trees and wildlife were carefully tended by a large staff of foresters, parkers and hunters - occupations which are still reflected in surnames. In addition to the oaks and deer (harts, hinds, bucks and does), the taking of partridges, hares, herons, wax, honey and bees was forbidden, as was the carrying of long-bows and the keeping of 'strange Greyhounds'. The southern fringe, which as late as the thirteenth century must have been in the vicinity of St George's Road, was gradually pushed back to reach the line of Watling St Road a century later. This was largely due to the townspeople's right to take timber for building. Though much of the fabric of the early Tudor town's buildings probably came from the forest, over 2,000 acres of primeval oak woodland still remained. This was gradually cleared to make way for farms and common grazings. Attempts to prevent this encroachment in 1623 led to rioting among the inhabitants of Fulwood and Broughton. A large expanse of cleared woodland south of the forest proper became 'Preston Moor'. This survived into the 1860s when it was developed for housing, with the central portion becoming Moor Park. Timbers from the forest must survive in a number of old houses and churches, but the forest is long gone (1817), and visitors to the Royal Preston Hospital are unaware that they are deep within the former glades of the Forest of Fulwood.

THE PERAMBULATION OF 1278

During the reign of Henry III a 'Perambulation of the Forest of the Lord King in the County of Lancaster' defined the bounds of his 'Fulewode':

> To wit from the Hay of Ravenkel (near Plungington House) unto the way of Dunepul (north of Preston Moor), and whence as the watercourse runs to Dupedale (Deepdale Road) and thence unto Lund to the upper head, and whence as that watercourse falls into Huctredescate (Ughtred's gate), and thence as the way goes to lower Coleford. And thence as it falls down to Cadileisahe (Cadley Shaw)

and thence unto the Hay of Ravenkil. And herein the men of Preston ought to have timber for their buildings and to burn, and pasture for their beasts.

R Cunliffe-Shaw, *The Royal Forest of Lancaster* (1956). W Farrer, *Lancashire Pipe Rolls and Charter* (1902).

FORMBY, GEORGE (1904-1961)

Real name George Hoy Booth; entertainer and 'big car' enthusiast. Born in Wigan, Formby trained as a jockey before joining his father in the music hall. In 1924 he married Beryl Ingham who became the driving force behind his career. With his toothy grin and banjulele he became a popular film star in the 1930s, and was a tireless worker during the war. Indeed the film *Let George Do It!* (1940), in which George clouts the Fuhrer personally, was reckoned to be one of the biggest morale boosters of the war. Though the public's film taste changed after the war, Formby scored a great success with the musical *Zip Goes a Million* (1951), and remained a tremendously gifted stage star. The modern appreciation of his genius should not be distracted by his dated and formulaic film appearances. He had strong links with Preston and announced his forthcoming marriage to local girl Pat Howson, but died in the town's Mount St hospital before the marriage could take place (March 1961). George Formby was a major figure in the popular social history of the country during difficult times and remained much loved thereafter: no mean achievement for a man who had been born blind and who had never learned to read and write.

D Brot, *George Formby: A Troubled Genius* (1999). *ODNB*: 'George Formby'.

FOUR AND TWENTY, THE

This was the name given to what was in effect the Parish Council, and is not to be confused with the Town Council, though members could serve on both bodies. It was so-called because eight men came from the town, and eight each from the upper and lower ends of the parish. It was responsible for the church's finances and its records survive from 1645. Much of its time was taken up with feuding with the vicar and discussing repairs to the building, and since most work was to be done 'as cheaply as can be got' these were fairly endless. Drawing its membership from the heart of the Preston establishment, this was thus one of the town's most influential bodies during the seventeenth century.

T C Smith, *Records of the Parish Church of Preston* (1892).

FRECKLETON AIR DISASTER (10.30 A.M., 23 AUGUST 1944)

A sudden and violent storm brought a Liberator aircraft down onto Holy Trinity C of E School and adjacent buildings in Lytham Road, where it exploded killing 38 children and 23 adults (including nine US servicemen and four RAF men). The wartime censorship could not hide the horror of a catastrophe which in recent years has been called 'Lancashire's Aberfan'. Eight local men serving in the Forces had to be told of their children's deaths, and a wife whose husband had earlier been killed in action had now lost her children. American servicemen ran from the adjacent airbase to claw through the rubble to rescue survivors, and many have since returned to visit the village memorial. Amazingly, 140 children in the upper school and their teachers escaped injury.

Lancashire Magazine (Sept. 1976). D Hunt, *A History of Preston* (1992).

FREEHOLD LAND SOCIETY

A scheme largely responsible for the growth of suburban Fulwood (essentially Victoria Road and Lower Bank Road) in the last quarter of the nineteenth century. The formation of land societies was a popular means of enabling the disenfranchised to qualify for the 40s freehold vote. In 1847-8 JOSEPH LIVESEY was a prime mover in the formation of the Preston society, and his son WILLIAM purchased the 45-acre Horrockses Farm in Fulwood for £5,000. The £50 plots were apportioned among the shareholders by lot in January 1851. Since at that time they lay outside of the Municipal Borough they carried no electoral advantage, but they duly turned out to be wonderful financial investments when the tram system reached Fulwood in 1879.

See J.Baker in I. Levitt (ed.), *Joseph Livesey of Preston: Business, Temperance and Moral Reform* (1996).

FRIARGATE

One of Preston's three great streets: it originated as the track leading away

Friargate from the roof of the Harris Library and Art Gallery, 2003 (photo: author)

from the market place onto both PRESTON MOOR (the great north road) and the way into the Fylde. The name is derived from the FRIARY built on what - in the twelfth century - was the edge of the town.
See BURGAGE.

FRIARY

The earliest reference to Preston's Franciscan friary comes in a grant authorizing the monks to cut the timber for their community from Henry III's royal FOREST OF FULWOOD. The monks must have been a familiar sight in the town, working among the poor and subsisting from bequests, charity and by begging from the townspeople. Though it later gave its name to FRIARGATE, the friary was located some distance away in the open fields off Marsh Lane (approximately 75 yards west of both Ladywell St and Marsh Lane). The site was explored in the mid-nineteenth century and pieces of stonework including a grave cover were recovered, but it seems that it had been extensively disturbed during the cutting of the canal fifty years earlier. Recent excavations ahead of the construction of the inner ring-road produced virtually nothing. This small establishment was dissolved in 1539, but an adjacent holy well - the Lady Well - survived for 300 years as a place of veneration for local Catholics. In the 1680s DR KUERDEN described 'the ruins of an antient Pryory ... But what is best thereof now standing is imployed for a House of Correction for the country's poor.' The site has now been dug away, and is occupied by the deep cutting on the ring-road to the south of Corporation St.

D Hunt, *Preston: Centuries of Change* (2003).

FULWOOD BARRACKS

Work on this large military establishment began in 1843, the year after the dangerously lawless events of August 1842. The site possessed easy and direct access to the manufacturing district, but was still some distance out from the suburbs. The initial cost of £137,921 2s 11d made it the largest government investment in the town prior to the two world wars, and can be compared in the private sector with the £40,000 cost of Stevenson's Ribble railway bridge. The site was steadily extended, and the barracks' 'spacious parading and drilling square' was to see much use: in August 1914 the site was utterly swamped by the crowds of servicemen, reservists and volunteers, with an additional 3,000 men reported to be 'sleeping rough' in outhouses and under hedges. Today the Barracks is the home of the QUEEN'S LANCASHIRE REGIMENT.

A Hewitson, *History of Preston* (1883). H Cartmell, *For Remembrance: An Account of Some Fateful Years* (1919).

The entrance to Fulwood Barracks c.1920.

G

GAS WORKS

The Preston Gas Company was founded in 1815, and by early in the following year the town had become the first in the provinces to be lit by gas. In 1839 the enterprise took over the Union Gas Company which had been formed by the town's leading textile manufacturers in 1827. The Glover St works was extended in 1828, and six years later the first gas holder was erected in Walker St. A third works (in Moor Lane) was added and by 1883 the company had 574 gas-making retorts and two large gas holder stations in Ribbleton Lane and at Walton, to supply around 330 million cubic feet of gas per year to the Preston district. Enormous local pride was vested in the undertaking and the company's spectacular head office in Fishergate (1872). In 1924 the company acquired 34 acres at Lostock Hall and within two years the site was consuming 52,000 tons of coal and 850,000 gallons of oil annually. It had its own branch railway and the enormous gas holders quickly became a familiar landmark south of the river.

F Harrison, 'Industrial Preston through Slump and War' (1994, unpublished).

GIBBET

A modified scaffold on which the executed person's corpse could be publicly displayed. The bailiffs were ordered to repair the town's gibbet in 1726. The Sheriff of Lancashire's accounts for 1716 record a payment of £12 0s 4d for the execution of the locals taken prisoner after the battle of 1715: 'January 27th. Erecting gallows and paid for materialls, hurdle, fire, cart etc. in executing Shuttleworth and 4 more at Preston *and setting up his head etc.*'. Preston also possessed a set of gibbeting irons; this was in effect an iron case in which a body could be suspended for a considerable time. William Whittle, having killed his wife and two children during an acute mental breakdown, suffered their use at the crossroads near his home in Farington in 1766. These irons were preserved along with other items in a museum of gruesome curiosities at the House of Correction, and can be viewed today in the museum at Peel Castle on the Isle of Man.

A Hewitson, *History of Preston* (1883); *Preston Court Leet Records* (1905).

See OLD PRETENDER

GLUBB PASHA: SIR JOHN BAGET GLUBB (1897-1986)

Army officer, Arabist and the last of the great military administrators of the British Empire. Born in Preston, the son of Sir Frederick Glubb a major in the Royal Engineers, Jack Glubb was posted to France in 1915 where he was wounded three times and won the Military Cross in 1917. A career soldier, he was sent to Mesopotamia in 1920, joined the military administration of Iraq in 1926, and four years later the Arab Legion in Transjordan. As commander (1939) he transformed the Bedouin tribesmen into a disciplined fighting force which performed well during the war. The difficult situation in the Middle East after 1945 brought him into prominence, but after the assassination of King Abdullah of Jordan (1951) Glubb found relations with young King Hussein more difficult. The world order was changing, and in 1956 the British pasha was abruptly dismissed along with the Arab Legion's British officers. As King Hussein later recalled, 'Glubb had to go!' He was given one day to get out and returned to Britain with just £5.

With no British or Jordanian pension Glubb took to writing and lecturing with alacrity, producing over twenty books mostly on Arabic subjects, to such effect that on his death thirty years later he could leave over £200,000. A shy man, who habitually wore his five rows of medal ribbons, Glubb was the last of the line of British officers which had effectively ruled large tracts of the remoter world for two hundred years.

J Glubb, *The Changing Scenes of Life* (1983). T Royce, *Glubb Pasha* (1992). *ODNB*: 'Glubb Pasha'.

GRAMOPHONE

An early form of record player, itself an archaic form of DVD player. In 1893 members of the Preston Scientific Society were loaned the machine belonging to Mr Henry Bell (Guild Mayor 1922), and were amazed when it 'reproduced songs and instrumental music which could distinctly be heard a few feet away'.

Preston Scientific Society Records.

GREAT ELECTION OF 1768

The election of 1768 is important because the subsequent proceedings established the principle of universal manhood suffrage in the town - a privilege that was long unique to only Preston and Westminster. Critically, only in these constituencies did a popular radical candidate stand any chance of winning a parliamentary seat, and Preston's radical tradition was born. In 1768 the fight was a straight Whig-Tory tussle, between the Stanley DERBY INTEREST and the Corporation. Lt Col John Burgoyne and Sir Henry Hoghton represented the former, and Sir Peter Leicester and Sir Frank Standish the latter. A canvass of burgesses put the latter ahead, and both sides imported thugs (delph men, colliers, etc.) to intimidate their opponents. The genteel Stanleys had the best of this work; the Mayor was put under the town pump and St Mary's Catholic church in Friargate was fired by the mob. Though a Tory fleeing for his life wrote 'God Knows where this will end . . . This is shocking work in a civilised country', these proceedings were quite normal parliamentary practice for the time! Men voted openly in party groups of ten until one of the sides could produce no further voters. A huge number of votes were rejected on the legitimate grounds that the would-be electors were not burgesses. Result: Whigs 489, Tories 565. The Stanleys, on appeal, then invoked a long-forgotten judgment from the election of 1661, that 'All the inhabitants...of Preston have voices in the election'. This had always been thought to refer to the Burgesses, but the decision now went in favour of all the male residents. New result: Whigs 1,147, Tories 567.

John Burgoyne (1722-92). Victor in the Great Election of 1768 and leading participant in the American War of Independence. His career really began when he eloped from Preston with Lady Charlotte Stanley in 1743; they were a devoted couple. This engraving was cut in Naples in 1760 (from J Burgoyne, Political and Military Episodes in the Latter Half of the Eighteenth Century, 1876).

The Poll Book for the election is preserved in the Lancashire Record Office. It contains the personal details of the electorate, among them those of RICHARD ARKWRIGHT, an obscure barber who was patiently perfecting his waterframe in Stoneygate. The father of the Industrial Revolution voted Tory.

J Burgoyne, *Political and Military Episodes in the Latter Half of the Eighteenth Century* (1876). C Hardwick, *History of the Borough of Preston* (1857). H W Clemesha, *History of Preston in Amounderness* (1912). LRO, DDPd 11/51.

GUILD MERCHANT

A formal meeting of burgesses to update the ordinances regulating a town's commercial life. Preston's Guild Merchant was probably already ancient when it was recognized in the charter of 1179. The first adequately recorded meeting is that of 1397, and only after 1542 were meetings held at regular twenty-year intervals. The sequence was broken in 1942, but has been held at the familiar interval since 1952. The proceedings of the Guild Merchant originally extended over several weeks to allow time for the burgesses to register their sons on the Guild Rolls, and to revise the town's statutes ('The Orders of the Guild'). As early as 1662 such gatherings of Prestonians had rather naturally become associated with merrymaking. This proved to be profitable, and in time it grew to overshadow the more formal proceedings and so transformed an ancient institution into a popular festival. Occasional prosecutions apart, the legal function of the Guild Merchant had ended by 1782 and the spectacular progress of the cotton industry by the Guild of 1802 heralded the rise of free trade.

All the usual suspects plus W A Abrams, *Memorials of the Preston Guilds* (1882). The definitive work is, of course, Alan Crosby's superb *The History of Preston Guild* (1992).

See BURGESS; BURGAGE STRIP; CHARTERS.

Preston Guild trades procession 1952. A Canberra fuselage leaving Lancaster Road en route for the Market Place: the rear fuselage was on the following trailer (photo: BAE Systems Heritage Group, Warton).

GUJARAT-HINDU SOCIETY

Established in 1965, charitable status 1975. During the 1960s Preston's small Hindu community held meetings in rooms in Glover St and later Great Avenham Lane, before moving into a part of the former St Stephens Primary School, South Meadow Lane, in 1975. The Prince of Wales visited the friendly though small centre in 1981, and in August 1997 celebrations were held to mark fifty years of Indian independence. Following a £1.64 million grant from the National Lottery, work on a new £3.28 million building began in 1998. Some 200 tons of white marble was carved in India to be assembled on site and the recreational and cultural centre opened in May 2001. It is now the largest of its type in the region, serving some 600 families in the Preston area. On the Centre's tenth anniversary in 1985 both the Prime Minister and the Leader of the Opposition had given their support to the venture. Neil Kinnock

The spectacular roofline of the Gujarati Hindu Centre, Broadgate, 2005 (photo: Gujarati Hindu Centre).

wrote: 'Your society and your centre . . . provide excellent means not only of enabling your community to sustain its cultural identity but also an opportunity to others to share in your culture and your tradition.'

GHS, *The Gujarat-Hindu Society* (1996); *Preston Mandir: Guidebook* (2004).

GY-82

A trawler, subsequently HMS *Preston North End* (1939-45). In the inter-war years the Grimsby trawler owners gave the tradition of naming their fleets on a popular theme a novel twist; 'Crampins' specialized in cricketers (with a *Hammond* and the *Don*), and 'Consols' in First Division football clubs. In June 1934 Sir John Marsden of the Consolidated Fishery Company informed the DEEPDALE board that a trawler had been named *Preston North End* (GY-82) - the sister ship of *Grimsby Town* (GY-81): a few weeks later a box of fish arrived! She was built at Smith's Dock in Middlesbrough, was 152 feet long with a breadth of 26.7 feet, weighed 419 tons gross, and carried a crew of around twenty. Other notable boats included *Arsenal* (GY-505: 1933-40), *Manchester City* (GY-53: 1934-40) and *Blackburn Rovers* (GY-102: 1934-40, 1962-70).

During the Second World War GY-82 and her sisters were commissioned by the Royal Navy, equipped with an artillery piece and used for a number of purposes. Many were lost, but HMS *Preston North End* (an anti-submarine trawler shepherding slow-moving convoys through the perilous western approaches) steamed on, and her battle ensign now has pride of place in the National Football Museum. She left Grimsby for the final time on 1 April 1950 but on the 14th ran aground on a submerged reef off the west coast of Iceland. In heavy seas skipper Jack East gave the order to abandon ship, one man lost his life and the boat was a total loss.

Half a century later, whilst visiting a small Icelandic museum, the writer's wife spotted relics salvaged from the *Grimsby Town* and it is thus possible that similar items were saved from her sister ship.

C B Cox, *The Steam Trawlers and Liners of Grimsby* (1989).

H

HANDLOOM WEAVING

Weaving by hand, usually in the weaver's home, was a long-established Preston handicraft. Economic specialization was a growing feature of medieval town life, and with ready access to lowland flax and upland wool it was natural that Preston's economy should develop a strong textile sector. Similarly, Chorley and Wigan grew from the exploitation of the coals lying a just few feet beneath them, and the communities along the Lancashire coast by shellfish collecting and fishing. Among the tolls the Prestonians were allowed to collect in 1314 were charges of 1d for 1,000lb of flax, quarters of canvas, silk and Irish cloth, and 3d for a cart of cloth. Weavers and cloth workers are frequently mentioned in Tudor deeds, the Guild Rolls and the later Court Leet Records. In 1561 the Mayor reported that 'clothes commonly maid nere about Preston and which be comonlie sold in the saide towne are narrow white kearses' (a coarse woollen cloth). The surviving wills and inventories of the leading burgesses reveal an extensive network of trade fed by local cloth workers; in 1565 a merchant tailor in the City of London sued William Hodgkinson for 100 bales of flax which he had ordered but apparently refused to pay for, and trade with distant towns such as Southampton was not uncommon.

Growth of the weaving trade was held up by the extremely labour-intensive nature of hand spinning. This bottleneck was made worse by improvements in loom productivity, but from 1770 access to machine-spun yarn made possible a great surge which would give Lancashire a world lead in cloth production that would last for 150 years. Within twenty years a rustic handicraft was transformed into the COTTON INDUSTRY, and as late as 1830 the home-based handloom weavers were still the largest sector of industrial workers! With runaway export demand for cheap cloth, people flocked into the industry; a set of looms was inexpensive and the trade was soon learnt. Lawrence Rawstorne of Penwortham later recalled these golden days: 'A good handloom weaver would then earn his 30s a week or even more: he would perhaps work half the week and drink the remainder'. It seemed that the weaving trade could never fail. In 1799 the residents of the town's House of Correction were put to it, and succeeded in transforming themselves from a cost to an asset for the ratepayers worth over £1,400pa by the 1820s. The elderly and juvenile inhabitants of the district's workhouses followed suit.

The early spinning factories of JOHN WATSON and JOHN HORROCKS thus grew up in response to the need for machine-spun yarn from weavers in and around the town. The resulting expansion of weaving in turn produced a further cycle of growth in the local cotton industry: large weaving colonies began to grow up both in the surrounding villages and within the town itself. The records of the Horrocks firm reveal an intricate system of weaving colonies around Preston, each with a local company warehouse from which the yarn was distributed or 'put out'. At Longridge (Club Row), Bamber Bridge (Club St) and Leyland (Union St) small 'building' societies were formed to erect purpose-built cottages usually with cellar workshops; aptly the Leyland speciality was the manufacture of slaves' clothing for the West Indies plantations. Similar if much larger colonies grew up in the town, where by 1830 perhaps 5,000 people were directly involved in the hand-weaving trade.

It was thus the construction of domestic weaver's housing which transformed the medieval geography of the town. The distribution of 'Step Houses' can be gauged from the 1847 60 inch to the mile OS map, and has been intensively studied by Nigel Morgan. He has identified two main zones of growth, clustering to the south of the mills in Stanley St (his 'Horrockses area'), and adjacent to the canal-side mills to the north of the town (his 'Friargate area'). Shortly before his death John Horrocks constructed a colony at NEW PRESTON in New Hall Lane; here the cottages had adjacent workshops specifically designed to someday accommodate power looms.

The large number of people entering the hand trade put a steady downward pressure on wages, power looms were expensive, and the introduction of power weaving was to be delayed into the 1840s. Thus what had long been a prosperous handicraft had by 1820 become associated with long hours and exploitation. The period of greatest crisis came in the 1830s and thereafter the hand trade began to die out. A Royal Commission gathered evidence from the town in 1834: it was estimated that the district (essentially Preston and South Ribble) still had about 13,000 handloom weavers, with perhaps 40,000 people dependent on the trade, wages continued to fall, and parents were encouraged not to put their children to the trade. The reformist political, religious and social movements of all kinds which abounded in the Preston of the 1830s found ready adherents among the struggling handloom weavers.

G Timmins, *The Last Shift: The Decline of Handloom Weaving in Nineteenth Century Lancashire* (1993). N Morgan, *Vanished Dwellings: Early Industrial Housing in a Lancashire Cotton Town* (1990). D Hunt, *A History of Leyland and District* (1990); *A History of Walton-le-Dale and Bamber Bridge* (1997).

For weavers who went on to greater things, see JANE LIVESEY; JOSEPH LIVESEY; RICHARD MARSDEN; THOMAS MILLER SENIOR; MOSES HOLDEN.

HANSOM, JOSEPH ALOYSIUS (1803-1882)

Architect and inventor. Born in York Hansom was apprenticed to a firm of architects, and in 1831 won the competition to build Birmingham Town Hall (opened 1833). This proved to be a financial disaster and the construction costs bankrupted Hansom and his partner Edward Welch. The following year he patented the safety cab which was to make him famous, and in 1842 established the influential *Builder* magazine. He then returned to architectural practice, specializing in Catholic churches in the Gothic style. Examples of his work are to be found virtually all around the world, and his ST WALBURGE'S CHURCH at Preston was noted (and not altogether accepted) for its enormous hammer-beam roof and colossal spire.

ODNB

HARRIS BEQUEST

Edmund Robert Harris (1803-77) was the son of the Reverend Robert Harris (1764-1862, headmaster of PRESTON GRAMMAR SCHOOL 1788-1835, incumbent of ST GEORGE'S CHURCH 1797-1862). He left the bulk of his half-million-pound-plus family fortune to be invested by trustees for charitable purposes. These were strongly educational, and the principal elements of the bequest – completed in lavish style – were the HARRIS LIBRARY AND ART GALLERY (£100,000), the Harris Orphanage (£100,000), and the Harris Institute (£40,000) with its schools of technology, science and art. The timeless question is of course, where had this money come from? Not from cotton; some was inherited, much earned in the family law business, but a very large part arose from investments by Edmund and his brother Thomas (d. 1875) in railway shares and real estate.

J Convey, *The Harris Free Public Library and Museum* (1993).

HARRIS LIBRARY AND ART GALLERY

Shortly after his death E R Harris's trustees decided to erect a purpose-built library and museum as the spectacular centre-piece of the Harris bequest, and in 1880 Preston Corporation duly obtained an Act of Parliament to enable them to purchase land along the eastern side of the market place.

Ironically, one of the historically most interesting areas of the old timber-framed maze-like town (Gin Bow Entry, Wilcockson's Court, Blue Anchor Court and the Strait Shambles) then disappeared to make way for the museum. The foundation stone was laid during the 1882 Guild celebrations, and local architect James Hibbert devised a modern steel-framed building within an amazing wedding-cake facade of classical styles. Work began towards the end of 1883 and by 1889 it was virtually completed, but legal problems delayed the opening until October 1893. The building's principal function was to house the town's main library; such care was taken over the planning of this service that even a century later the library was circulating over 800,000 books a year! The cost of the building was estimated in 1893 to have been £30,000 for the land (paid for by the ratepayers), £79,609 for the structure and £22,947 for books and museum objects.

J Convey, *The Harris Free Public Library and Museum* (1993).

HARRIS TECHNICAL COLLEGE
See UNIVERSITY OF CENTRAL LANCASHIRE.

HASLAM PARK
See PUBLIC PARKS.

HIBBERT, JAMES (1833-1903)
Preston architect. See HARRIS LIBRARY AND ART GALLERY.

HIGGINSON, ELEANOR BEATRICE (NEE ELLIS) (1881-1969)
Suffragette. Born in London, her family settled in Preston where she taught at St Mark's school until her marriage in 1905. As a prominent local member of the Labour Party she was a natural recruit for EDITH RIGBY and the Preston branch of the WSPU which she joined in 1913. The following year she served as secretary whilst Rigby was 'on the run' from the police after her excursion into bombing and arson. In May 1914 she was one of the deputation of suffragettes to put their case to the King, and though handled roughly in the subsequent disturbance she was not arrested until she put a brick through a pub window, joining the sixty-five other women and two men taken into custody. She was sentenced to four months' imprisonment, went on a hunger strike in Holloway Prison, and was released after two weeks under the Cat and Mouse Act. The First World War broke out before she could be arrested again, and she spent the war doing good deeds for the poor. With the vote for women won, Eleanor Higginson returned to local politics. She was a WEA tutor, magistrate and served on the council in 1940-5. Her husband died in 1938, she moved to Bognor Regis in 1954, and died at Chichester.

ODNB

HMS *PRESTON NORTH END*
See GY-82.

HIPPODROME
Royal Hippodrome Theatre, Friargate (1905-1957). The opening of the 2,500-seater Hippodrome in 1905 for popular entertainment marked an important stage in the social development of Preston; in contrast to the grim days of just thirty years earlier local people had increasing leisure time, and more importantly money which they were prepared to spend in order to enjoy it. The coming of the Hippodrome is clear evidence of the improving social conditions in the early years of the twentieth century. The *Lancashire Daily Post* managed to convey the general impression:

> The ceiling is divided into eight oblong panels with splendid Egyptian mountings in fibrous plaster, and these are bordered by friezes representing garlands of flowers. The proscenium is in Ionic style with Renaissance panels and friezes and on each side are statues representing 'Repose' and 'Silence', supported by brackets, imitative of the heads of Satyrs...

Though the ubiquitous 'WILL ONDA' experimented with his early picture shows, the Hippodrome remained the home to live theatre and popular entertainment. In 1911 Marie Lloyd appeared here, in 1922 Gracie Fields, and in September 1941 the great Richard Tauber appeared in *The Land of Smiles*. Harry Lauder's song, 'Keep right on to the end of the road' became the Prestonians' Wembley anthem. The encroachment of the cinema into Preston's theatre land was resisted, 'Living Artists Not Talking Pictures' was the battle-cry, and the Hippodrome introduced a continuous live programme (10 a.m. to 10 p.m.) in 1934. After 1947 an initially short run of plays performed by the (Reginald) Salberg Players extended for eight years, and came to mark a real high point in the town's cultural life. A whole generation of British talent made early appearances here in 'Good Plays, Well Presented', including Peggy Mount, John Barron, John Dearth and the future father-in-law of a Premier of Britain. Many years later when Leonard Rossiter was appearing at the Guild Hall he remarked to David Hindle, 'I started here you know, at the Hippodrome down the road': the comic genius had been ninth on the bill (September 1954).

The grim words of Claude Talbot on the theatre's closure in 1957 were widely reported at the time, but thankfully – as things turned out – incorrect: 'The date of 25 May 1957 should be remembered with shame by every citizen of this town. I don't think there will ever be a live theatre in Preston again.' In two years Preston had thus lost both the PALACE and the Hippodrome, and in 1959 the building was demolished to make way for a C&A store.

J Cotterall, *Preston's Palaces of Pleasure* (1988). D.Hindle, *Twice Nightly: An Illustrated History of Entertainment in Preston* (1999).

HOLDEN, MOSES (1777-1864)

Handloom weaver turned astronomer. Born in Bolton, Holden was 5 years old when his family moved to Preston. After working as a handloom weaver he became a landscape gardener, but his real interest since early childhood had been in astronomy, where he found a ready patron in SAMUEL HORROCKS. An illustrated public lecture at the THEATRE ROYAL (April 1815) proved a great success, and for the next eleven years he toured England with his slide show and Orrery. He was a skilled instrument maker, and also published a small atlas of the fixed stars in 1816 and an almanac after 1835. In 1828 he settled once more in Preston, was one of the founders of the Institution for the Diffusion of Knowledge, and gave courses in astronomy until 1852. Holden was given the Freedom of Preston in 1834 and became a member of the British Association for the Advancement of Science in 1837. He died at his home in Jordan St.

Obituary: *Preston Guardian* (11 June 1864). *ODNB*.

HORROCKS, JOHN (1768-1804)

The Greatest Name in Cotton: MP for Preston 1802-4. Born at Cockey Moor, Bradshaw, on the outskirts of Bolton, Horrocks was one of the two surviving sons of a Quaker and prosperous quarryman at Edgeworth. As a child he was put to work with one of the very early factory pioneers, Thomas Thomason, who, it has been said, was the first person to become aware of the child's remarkable gifts. Thomason died in 1782 and some time later Horrocks began to employ his sisters at the hand production of fine yarns in the quarry buildings. These found a ready market at Preston, where the youngster became a supplier to JOHN WATSON. The latter was the leading spirit of his day in the establishment of factory-based spinning in Preston, and a man for a hard bargain. It could only have been a matter of time before the two fell out, with the young businessman refusing to have anything more to do with him.

Horrocks married and the young couple moved to Preston in the New Year of 1791. The town was changing fast, it was to be linked to the CANAL network and had an enormous hinterland of handloom weavers whose demand for yarn could not be met by the local spinners. From a small building at the bottom of Turks Head Court he employed local spinners working in their own homes (as well as the folks at Edgeworth) and began directly to employ weavers in his own right. This was clearly impressive yet still small-scale. How was he able to overtake John Watson & Sons within five years, and become the largest spinner and manufacturer in the world just thirteen years later? He convinced Richard Newsham and the Preston banking fraternity that he was a good bet! Work began on the first mill in what would become the world-famous Yard Works site off Stanley St. The 'Yellow Factory', though minute by later standards, was thought to be an enormous undertaking at the time and caused a wobble among the bankers, but was the prelude to a remarkable burst of mill building. Within ten years the firm had seven spinning mills on three sites in the town (Yard Works, Spittals Moss and Frenchwood). The organization of the firm kept pace with its growth; his brother Samuel was brought into the business, to be followed by fellow partners John Whitehead and Thomas Miller.

In 1796 Horrocks contested the parliamentary seat on behalf of the Corporation's Tory interest, and though narrowly defeated by the Derby Whig interest it was clear that he would be successful in 1802. The result - in this most 'democratic' of boroughs - was for the two parties to each put forward one of the town's pair of MPs! The 'Grand Alliance' held until 1826 when SAMUEL HORROCKS retired and the Corporation withdrew from parliamentary politics. Duly 'elected', Horrocks became one of the first 'cotton' MPs. He opened company offices in the City of London and became an associate of William Pitt. His mother thus lived to see her sons enter church together as Preston's MP and Mayor. Their impact on the town had been enormous: in the ten years from 1792 the population had doubled, the skies above had become clouded with smoke, and the great barracks of their workers' housing had begun to submerge the gentrified market town.

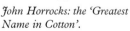

During these years the firm was spectacularly profitable. In 1799 the company's capital of £105,541 1s 8d produced a profit of £55,775 17s 4d; John's share was almost £45,000, and Sam's £11,000. The brothers were well able to afford their mansions at Penwortham Hall and Lark Hill, and in 1806 the capitalization of Horrockses & Co. exceeded £200,000. John Horrocks died suddenly at his house in New Bridge St, Blackfriars, London, on 1 May 1804, leaving a fortune in the order of £150,000. His body was brought back to Penwortham and interred beside the Parish Church, overlooking the new Preston he had done so much to create. Executive control of the firm passed to Samuel, with THOMAS MILLER SENIOR company manager.

John Horrocks: the 'Greatest Name in Cotton'.

Anon., *Fortunes Made in Business* (1887). Consolidated Cotton Mills Trust, *Concerning Cotton* (1925). S Birtles, 'Horrockses: The Development of a Cotton Enterprise' (1980, unpublished dissertation, LRO). M Burscough (2004) *The Horrockses: Cotton Kings of Preston* (2004).

See COTTON INDUSTRY; HANDLOOM WEAVING; NEW PRESTON.

HORROCKS, SAMUEL (1766-1842)

Cotton master, Mayor (1802) and MP for Preston (1804-26). In death as in life it has been Sam Horrocks's lot to be overshadowed by his meteoric younger brother. This is not very fair for a former delph-man who went on to become a close friend of William Wordsworth, built a palatial mansion at Lark Hill and survived an assassination attempt. Critically, he steered the firm through the difficult years at the close of the French Wars, and oversaw its emergence as an essentially modern manufacturing concern. Power weaving was steadily introduced in the 1820s, and a web of offices was opened throughout the Far East. The company was thus well placed to exploit the growth of the Indian market on which the industry's Victorian prosperity was to be based.

Much has been made of Sam Horrocks's parliamentary reputation - or rather the lack of it! Having been Mayor of Preston in 1802 he inherited his brother's seat in 1804, and was held in place through subsequent elections by the 'Grand Alliance'. Hewitson recalled the story of how people crowded to buy copies of his recent speech in the House, only to find that they had been sold blank sheets of paper. When they complained they were told 'Well he said Nowt'! Radical opponents claimed that in all his years representing the interests of the Prestonians in the Mother of Parliaments his only contribution to proceedings was a feeble 'Ohh...', and his opponents sported cards with a large 'O' painted on them.

W Dobson, *Parliamentary Representation of Preston* (1868). Margaret Burscough, *The History of Lark Hill, Preston, 1797-1989* (1989); *The Horrockses: Cotton Kings of Preston* (2004).

HORSE RACING NEWS

In June 1932 staff at the Harris Reference Library began to obliterate horse racing news from the newspapers for, as a spokesperson explained:

> It was no uncommon experience to find five or six men scanning the pages containing turf gossip in a morning paper for an exceptional length of time, and so no-one who was not directly interested in this had much of a chance of even approaching the reading desk.

Lancashire Daily Post (26 March 1932).

HOUDINI, HARRY (1874-1926)

Escapologist whose real name was Eric Weisz. The Great Houdini performed in Preston on a number of his British tours. He escaped from the Public Hall, but a visit in 1906 (to the HIPPODROME) proved more difficult. No prison in the world could hold him, but Preston's posed problems when it transpired that it possessed 'unusual locks and handcuffs'. After some hours of struggle he was seen noticeably to renew his eventually successful efforts to escape from the place when a guard confidentially told him that if he became peckish a prison tea would be provided for him. Houdini duly gave the prison the ultimate compliment: 'Preston should be equally proud of its prison as of its North End football team' (who are, of course, notorious escapologists themselves).

D Hindle (1999) *Twice Nightly: An Illustrated History of Entertainment in Preston* (1999).

HOUSING
Sheltering the workers (1790-1914)
In his series of lucid and detailed analyses Nigel Morgan has traced the emergence of the Victorian townscape - a major contribution to the 'History of Preston'. He has identified three key chronological stages in this process.

1790-1815. A period of overcrowding and internal expansion which saw the emergence of two large clusters of HANDLOOM WEAVING houses, off Friargate and to the south of Church St (his 'Horrockses' grouping). There was no civic control over house building.

1850-80. This period was marked by large-scale terraced-housing development around the old medieval core, notably in Plungington, along the western edge of the town, and along the Ribbleton-New Hall Lane axis. This was a period of slowly creeping civic control.

1880-1914. Preston pushes further out to the suburbs at Fulwood and Ashton. The 'Canary islands' in Deepdale are built. Civic control brings about a major improvement to Preston's housing stock. The ground floors of new houses now have to be higher than the pavement outside, and the 'good' housewife demonstrates her respectability by drawing attention to her improved home by regularly donkeystoning the front doorstep. Yet throughout the nineteenth century (and for long thereafter) houses were built not for the comfort of their inhabitants but for the profit of the developer.

The standard of new housing - which had such a profound effect on the quality of life in Preston - was thus closely related to immediate housing shortages and the emerging regulatory framework. Population growth was at its greatest in the first half of the century, whilst building control was non-existent in 1800, little improved by 1850, but increasingly important thereafter. The population rose from around 10,000 people in 1800 to almost 70,000 fifty years later, with shelters for almost 20,000 people required in the 1840s alone; the Reverend JOHN CLAY adequately documented the horrific consequences. It took Preston well over a century to overcome the worst of these problems, but the establishment of the Board of Health (1850) and particularly the Preston Improvement Act (1880) led to their very slow amelioration; the Longridge reservoirs brought piped fresh water, sewers were built and the post of Medical Officer was made full-time in 1882. With piped water and sewers in place flush toilets could be introduced, and slum clearance got under way in the 1880s with the construction of Corporation

Late 19th-century development along New Hall Lane c.1925. This is one of the classic images of industrial Lancashire, and although the grid rows of terraces became something of a music hall cliche they were essentially modern houses. The Yard Works can just be seen beyond London Road in the top left-hand corner.

St. Significantly, virtually all of the town's surviving terraced housing dates from the period after 1880.

N Morgan, *An Introduction to the Social History of Housing in Preston* (1982); *Vanished Dwellings: Early Industrial Housing in a Lancashire Cotton Town - Preston* (1990); *Deadly Dwellings: Housing and Health in a Lancashire Cotton Town* (1993). D Hunt, *A History of Preston* (1992).

See COTTON INDUSTRY; JOHN CLAY; NEW PRESTON; JOHN HORROCKS.

A land fit for heroes (1918-1939)

Between the wars Preston's population began to relocate to new housing estates both within the borough and in the adjoining districts of Fulwood and Penwortham: a process which continues to this day. Slum clearance, which had begun in the 1890s, was pushed ahead and 4,347 new houses were built in the borough. Of these 2,847 were erected by the council, many on the improved semi-detached plan. They formed the basis of the later Larches, Home Slack, Ribbleton and Farringdon Park developments. The imprint of the art-deco planners can best be seen in the Fishwick Parade and Downing St district. By 1948 5,981 houses had been built, accommodating 21,000 people. During the 1930s alone Preston's population fell by 8,000, whilst that of Penwortham-Fulwood rose by 10,000. The housing programme gave an important boost to the economic recovery building from 1935, and for many people home ownership became a realistic aspiration:

> The Gammull Lane Estate Ribbleton (near Messrs.Courtauld's new works) Freehold Houses at £499, £560 and £720 each. The Clifton Park Estate: Healthy, Sunshine, Semi-detached houses for sale. Price £355.

At Penwortham a new home could be had for £25 down and payments of 12s a week. Having peaked at around 120,000, the old town's population now began the steady and irreversible move to the suburbs.

D Hunt, *A History of Preston* (1992). C Stansfield, *Beside the Seaside* (1986).

Suburbia (1945-2005)

The war had seriously disrupted redevelopment plans. It was estimated in 1946 that of the town's stock of 32,000 houses, half had been built in the fifty years after 1840. Post-war development owed much to two central analyses: *Towards a Prouder Preston* (1946) and the *Development Plan for the Borough of Preston* (1951). These recognized the failures of the past and anticipated extensive house clearance, construction of double the number of pre-war new homes, and the extensive remodelling of the town centre. In 1955 it was claimed that at the current rate it would take two hundred years to clear redundant housing, and the first large-scale clearance drive began with 209 houses in the Pleasant and Brunswick St areas. Soon enormous areas of the town resembled bomb sites and distinct communities such as Bow Lane, Adelphi and Queen St were demolished. To house the dispossessed large estates were developed, and Brookfield, for example, which was to have an initial 1,200 houses (for 5,000 people) was to grow to 2,500 'luxury dwellings' (to house 7,500), whilst new housing at Ingol was said to 'be a dream come true'. The first multi-storey flats appeared in 1957, and the high-rise blocks on Avenham and Moor Lane were built in 1963-4.

At this point the local effort was swept up in the grandiose scheme for a Central Lancashire New Town. In 1965 the Preston-Chorley belt was designated as the site of the last of Britain's new towns. Futuristic plans appeared, the project received the official go-ahead in 1970, and it was hoped that it would stimulate sufficient growth to offset the economic decline of East Lancashire and Manchester. Though an enormous 'bank' of farm land was acquired for future development (8,000 acres) the whole planning climate was steadily moving against the post-war New Town concept, in favour of direct investment into the 'inner city areas'. Significant cuts were made in 1977, and it was announced in 1981 that the scheme would end in 1985. During its fifteen-year existence, around £200 million of central government cash was spent creating almost 10,000 new houses, industrial estates and a new and extensive road system.

Few mourned its passing, and it is perhaps a wonder that the scheme survived as long as it did. The consequences cannot however be avoided: by the start of the twenty-first century this district of mutually suspicious communities (often with individual histories of their own extending back for a millennium) had indeed become the single sprawling metropolis the planners had anticipated. For the first time the Broughton-Chorley belt began to acquire a growing sense of identity which - for good or ill - will play no small part in the future evolution of its government.

Preston Borough Council, *Towards a Prouder Preston* (1946); *The Development Plan for the County Borough of Preston* (1951). G L Woodcock, *Planning, Politics and Communications: A Study of the Central Lancashire New Town* (1986). D Hunt, *A History of Preston* (1992).

Property along Chapel Walks looking south to Fishergate, seen from the roof of St George's Shopping Centre 2004. The narrow buildings to the rear of their much wider frontages on Fishergate indicate the consolidation of the medieval burgage plots to form land holdings more suited to modern building (photo: author).

HUNT, HENRY 'ORATOR' (1773-1835)

Radical politician and MP for Preston 1830-4. Most celebrated for his participation in the great suffrage meeting on St Peter's Fields, Manchester, on 16 August 1819. The broad Preston franchise gave Radicals like Hunt some hope of election, and he contested the seat in 1820 whilst awaiting trial for his radical views. He failed and was sentenced to two years in Ilchester gaol. He failed to dislodge the DERBY INTEREST again in July 1830, but won a remarkable victory at a by-election the following December. After their win in the summer the Stanleys were complacent, fraud was rife and an electorate of 6,291 managed to poll 7,122 votes! Hunt won by 338 of them, and modestly presented silver medals to his supporters bearing the inscriptions 'H.Hunt esq. MP for Preston, Dec 24th 1830', and 'One of the 3730 electors of Preston - The Grateful tribute of the People of England'. He was now free to play a full part in the Reform Bill campaign.

Henry Hunt (1771-1835) Radical MP for Preston 1830-4 (from R Huish, The History of the Private and Political Life of Henry Hunt Esq, MP for Preston, *1835.*

Historians have made much of Hunt's defeat in 1834, following the reforms he had himself promoted. The truth is rather prosaic; the measure had less impact on Preston's wide franchise, and many of Stanley's Tory supporters had voted for the extremist Hunt in 1830 in disgust at Stanley's support of even a very moderate measure of reform! In 1834 they simply 'came home'.

W Proctor, 'Orator Hunt: MP for Preston', *TLCHS* 114 (1962). R Huish, *The History of the Private and Public Life of Henry Hunt Esq, MP for Preston* (1835).

See BLACK FEET: BOB'S BONES.

I

INSTITUTION FOR THE DIFFUSION OF KNOWLEDGE

See UNIVERSITY OF CENTRAL LANCASHIRE.

ISLAM IN PRESTON

Though Muslims were frequent visitors to the Port of Preston their modern communities date from the late 1950s when their founders were attracted by plentiful - if often badly paid - work in the mills. Gujarati Sunni Muslims from India are the largest non-white ethnic group in Preston (accounting for 5,500 people in 1986), and with the Gujarati Hindus form the biggest linguistic grouping. Pakistani Sunni Muslims accounted for a further 1,500 people in 1986. In the 2001 Census, Christians (71.5 per cent) comprised Preston's largest religious group, followed by Muslims (8.2 per cent: 10,629 people), Hindus (2.6 per cent), and Sikhs (0.6 per cent). By contrast, nearly 10 per cent of Prestonians had 'No Religion', and 7 per cent failed to state their religion.

Early progress was slow and fraught with difficulty. In 1960 a dance hall in Starkie St was hired for Friday prayers, and two years later the Preston Gujarati Muslim Society took a house in Great Avenham St. Other premises followed as needed, the former vicarage in Clarendon St became the town's first mosque, and the first purpose-built mosque followed in 1972. By 1975 the town was home to around 6,000 predominantly Indian Muslims but still had just three mosques. Provision has been greatly improved in recent years: for example Fishwick has the Aqsa, Medina and Quba Mosques, Avenham the Jamea Mosque, and Deepdale the Quwatul, Noor and Raza Mosques.

D Shepherd and S Harrison, *Islam in Preston* (1979). HMSO, *2001 Census* (2002).

See MASJID-E-NOOR; RAZA MOSQUE.

J

JACOBITES
See OLD PRETENDER; MOCK CORPORATION OF WALTON-LE-DALE; BONNIE PRINCE CHARLIE.

JAMES, ALEC (1902-1953)
Pre-eminent Scottish footballer: a PRESTON NORTH END player 1925-9. Born at Mossend, North Lanarkshire, the diminutive James signed for Raith Rovers in 1922, and was 'bundled unceremoniously across the border' to sign for North End in September 1925. His uncanny ball skills and perceptive tactical play made him a firm favourite, he increased gates both home and away, and he was one of the first players to appreciate fully his own 'box office' value. Despite J I Taylor's extravagant team-building, the 'school of 1925' failed to escape the Second Division, and when the club refused to release him from an important League match to play for Scotland James became disenchanted. In March 1928 'Wee Eck' starred in the 5-1 demolition of England by Scotland's 'Wembley Wizards', and cheekily presented the Preston board with a photograph of himself cheerily shaking hands with the Duke of York before the game! In 1929 he eventually left Preston for Herbert Chapman's great Arsenal 'team of the thirties'. Yet though he went on to become one of the world's greatest players it has generally been accepted that he played and enjoyed his most creative football at DEEPDALE.

John Harding, *Alex James: Life of a Football Legend* (1988). D Hunt, *A History of Preston North End Football Club: The Power, the Politics and the People* (2000).

JAMES VI OF SCOTLAND, JAMES I OF ENGLAND

'Scotch Jamie' visited Preston en route to a short but celebrated stay at Hoghton Tower, in August 1617. Nicholas Assheton of Downham maintained a diary of the visit:

August 15. King came to Preston. Ther, at the Crosse, Mr.Breares, the lawyer, made a Speache and the Corporation presented him with a bowle; and then the King went to a banquet in the Town hall, and so away to Houghton; ther a speeche made. The King killed a stag. We attended on the Lord's table.

Three days later Sir Richard Hoghton and his party were back carousing in Preston, 'as merrie as Robin Hood, and all his fellowes'. No doubt he was celebrating the success of the hidden agenda which lay behind his lavish entertaining of the King - the agreement with the Crown to exploit the Pleasington alum mines. James had taken a break from hunting to view them 'preciselie' on the second day of his visit. Perhaps significantly, the otherwise attentive Asheton makes no reference to the knighting of the Loin.

G Miller, *Hoghton Tower* (1949).

K

KUERDEN, DR (REAL NAME RICHARD JACKSON) (1623-?1701)

Physician, Royalist, supervisor of Preston's roads, and a 'Paineful gatherer and lover of Antiquities'. Born at Cuerden, Richard was educated at Leyland Free Grammar School under Mr Sherburn; his parents Gilbert Jackson and Ann Leyland are buried in the adjacent cemetery. After a highly successful university career at Oxford and Cambridge he took up medicine, which he was practising in Preston by 1662. An ardent Royalist (and possibly a Catholic) his refusal to take various oaths hindered his progress at Oxford and delayed his 'graduation' as MD.

Nothing is known of his medical prowess, and local history was his great interest. With Christopher Towneley he planned a large-scale 'History of Lancashire', but the latter's death in 1674 dealt the project a massive blow. The pair gained access to many collections of civic and family records which Kuerden never succeeded in assembling, though he advertised publication of 'Brigantia Lancastriensis restaurata' in five volumes in 1688. Despite Kuerden's anxiety about the archive's survival after his death, much of it has been preserved, and the pair were literally centuries ahead of their time. An anonymous fragment published in 1818 became the first published 'History of Preston', and Edward Baines published the first *History of Lancashire* in 1836, almost 150 years after Kuerden's rather premature announcement!

Kuerden seems to have enjoyed good relations with Preston's RESTORATION town council, fostered their sense of tradition and love of ceremonial,and went to great pains to present their town in as good a light as possible. This did not protect him from the angry ratepayers, however, for in 1675 'Edward Rigby and Richard Kewerden Dr. in phisicke', unpaid Overseers of the Roads, were arraigned before the COURT LEET 'upon paine of Vs. apiece...for not repairing ye highways belonging to this Corporation'. In 1701, the town clerk was ordered to get back papers 'formerly lent to Dr. Kuerden'. Preston's 'Great Doctor' spent his final years in great poverty, and the precise date and place of his death are not known. Such is the lot of the historian of Preston.

Kuerden's 1682 manuscript was published with notes by John Taylor, *A brief Description of the Burrough and Town of Preston, and its Government and Guild* (1818): Taylor was ignorant of who had written it! Extracts have been used by virtually all the subsequent writers on this subject. C W Sutton (2004) *ODNB*: 'Richard Jackson'.

L

LAMP LIGHTERS

Preston had no street lights before 1699, when the council decided to provide 'lamps or convex lights' for 'the better going in the streets of this town, in the winter evenings, in the decrease of the moon or when the cloude interfere'. Even after the advent of gas in 1816 Preston continued to employ large numbers of oil lamps, and in 1821 had 350.

The children's lampleeter's street song was recorded in 1942:

Oily, oily Peter, best lamp leeter,
Oily, oily Bob, stole a tiny cob,
Oily, oily Jack, with the Devil on his back.

Preston Herald (11 Dec. 1942).

LANCASHIRE COTTON FAMINE OR 'THE GREAT COTTON PANIC' (1861-1864)

A long period of mass unemployment and poverty brought about by the failure of the textile industry in what was essentially a single industry town. Though popularly associated with the disruption of raw cotton imports by the American Civil War, the crisis had its origins in an orthodox but steep economic depression resulting from over-production (1859-61), speculation and the failure of markets in India and the Far East. This situation was exacerbated and prolonged by the uncertainties and high prices brought about by the war. To assist the Board of Guardians a Preston Relief Committee was established under the auspices of JOSEPH LIVESEY. In December 1863 the Poor Law Guardians relieved 9,550 cases representing 22,302 people, and the Relief Committee 10,571 cases representing 40,627 people. Many people would clearly be helped by both parties, but the best estimate at the time was that 49,000 Prestonians were receiving outside relief of some sort. The number of people wholly unemployed peaked at 14,500 in April 1863. To the foresighted it was a taste of what could befall the region if the economy was not diversified in preparation for the day when other countries would capture Lancashire's pre-eminence in the COTTON INDUSTRY.

D Hunt, *The Silent Mills: Preston and the Lancashire Cotton Famine* (1991).

LANGLEY LANE, GOOSNARGH
Nuclear bunker; see TOP SECRET PRESTON.

LEASES
An interesting selection of early Preston leases has survived; they tell us much about the evolving geography of the town and something of the activities of its inhabitants.

For example, in 1331 John of Ashton needed a narrow strip from his neighbour Ralph to enable him to complete his house. Ralph agreed that this was reasonable but insisted that John 'keep him from damage done by water', and make a gully between their houses 'so that the water may have free exit into the highway' - where of course it became someone else's problem.

J H Lumsby, *De Hoghton Deeds and Papers* (1936); an enormous selection of leases and deeds from the 1280s to the present can be viewed in LRO.

See BURGAGE.

LEPER HOSPITAL
Characterized by lesions of the skin, leprosy is caused by the bacillus Mycobacterium Leprae. In Europe the disease was particularly prevalent during the Middle Ages but tended to die out thereafter. Preston's leper hospital is first recorded around 1178, but it may have been founded in 1127 when monks from the very early but short-lived house at Tulketh migrated to establish Furness Abbey. In 1373 Sir Adam de Houghton was authorized to take four great oaks from the FOREST OF FULWOOD to construct a fence around the mission. Styled the 'Hospital of the Brethren of Saint Mary Magdalen of Preston' it stood within its small estate - the MAUDLANDS - on or close by the much later site of ST WALBURGE'S CHURCH. It was probably only a small building, but had its own chapel and a warden who supervised the nursing staff of monks and sisters. As the town's only medical facility these restricted resources were obviously overwhelmed by the pandemic of 1349-50, but although the staff themselves suffered severely the enormous sum (£32) was received in alms to support their extended efforts. With the general decline of leprosy in the following centuries the hospital fell out of use, and was in 'grete ruen and dekey' at the time of its dissolution in 1548. Though absent from Europe, it is estimated that there may still be as many as two

million cases of leprosy in the world today.

H Fishwick, *History of the Parish of Preston* (1900). T C Smith (1892) *Records of the Parish Church of Preston* (1892).

See BLACK DEATH.

LISZT, FRANZ (1811-1886)

Composer and pianist. Liszt appeared at the THEATRE ROYAL during his English tour of 1840-1. His Preston visit on Wednesday 2 December 1840 was musically stupendous but was not a sell-out. As the *Preston Chronicle* lamented, the attendance was

> By no means worthy either of the musical reputation of Preston, or commensurate with his high deserts. Nevertheless there was a fair sprinkling of the fashionable and respectables of the town and neighbourhood.

The great man was 'heartily welcomed' indeed 'it was next to impossible to describe the enthusiasm he excited throughout'. Finally the reporter gave up: 'The attempt at description on our part would be at once vain and presumptuous'! In short Liszt's visit must rank alongside that of the Beatles and Paganini as one of the high points in the whole of Preston's cultural history.

D Hindle, *Twice Nightly: An Illustrated History of Entertainment in Preston* (1999). *Preston Chronicle* (5 Dec. 1840).

LITTLE AMERICA (1942-1945)

The name given to Kirkham and the Fylde villages adjacent to the enormous US airbase at Warton. Around 20,000 men were stationed here in what became a vital staging post between America and the invasion of Europe.

See YANKS; FRECKLETON AIR DISASTER.

LIVESEY, JAMES (1831-1923)

Railway Engineer, son of JOSEPH AND JANE LIVESEY, and brother of WILLIAM. After a railway apprenticeship with the Caledonian Railway Co. and work with a number of leading engineering firms including Beyer, Peacock & Co. of Manchester, James was employed on the Queen Isabel II Railway in Spain. Returning to Manchester the Livesey newspaper interest asserted itself and he founded a company to manufacture newspaper-folding machines - one of a number of his mechanical inventions. He founded one of the world's leading engineering consultancy businesses, with railway interests all over the world but particularly in Canada and South America. His extremely colourful life is in marked contrast to those of the other members of his family; details of his Spanish marriage are less than clear, though his son Fernando Harry (Sir Harry Livesey, 1860-1932) himself became a leading engineer. Livesey survived the catalogue of rail accidents then a part of the empire-building

railway engineer's lot, and his father would have no doubt found many of his associates - such as George Hudson and Andrew Carnegie - unsuitable companions of first choice. He died in his nineties at his Westminster residence, the possessor of a Sussex estate, homes in Norway and France, and a fortune exceeding a quarter of a million pounds (*ODNB* - another account places him on his yacht off Monte Carlo!). Though little known in Preston, Joseph Livesey's youngest son was thus a key player in the opening up of enormous tracts of North and South America to economic development.
ODNB

LIVESEY, JANE (1799-1870)
The wife of JOSEPH LIVESEY and mother of JAMES and WILLIAM. When Joseph Livesey abandoned Anglicanism to become a 'Scotch Baptist' Jane came to his attention as 'an amiable and religious girl', and she came to hear of him 'as a preacher'. Without ever meeting the strikingly handsome Liverpool girl Livesey decided that she was the wife for him, and he proposed after a speaking engagement in Manchester: the lady accepted. Their courtship then ensued by post and the young couple (he was 21, she was 19) had a very plain wedding in the vestry of St Peter's Church, Liverpool. The couple lived for a short time at the weaving shop at Walton-le-Dale, before moving to Preston. Here Livesey was taken seriously ill and was advised to eat plenty of cheese, and so the couple stumbled across the enormous profits to be made out of selling Preston's culinary speciality.

Jane manned their stall whilst Joseph went from farm to farm buying whole Lancashire cheeses and in a few years they had cornered the enormous market. This provided the foundation for their large family and the importance of domestic bliss was a subject with which Livesey never tired of regaling his readers. Jane took as large a part as her family commitments would allow in her husband's activities, visiting the poor, supporting their educational ventures, and working in the women's section of the temperance cause where the Preston ladies established the world's first Temperance Hotel. In short she played a full part in what are usually regarded as solely her husband's activities, but in addition gave birth to thirteen children between 1816 and 1837. Joseph seems to have suffered a complete breakdown when their fifty-two-year marriage was ended by her death in 1870.
See M Clark in I Levitt (ed.), *Joseph Livesey of Preston: Business, Temperance and Moral Reform* (1996).

LIVESEY, JOSEPH (1794-1884)
One of the most influential men in Preston in the years (1830-80); a prosperous cheese factor and social reformer. A self-educated self-made man,

Joseph Livesey, (1794-1884). Cheese merchant, newspaper magnate, dietary experimenter and social reformer (from J Pearce, The Life and Teachings of Joseph Livesy, *1887).*

Livesey's fortune came from the local cheese trade which he stumbled into quite by accident. His strong individualism, primitive Christianity and antipathy to authority was ever apparent. In the 1820s he supported Preston's Radical parliamentary candidates, was a strong advocate of the 1832 Reform Bill and took a leading part in opposition to the New Poor Law (1834). His dislike of committees meant, however, that his sojourns on the Town Council and Board of Guardians were relatively short. Once the temperance movement began to develop tendencies not to his liking, he poured his considerable energies into the successful fight for free trade (1841-6). His role in the early history of the temperance movement should not therefore distract from the much wider interests of his life, and he left a mark on all the progressive movements and institutions of his time. Indeed, in later life he seems to have realized that his very strong position on the drink issue had been to some extent counter-productive.

Obituary: *Preston Chronicle* (6 Sept. 1884). J Pearce, *The Life and Teachings of Joseph Livesey* (1887), which includes Livesey's 'Autobiography'. I Levitt (ed.), *Joseph Livesey of Preston: Business, Temperance and Moral Reform* (1996). ODNB. The Livesey Historical Society is based in Tennessee: http://www.lhsociety.org. Many family and related papers are preserved in the Livesey Collection held by the University of Central Lancashire.

See THOMAS BATTY ADDISON; MALT LIQUOR LECTURE; PRESTON TEMPERANCE SOCIETY; SEVEN MEN OF PRESTON.

LIVESEY, WILLIAM (1816-1909)

Son of Jane and Joseph Livesey, leading light of the Preston FREEHOLD LAND SOCIETY (1851) and newspaper proprietor. As firstborn (and like his father the only survivor of twins) it was William's lot to play a full if 'Jack of all trades' role in all the family enterprises, and needless to say he was an acknowledged authority on cheese. Joseph was living with William and his wife when he died, and William took great pains to oversee the publication of his father's memoirs which established his lasting reputation.

J Pearce, *The Life and Teachings of Joseph Livesey* (1887). M Clark in I Levitt (ed.), *Joseph Livesey of Preston: Business, Temperance and Moral Reform* (1996).

LOCK-OUT OF 1853-4

Preston's most celebrated labour dispute. The early 1850s were one of the most prosperous periods in the history of the cotton trade, and the spring of 1853 was marked by labour unrest in all of the Lancashire towns as the workforce sought to share in the prosperity. The battle was for the restoration of the 'Ten Per Cent', won and lost in earlier disputes. Amidst national strike fever the employers gave way, but it became clear that the success of the whole movement would depend on victory at Preston, which became the principal battleground. By mid-August it appeared that the Preston mill owners would give way and only half a dozen firms held out. But the Preston Masters Association (under the astute leadership of THOMAS MILLER JUN) comprised thirty-five of the Preston firms, each strongly committed to group action through the deposit of a £5,000 bond. Though industrial action was restricted to only a small number of mills the Association now amazed everyone by ordering that all workers be locked out. After all, were they to be dictated to in their own mills?

The Preston Lock-Out officially began on Saturday 15 October when 80 per cent of the town's production was switched off, throwing a similar proportion of the 25,000 'operatives' out of work. A long war of attrition now began, with support for the Preston workers coming from neighbouring towns, particularly Blackburn. Rather alarmingly, an obscure journalist writing in an American newspaper - Karl Marx - thundered: 'Our St. Petersburg is at Preston!' As Christmas approached, it became clear that the dispute had come at too late a stage in the trade cycle, cotton markets began to deteriorate, a poor harvest drove up food prices and troubles in China disrupted Preston's markets. Now it was the lock-out that began to spread from town to town and by the end of October 183 mills were closed and 47,000 people thrown out of work. Across the county the masters agreed to pay a levy of 5 per cent of their wage bills in support of their Preston compatriots.

The winter of 1853-4 was a harsh one, a bleak Christmas passed, and at the end of January Charles Dickens began a two-day visit to collect material for a forthcoming book. On Thursday 9 February the lock-out officially ended and the mills reopened. Work began in the twenty mills which had met their workers' demands but a strict strike was maintained at those which had not. The masters now panicked and began to import 'blackleg' labour into the town. When a party of 'Knobsticks' duly arrived at Preston station they were kindly spirited away by the union leaders. Though the employers' ruse failed, the depression in the trade deepened and was further disrupted by the outbreak of the Crimean War. A new round of wage cuts thus began, and the withdrawal of the 'Ten Per Cent' from the Blackburn workers spelled certain defeat for their Preston allies. On May Day 1854 a meeting at WALTON BRIDGE attended by 10,000 people ratified a return to work. The Preston masters ruthlessly blacklisted agitators, among them John Huntington who left for America and, with a certain Mr Rockefeller, went on to found Standard Oil of Ohio.

During the dispute the number of convictions for drunkenness fell, enthusiasm for sports of all kinds proliferated and a high level of order prevailed. The Reverend Clay by contrast was concerned at the 'evil consequences' arising from the large number of young men and woman associating with too much time on their hands. Dutton and King drew an inescapable conclusion: 'Deprived of their beer the operatives could still enjoy sex and football'!

H I Dutton and J E King, *Ten Per Cent and No Surrender: The Preston Cotton Strike of 1853-4* (1981). For Huntington's story see *Preston Herald* (10 March 1950).

See AGITATION; SPINNERS STRIKE.

LONG PRESTON PEGGY

According to the ballad of the same name, she was an inhabitant of Long Preston who made her way to Preston to see the Jacobite army:

Long Preston Peggy to Proud Preston went,
To see the bold rebels it was her intent:
For in brave deeds of arms she did take much delight,
And therefore she went with the rebels to fight.

The Victorian romantics did their best for the lass, promoting her many attractions and devising a love interest with the Young Chevalier - until Charles Hardwick investigated further: it is not clear whether the ballad refers to 1715 or the 1745, and in later life she is said to have been overly fond of singing her 'hit' song whilst 'indulging in spirituous liquors'. Perhaps Charles went too far, and after an interesting life the fair Margaret simply enjoyed a sociable old age.

C Hardwick, *History of the Borough of Preston* (1857).

LORD, CYRIL (1911-1984)

Last of the local cotton tycoons and subsequently 'Mat Man: Karpet King of Europe' in an episode of the 1960s American TV series *Batman*. Born in Manchester, Lord entered the expanding man-made fibres trade and was an adviser to the Cotton Board during the Second World War. A brave if not reckless businessman he acquired considerable experience of both the manufacturing and merchandising sides of the textile business and was a gifted publicist. These talents he employed to great effect after 1945, when with the backing of the Irish banks and the buyers market for cotton mills he quickly built up a considerable business centred around mills in Chorley, Leyland and Preston. Then the darling of the city financiers his flotation of a part of his company in 1954 was oversubscribed twelve times. The late 1950s saw renewed and rapid contraction and Lord became a leading advocate of 'protection' for the industry. As ever his publicity was highly effective: he circulated 1,200 members of the establishment with wallets stuffed with cotton and Japanese money, and sent every MP a photograph of the smashed machinery in the interior of Embroidery Mill (June 1958).

Against this depressing and irreversible background and an unsuccessful attempt to transfer production to South Africa, Lord had developed the enormous carpet factory at Donaghadee, Northern Ireland. He applied himself to selling the five yards of carpet the plant produced each minute with gusto: 'This is luxury you can afford with Cyril Lord!' By the early 1960s Lord was a millionaire, but great controversy surrounded a second share issue in 1965, and the empire collapsed spectacularly in 1968. By this time he had retired to the West Indies. Lord was a colourful character, with three wives, a yacht and a Caribbean home: his friend Ian Fleming is reputed to have based the character of Pussy Galore (of 'Gold Finger' fame) on his second wife, the novelist Shirley Hussey. He died at his home in Barbados in May 1984, and the final payment to his creditors was made in 1987. *ODNB.*

LOYAL NORTH LANCASHIRE REGIMENT
See QUEEN'S LANCASHIRE REGIMENT.

LUDDISM
The deliberate smashing of machinery perceived to be a threat to employment. The fear of attacks on his machinery induced RICHARD ARKWRIGHT to work amidst great secrecy in Preston and subsequently to establish his mills in the Midlands. His early factory at Birkacre near Chorley was destroyed by Luddites and the magistrates did nothing to prevent this. Forty years later the introduction of powerloom weaving (always a potent psychological threat to HANDLOOM WEAVING) led to serious rioting in Blackburn. The Preston masters armed their loyal men and stored the upper floors of their mills with paving stones to throw onto potential intruders. Widespread panic broke out when a large revolutionary host was reported to be gathering on Preston Moor; the military ('a troop of the 2nd Dragoon Guards and a detachment of the 73rd Regiment of Foot') stood by as what turned out to be enthusiastic spectators attending a boxing match returned home.

In 1831 more serious disturbances in the town resulted in the smashing of the new machinery in Birley's 'Big Factory' at Fishwick. Hewitson described the subsequent events of 7 November which he blamed on a visit by HENRY HUNT:

A mob marched up and down the town; workshops and mills were entered, and machinery stopped; the old lock-up (an 'overnight' prison), in Turks Head Yard was broken open, the prisoners were let out, and the books and coats of the constables thrown onto the fire.

An attack on the House of Correction in Stanley St penetrated the outer gate and was only thwarted when Captain Anthony - the governor - standing before the mob with burning fuse in hand, threatened to fire a cannon from point blank range at the rioters. Soldiers of the 80th Regiment arrived the next day, and four 'Martello Towers' were erected the following year to strengthen the house's defences! Sadly, this Preston Bastille did not survive long; three towers were demolished in 1864 and the final one was removed from what had become the Preston Prison site in 1877.

Preston Chronicle (6 May 1826). A Hewitson, *History of Preston* (1883).

    See CHARTISM; SPINNERS STRIKE.

M

MAINSPRIT WEIND OR PETTYCOAT ALLEY
    See WELLS.

MALT LIQUOR LECTURE
A lecture on the chemical nature of beer devised by JOSEPH LIVESEY and first delivered in Preston in February 1833. It quickly became a leading manifesto of the temperance cause and was delivered by missionaries throughout Britain, Europe and North America for many years. It purported to show - wrongly as it turned out – that fermentation destroyed the food value of the original ingredients. With a table festooned with interesting-looking scientific implements of all kinds, Livesey carried the whole thing off with great aplomb, finally reducing a quart of the resulting beer to water, mash and pure alcohol which Livesey then burned off in a lamp. On one occasion a 'reformed drunkard' cried out mournfully at this point – 'I could have lit all the lamps in Salford!'

J Livesey, *The Malt Liquor Lecture* (1834, repr. 1870). B Harrison, *Drink and the Victorians* (1971).

The Malt Liquor Lecture - under way in the Cock Pit, Preston, 1830s. Top-hatted Dickey Turner is seated on the front row looking straight at the engraver (from J Pearce, The Life and Teachings of Joseph Livesey, *1887).*

MANOR OF PRESTON

After the Norman Conquest Roger of Poitou succeeded Earl Tostig of Northumbria as Lord of the Manor of Preston, who in turn may have 'replaced' the churchmen of York whose diocese had been granted lands here in 903. When Roger fell from grace, the manor passed with his other lands to the Duchy of Lancaster and ultimately to the Crown. The Corporation was then able to rent the feudal charge due to their Lord (the King - as Duke of Lancaster) for £15 per year. This was a shrewd piece of business for the Prestonians since in 1244 it was estimated that the rental would have been worth £20 if it had remained in the King's hands! With an absent lord the townspeople were not so prone to external interference in their affairs as would have been the case if the lordship had been in the private hands of the Hoghtons, the Langtons or the ffaringtons. Preston Corporation became in effect Lord of the Manor when it purchased the rental outright in 1676.

D Hunt, *A History of Preston* (1992).

MARKETS

Preston grew out of its ideal location as the central place in which country people could meet and mutually exchange the natural produce of a large area of Lancashire, and the right to hold markets was one of the principal freedoms sought and granted through the succession of royal charters. Writing in the 1680s DR KUERDEN left a vivid picture of Preston's thriving market scene. The meat market was held every day apart from Sunday in the butchers 'shopps' and stalls beneath the TOWN HALL, and Wednesday, Friday and Saturday were the market days. The proceedings were carefully regulated by bells to ensure that the Prestonians had the first choice of the goods for sale. On busy days the main streets and thoroughfares would be jammed with jostling traders and their eager customers. Buildings adjacent to the market place were used to store samples (particularly of grain and cloth), and bargains were usually struck in one of the twenty-eight public houses which as late as 1882 stood within the space of a 150-yard walk; the construction of the Harris building alone removed seven of them.

Kuerden's account reveals a rich assortment of highly specialized markets:

Wednesday, and Saturday, and Friday being ever a market for fish, butter, and cheese, as likewise in the evening for yarn...And upon Saturday, as soon as light appeare, is the market bell for linnen cloth: when ended, yarn appears, bread and fish all in a row upon the fish stones, and places adjacent; there butter, cheeses and pullen, and potters about the butter crosse, in the end of Cheapside market; and bread neare unto the fish market.

The market for corn and other foodstuffs moved to the new CORN EXCHANGE in Lune St in 1824, and the opening of the great 'covered market'

Preston's covered markets c.1920. Though general goods were on sale on the day that this photograph was taken, the smaller market area to the right was normally the town's fish market.

led to a further reordering of the town's markets in 1875. The market for grain and dairy products (particularly cheese) continued to be held at the Corn Exchange on Saturdays, but the great market square was used only for the sale of cloth and small domestic items, and the 'covered market' became the centre of activity which it essentially remains to this day.

R Kuerden, *A Brief Description of the Burrough and Town of Preston* (1682, published by J Taylor, 1818). A Hewitson, *History of Preston* (1883).

See CELIA FIENNES.

MARSDEN, RICHARD (1802/3-1858)

The leading figure produced by Preston in the nineteenth-century movement for working-class emancipation. Apart from occasional mentions in the local press, the record of the career of this genial, light-blue-eyed fiery mass orator is almost entirely restricted to his letters to the working-class press of the day, notably the *Northern Star*.

Probably a native of South Lancashire, Marsden moved to Bamber Bridge from Manchester in 1829 to find work in the local handweaving trade, and in his early letters he frequently refers to the hardships endured by the 'White slaves of Bamber Bridge'. An associate at this time of JOSEPH LIVESEY, the two would ultimately be drawn apart on the issue of trade union militancy, which the more moderate Livesey could never countenance. With the formation of the Preston Radical Operatives Association in 1837 Marsden himself emerged as a leader of local opinion, and was a natural candidate to represent the town at the Chartist National Convention held in London in February 1839. Animated by strong feelings of social injustice and the severe hardships endured by his wife and daughters, he soon became frustrated by the convention's tame proceedings. For a time he held centre stage and was elected 'Chairman for a day', and not until the emergence of George Woodcock of the TUC in the 1960s would a 'Prestonian' hold such a position again. Yet March saw him saddened, disappointed and back in Preston; here twenty muskets had been bought by the inhabitants of one street alone!

The rejection of the first petition and the general strike which followed led to the issue of a warrant for Marsden's arrest, and he was 'on the run' until his incarceration in Newcastle prison in July 1840. On his release, and starving, he returned to his family in Marsh Lane, Preston, but financial help was forthcoming from supporters throughout the North, attesting to the high esteem in which he was held. May 1842 saw the failure of the second petition and Marsden was a frequent speaker at the meetings which followed. His role in the 'Plug Riots' of August is less than clear, and although the Preston Chartists tried to distance themselves from local events, it is hard to believe that he was not about in Lune St during Bloody Saturday. He was briefly arrested but released without charge following the debacle at Walton Bridge a few days later.

The onset in 1846 of the third serious economic depression in ten years saw a third and final revival of CHARTISM. The collecting of signatures began for a massive petition, and the French Revolution of February 1848 gave a tremendous boost to the reform movement. An enthusiastic throng in the Temperance Hall sent the French people the Fraternal Greetings of the 'Industrious Classes of Preston' and elected Marsden to represent the town in the forthcoming London convention. Here he was once again a prominent figure and was probably present to see the failure of the great demonstration at Kennington Common. Chartism as an organized movement never recovered, and references to Marsden's activities seem to end in 1850. He played no part in the strike of 1853-4, and it had been assumed that he was dead by this time. Like the majority of working people at this time he and his family simply slip from the pages of history.

Richard Marsden's political views have been brilliantly analysed by J E King: a man of strong religious beliefs, he was no 'Marxist' and 'never sought the elimination of other social classes'. He came to accept the central importance of trade unions to advance and defend social conditions within what today would be seen as a mixed economy. Like the central tenets of

Chartism itself, this view or at least a modified version of it still had an important role to play in the emergence of modern Britain in the years before 1945.

J E King, *Richard Marsden and the Preston Chartists, 1837-1848* (1981). *ODNB*: according to which Marsden died at 16 Club St, Bamber Bridge, on 28 January 1858. *Peoples Paper* (27 Feb. 1858).

MASJID-E-NOOR

The 'Mosque of Light', Noor St, serves the town's 9,000-strong Gujarati Sunni Muslim community. The land on the former ROYAL INFIRMARY site was acquired in 1990 and the south-east-facing Mosque with its spectacular copper dome was opened in 2001. This architectural masterpiece has two prayer halls each accommodating 250 worshippers.
See ISLAM IN PRESTON.

MAUDLANDS

An early medieval estate in Preston belonging to the Brethren of the Hospital of St Mary Magdalen, from which the adjacent Spittallers Moss also derived its name.
See LEPER HOSPITAL; ST WALBURGE'S.

MAUDLAND BANK

A large railway embankment in the MAUDLANDS. The halting of down Scottish Expresses here on their approach to Preston Station became a local joke, drawing the laconic remark: 'Another player for North End!'

MILLER PARK

See PUBLIC PARKS.

MILLER, THOMAS, SENIOR (1768-1840)

Cotton Manufacturer. Miller, a 'good practical weaver' and 'small manufacturer' at Bolton, was brought in by JOHN HORROCKS to manage a part of the Preston works. His value was quickly appreciated and he became a partner in 1802 on a wage of £300 per year. More importantly he was given a 5 per cent share in the profits of 'Horrocks, Whitehead & Miller' - worth well over £2,000 that year. His profits were used to acquire further stock in the firm, and his share grew to around a quarter. On the founder's death, executive control passed to SAMUEL HORROCKS, with Thomas Miller the works manager. In the 1830s he was joined on the board by his son Thomas who, after the deaths of his father and Sam Horrocks, became the largest single shareholder himself in 1846. Under his management the company made great progress, pioneering the development of foreign agencies

(Portugal 1823, India 1830), and mechanizing the weaving side. In June 1840 a new weaving shed was opened and the firm's agents were asked 'To look out for and send any examples of power loom cloth to Preston'. Much of Horrockses' eastern trade was conducted by barter, and remarkably the Preston firm became an important trader in sugar, coffee, tea and spices! By the time of his death the balance on his stock account stood at £136,205 11s 0d, and control of the firm ultimately passed to his son and namesake.

D Hunt, *A History of Preston* (1992). Margaret Burscough, *The Horrockses: Cotton Kings of Preston* (2004).

MILLER, THOMAS, JUNIOR (1811-1865)

Greatest of the Cotton Lords of Preston. Educated at Preston, Manchester and Paris, Miller followed in the footsteps of his father and became sole proprietor of 'Horrocks, Miller & Co, Yard Works, Preston', in 1860. As the town's wealthiest resident and the leading light of the local Liberals it might have been expected that he would have pursued a political career, but this was not the case. He served as a magistrate and represented Fishwick Ward on the Town Council, becoming an alderman in 1846. After a dispute in 1845 Miller bitterly refused repeated offers of the mayoralty, and though enormously influential he rarely took the initiative in politics himself. In labour affairs, however, he opposed the Ten Hours Bill and took the lead in the Masters Association; in him the operatives had 'a stubborn and unforgiving opponent'. In the words of George Cowell, labour leader during the LOCK-OUT OF 1853-4, he was 'notorious for screwing down the operatives in his employ', and paying miserly wages.

Not surprisingly his obituary published in the *Preston Guardian* (1 July 1865) saw him rather differently:

He took a warm and unaffected interest in all that concerned the welfare of the working classes. Brought into constant contact with thousands of operatives working in his mills, he knew well the class from which his ancestors had sprung. He studied their wants, and he did not a little to supply those wants.

Faced by the problem of what to do with his enormous wealth after his father's death Miller began to invest heavily in land and paintings. He purchased the manor of Singleton for £40,000 in 1853, developed Singleton Hall and steadily extended his estate in the Fylde. His large town house still broods over the north-east corner of Winckley Square, and he filled his properties with works by Millais, Landseer and Whistler.

The year before his death his stock in the company ledger passed the half a million pounds mark. His death was reported to have caused great consternation among his workforce and his interment was the occasion of perhaps the greatest of the set-piece funerals of a Cotton Lord: his workers massed at the Yard Works before proceeding to line the streets from the Corn Exchange to his house in Winckley Square on the processional route around the town. Thomas Miller junior is perhaps best remembered today for his gift of the land on which Miller Park was created (1864).

D Hunt, *A History of Preston* (1992). Margaret Burscough, *The Horrockses: Cotton Kings of Preston* (2004).

MINSTER, THE

Preston Parish Church. From early times the church was dedicated to ST WILFRID, and from the late sixteenth century to the apostle St John the Divine. A church has probably existed on this prominent site on the CHURCHGATE-FISHERGATE ridge from early Saxon times, and the curvilinear field layout in which it stands seems to underlie the regular medieval town plan. 'Atticus' (Anthony Hewitson, *Our Churches and Chapels*, 1869) dismissed the inevitable squabble about the building's origins with fine journalistic scepticism:

It doesn't particularly matter when the building we call our Parish Church was first erected; and, if it did, the world would have to die of literary inanition before it got the exact date. None of the larger sort of Antiquarians agree absolutely on the subject, and the smaller fry go in for all sorts of figures.

The church is definitely recorded in 1094, but its existence can be inferred from before 670.

Successive generations of Prestonians do not seem to have been prepared to fund the fabric of their church properly, making repairs only when the building's condition had become a scandal in the neighbouring towns, and then usually at the cheapest cost. The seventeenth-century church seems to have been a low, clerestoried, four-bay building with north and south aisles, and a tower at the west end. It possessed two chapels (Lea Chapel and Wall's Chapel), and before the Reformation had a succession of chantries, including those of 'Jesus' and 'St Mary'; these and the outlying chapels required a staff of around a dozen priests.

The building particularly suffered during the Civil War, and for a period of 450 years - on and off - at the hands of the Scots. In 1671 it was described as 'foule and uncomely', and although DR KUERDEN could always be depended upon to put a fine spin on Preston life (describing the region's mother church as 'spacious, well-built, or rather re-edified'), the entire roof eventually fell in (1770). In 1811 the perennially dangerous tower had to be pulled down, and the chancel had to be rebuilt six years later. Charles Hardwick thought the structure little more than an exercise in 'Joiner's Gothick', and in 1853 the entire building was demolished (apart from the lower part of the tower) and rebuilt in a fourteenth-century style. Following

Preston Parish Church c.1910. Located high on the Church St-Fishergate ridge, the ancient church of St Wilfrid has been at the centre of town life since at least the 7th century.

the grant of city status the church was reordered, and the 'Minster' was opened in 2003. The site has thus been at the centre of the lives of the Prestonians for almost 1500 years.

T C Smith, *Records of the Parish Church of Preston* (1892).

MOCK CORPORATION OF WALTON-LE-DALE

A group of leading local Tories who began to meet for fraternal and very sociable dinners at the Unicorn Inn in 1701. They went to great pains to mock the proceedings of Preston's Whig-dominated Town Council, and amidst much hilarity appointed a long list of officers (all equipped with staves, chains and medals of office). However the body soon developed a deeper and more sinister aspect, for the Tory interest - in 'opposition' since the 'Glorious Revolution' - came to favour the restoration of the Stuarts. In 1711 the Earl of Derwentwater was elected Mayor of the Mock Corporation: four years later he led the Jacobite army to defeat at Preston, and two members were subsequently executed. Yet the treason of the majority of members probably went no further than drunken toasts to 'The King Over The Water' - certainly the majority of the 'Walton Ale-house Tories' wisely kept their heads down during the events of both 1715 and 1745. By 1750 the august body had become a well-heeled diners' club, and was a popular feature of the 'Walton Wakes'. In 1791 Robert Hilton was the final Mayor to be appointed, up to the present time. The fund raised by selling the 'Freedom of the Borough' was not dispensed in the purchase of powder and guns but went instead to the accumulation of a great store of more useful civic paraphernalia. Happily these 'crown jewels' were purchased at the initiative of Walton people, and presented to the Harris Museum in 1947. The Minute Book and list of regulations also survive. The old Unicorn Inn remains more or less intact, and is currently a popular Italian restaurant. It is quite possible, therefore, that the world has not heard the last of the celebrated Mock Corporation of Walton-le-Dale.

D Hunt, *A History of Walton-le-Dale and Bamber Bridge* (1997). The records are held by the Harris Museum. Despite its local notoriety, there is no tradition that Bonnie Prince Charlie visited the inn during his two marches past it: this seems an unlikely omission for a prince so interested in the district's Jacobite history.

See BONNIE PRINCE CHARLIE; OLD PRETENDER.

MOOR BROOK, DEEPDALE BROOK, SWANSEA GUTTER
A now covered stream which flowed west from the Deepdale area across PRESTON MOOR to join the RIBBLE at the boundary with Ashton.

MOOR PARK
See PUBLIC PARKS.

MORMON MISSION (1837-1838)
On 22 July 1837 a party of seven Mormon missionaries arrived at Preston where the brother of one of their number was the minister at Vauxhall chapel. Here Herber C Kimball preached their first sermon in Europe, 'I declared that an angel had visited the earth, and committed the everlasting Gospel to man'. Sunday 30 July was a momentous day: the missionaries were lodging in a house in St Wilfrids St and by their own account were awakened

when a vision was opened to our minds, and we could distinctly see the evil spirits, who foamed and gnashed their teeth at us...However the Lord delivered us from them.

At 9 a.m. Kimball baptised nine converts in the River RIBBLE:

The circumstance of baptising in the open air being somewhat novel, a concourse of between seven and nine thousand people assembled on the banks of the river to witness the ceremony.

Branches were established in a number of the villages around the town, and when the 'freshwater streams were frozen with ice' ten people were baptized 'in the open sea' at Longton. By their departure for the United States in April 1838 a small but pioneering mission had been established in Britain, and Kimball later returned with Brigham Young to attend a 'general conference'

held in Preston on 14-16 April 1840.
R L Evans, *A Century of 'Mormonism' in Great Britain* (1937). D M W Pickup, *The Pick and Flower of England* (1997).

MORRIS, (JOHN) MARCUS HARSTON (1915-1989)

Clergyman, magazine publisher and one of the parents of 'Dan Dare'. Born in Preston, Morris was educated at Cheltenham and Oxford. Destined for the church, he was ordained in 1940 and became vicar of St James at Birkdale in 1945. Here work on a church magazine brought him into partnership with the artist Frank Hampson, with whom he devised a new type of cartoon magazine for boys; it was called the *Eagle*. 'Dan Dare' with full supporting cast duly appeared on the magazine shelves on 14 April 1950. A number of related titles followed (including *Girl* in 1951), and Morris ascended the publishing ladder at Hulton Press, and later with the National Magazine Co. in America for whom he launched *Cosmopolitan Magazine* in Britain. From 1952 to 1983 he was honorary chaplain at St Brides, Fleet St.
ODNB.

MOSNEY

An early cloth-printing complex at Walton-le-Dale with extensive interests in Preston (1780-8). Many historians contend that the mechanization of cloth printing was just as important a leap forward as the 'invention' of the water frame by RICHARD ARKWRIGHT. It was first achieved at Mosney - a water-powered site on the River Darwen at Walton - by the firm of Livesey, Hargreaves and partners. Though short-lived the concern employed perhaps 200 cloth printers (many of them women 'pencillers') on the site, and a much larger number of ancillary workers and weavers in the surrounding district. In 1792 O'Brien claimed - perhaps extravagantly - that the firm 'was a means of giving bread to near 20,000 persons'. The concern expanded rapidly and quickly mechanized many aspects of the printing process for which important patents were obtained in 1783 and 1785. To fund their business the firm issued very large quantities of £5 notes, which became 'the circulating medium of the country in and around Preston'. This led to the collapse of the firm in 1788 - the Preston district's first great commercial failure. It would be but the first of many, and the once considerable site at Mosney had virtually vanished from the landscape by 1850.
W A Abram, *History of Blackburn, Town and Parish* (1877). D Hunt, *A History of Walton-le-Dale and Bamber Bridge* (1997).
See COTTON INDUSTRY.

M6 MOTORWAY OR PRESTON BYPASS

The First World War saw great advances in the design of motor transport, and particularly of commercial vehicles. When the ABC road classification system was introduced, the Wigan road became the A49 and the key Preston-Carlisle route over Shap the A6. Initially the aim was to improve existing routes by removing meanders to enable a 'fast' speed of 30mph to be sustained on the 'better stretches' of road. Garstang was bypassed in 1924, and improvement of the line of the Liverpool Road (A59) saw Walmer Bridge and Hoole bypassed two years later, though the tortuous road through Longton was only improved in the late 1950s. A national programme of road building during the depression would have done much to reduce unemployment and promote recovery, but it was not until 1936 that a new through road from Warrington to Lancaster to pass to the east of Preston was put forward in earnest. This would have the great advantage of taking much of the through traffic away from the town's medieval central area.

The war caused further delays, and it was not until 1953 (twenty years after the German autobahnen programme) that construction of the £15 million Preston and Lancaster sections of the Warrington-Lancaster trunk road was announced. Work began in June 1956, and the giant girders of the Samlesbury bridge were lowered into place in March 1958. On 5 December Prime Minister Harold Macmillan opened the (unfinished) road, drove along it in style from Bamber Bridge, and declared the Preston Bypass to be Britain's first 'Motorway'. Many Prestonians were sceptical, the road was initially little used and was believed by many to be a white elephant. Work to link the Preston and Lancaster roads began in 1962, and the M6 was born. This was soon followed by the M61 (Preston to Manchester), the M55 (Preston to Blackpool), and the M65 (Preston to Colne), requiring the enormous road intersections at Broughton (via the spectacular 'Fylde Junction Higher Bridge') and Cuerden. In the 1980s an intermediate system of inner-ring dual-carriageways was developed (the Tom Benson Way, Eastway, Schleswig-Flensburg Way, etc.) to alleviate more localized bottlenecks. It is doubtful if any politician ever spoke truer words than 'Super Mac', for as he opened the rather quaint Preston Bypass he remarked that, although it was a fine road, 'we will soon have to be extending it'!

D Hunt, *A History of Preston* (1992). A Crosby (ed.), *Leading the Way: A History of Lancashire's Roads* (1998).

NEW PRESTON
The name given to a colony of handweavers' houses built among the open fields along the north side of New Hall Lane by JOHN HORROCKS. Their revolutionary design, comprising alternate rows of houses and loomshops, allowed for the future introduction of transmission-shafts for steam power-

weaving. They were demolished to make way for the New Preston Factory and subsequently the Centenary Works. Anthony Hewitson left a colourful description of the residents during their golden age:

The male denizens of 'New Preston' were...an exceedingly rough lot. They could earn good wages after playing two or three days a week. In their leisure time, or the time in which they did not care to work, they used to swagger about in top boots, and often extract what to their minds was enjoyment, from badger-bating, dog-worrying, cock-fighting, poaching and drinking. A pack of hounds was kept in 'New Preston' for the recreation of the people.

By the late nineteenth century 'New Preston' had given its name to the entire district along Ribbleton Lane and New Hall Lane.

A Hewitson, *History of Preston* (1883).

See HANDLOOM WEAVING.

NEW VICTORIA

Cinema and cafe, Church St, subsequently the Odeon cinema, and Top Rank ballroom (itself subsequently Tokyo Joes). Preston's first 'super-cinema' opened in 1928, the year after the success of Jolson's part-talkie *The Jazz Singer*. The statistics of this graceful art-deco building were impressive; 1,250,000 bricks, 550 tons of cement, a balcony arch 75 feet wide supported by a girder weighing 30 tons, 10,000 electric lamps, 50 miles of electric wire and an air conditioning system delivering two and three-quarter million cubic feet of air an hour! Here was Preston's temple of escapism, a point made in the opening-day souvenir:

Always there will be pictures that grip your interest, pictures which will make you glad, will fill your soul with laughter, and will eliminate from your system the day's accumulation of household or business anxieties.

The auditorium also accommodated stage shows and could boast an enormous Wurlitzer Organ which emerged from beneath the stage along with the young Reginald Dixon. The New Victoria was taken over by the Rank Organization in 1964, renamed the Odeon and developed as a broad-based entertainment centre. The former stalls area was roofed over to form the Top Rank dance hall, reducing the capacity of the cinema above from 2,000 to 1,200 patrons. In 1970 the popular cafe and meeting place was converted into 'Odeon Two' - an early multi-screen cinema. In 1992 the Odeon became the final Preston cinema to close, ironically as a result of competition from the vast, new and hugely successful out-of-town multi-screen cinemas at Riversway (1990) and the Capital Centre, Walton-le-Dale (1991). After forty years of decline Preston cinema had entered a new golden age, and the New Victoria lived on as 'Tokyo Joes' nightspot.

J Cotterall, *Preston's Palaces of Pleasure* (1988). D Hindle, *Twice Nightly: An Illustrated History of Entertainment in Preston* (1999).

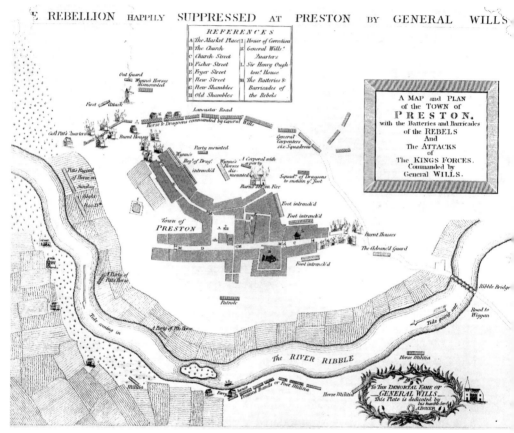

A contemporary plan of the 'Rebellion Happily Suppressed at Preston' in 1715. Note the line of the road as it enters the town from the south. The old Ribble bridge lay some way downstream of the present structure, and the road - Swillbrooks - ascended the escarpment to the west of 'London Road', crossed the Syke and entered Church St along 'Manchester Road' (from E Baines, History of the County Palatine of Lancashire, 1838).

O

OLD PRETENDER

James Edward Stuart (1688-1766) was the son of James II (deposed 1689), on whose death (1701) he was styled by his supporters James III of England, James VIII of Scotland. His followers were known as Jacobites - from the Latin for James. An attempt to install him failed in 1708, and

September 1715 saw the celebrated muster of the clans at Braemar. Led by Thomas Forster and the Earl of Derwentwater the force of less than 2,000 Scots set out for London and had reached Lancaster by November. No attempt was made by the government forces to defend Preston, and on 10 November amidst a sea of blue and white rosettes the Pretender was duly proclaimed King James III on the Market Place. As at Lancaster the Scots were quickly distracted by the genteel country town's delights, enabling their opponents to mass south of the Ribble and to bring in reinforcements from Yorkshire:

> The Ladys in this towne . . . are so very beautyfull and so richly attired, that the gentlemen minded nothing but courting and ffeasting.

Critically, the promised support of local Catholics simply did not materialize, there was no general uprising and the dispirited Forster knew his certain fate.

To their amazement government troops under General Willis crossed the RIBBLE BRIDGE unmolested and were able to reach the town itself. They found Church St, Friargate and Fishergate defended by barricades, and the Scots quickly proved themselves to be fine street fighters. Government losses were considerable, and with houses at both ends of the town on fire both sides 'lay upon their arms, but General Forster went to bed'. A force of 2,500 men under General Carpenter now completed the encirclement, and Forster decided to surrender. The disgust of his troops knew no bounds, 'nothing could quiet them for a great while'. Such locals as had joined the adventure now made good their escape by fording the river below Fishergate Hill. The Highlanders laid down their arms in the Market Place and were then locked in the Parish Church. Their officers were held in the White Bull, the Windmill and the Mitre - the alehouse which had been their headquarters. In the battle they had lost barely 20 men, but nearly 300 government troops had been killed. The latter now took their revenge by going on a rampage and looting the town, and

> with force of armes broke open doors and locks of chambers and closetts, and the moneys, plate, goods and chattles of most of the inhabitants...did steal, take and carry away.

Although to impress the Prestonians a number of locals were executed (on the later site of English Martyrs church in Garstang Road), the majority of Forster's army was shipped out to labour on the West Indies plantations. As in 1648 the Stuarts had paid a heavy price for their failure at Preston.

S Hibbert-Ware, *Lancashire Memorials of the Rebellion of 1715* (1844). C Hardwick, *History of the Borough of Preston* (1857). H W Clemesha, *History of Preston in Amounderness* (1912).

See BONNIE PRINCE CHARLIE; MOCK CORPORATION OF WALTON-LE-DALE.

OPEN AIR SCHOOL
See PUBLIC PARKS.

P

PAGANINI, NICCOLO
The great musician, whose frenetic piano playing was popularly thought to be under diabolic inspiration, thrilled crowds at the THEATRE ROYAL on 27 August 1833.

PALACE, THE
King's Palace Theatre (1913-55), Tithebarn St. Built on the site of a skating rink, the Palace had a capacity of 3,000 people (2,550 seated, 450 standing) and - decorated in the preferred French seventeenth-century style - was a real wonder. David Hindle has recalled: 'I can remember the large gaping boxes on either side of the proscenium, and the cavernous nature of the auditorium, with a single-tier circle'. Though converted for cinema use in the 1920s the Palace returned to live shows, becoming one of the region's great centres of Variety. GEORGE FORMBY was a popular and regular star and both Ted Ray and Donald Peers made their debut here. Perhaps rightly it was as a theatre (and not a cinema or worse a bingo hall) that it bowed out in 1955.
J Cotterall, *Preston's Palaces of Pleasure* (1988). D Hindle, *Twice Nightly: An Illustrated History of Entertainment in Preston* (1999).

PALLADIUM CINEMA
Opened in Church St in 1915 the Palladium was Preston's first purpose-built cinema, and was at the centre of a group which came to comprise the Empire (cinema 1930), the NEW VICTORIA (1928) and the RITZ (1937). In 1968 it closed, was purchased by the borough council and demolished.
J Cotterall, *Preston's Palaces of Pleasure* (1988). D Hindle, *Twice Nightly: An Illustrated History of Entertainment in Preston* (1999).

PALS COMPANY (1914)
The Preston Pals were not a classical 'Pals' formation. They were formed in late August 1914 for 'young businessmen, clerks etc' who had been put off enlisting by the chaos and crowds at FULWOOD BARRACKS. Many wore smart suits and straw hats as they proudly lined up on the Market Square in the warm August sunshine, thinking that they would be home again in a few months. They duly served in the 250-strong 'D' Company of the 7th Battalion of the Loyal North Lancashire Regiment, whereas the majority of local recruits served in the 1st/4th Battalion. The company suffered heavy casualties, particularly on the Somme, and gradually lost its local identity. In May 1915 Meyrick Hollins formed a second company. In a moving speech in November 1916 Harry Cartmell spoke of the 'handful of men' left from 'whole Battalions from our town': in particular:

How could we bear the knowledge of what has happened to the Preston Pals, that splendid company of fine young fellows, full of fire and life and energy, that left the town in the very early days of the war. On a morale-boosting visit to their section of the line in late 1915 he was greeted by the Assistant Borough Surveyor but was shocked to discover their depleted numbers.

I Birwistle, 'The Life of the Preston Pals (1914-18)' (1987, dissertation). H Cartmell, *For Remembrance: An Account of Some Fateful Years* (1919).

See DECLARATION OF WAR (1914); SOMME.

PARISH CHURCH
See MINSTER.

PATESON, ROBERT (1827-1910)
Self-educated scientist and photographer 'well versed in chemistry and electricity'. Pateson, himself a successful product of the Institution for the Diffusion of Knowledge, remained a committed working-class educationalist and self-improver all his life. Leaving Bow Lane school at 13 he worked initially as a druggist's assistant at a shop on the corner of Lune St and Fishergate. Here his interest in chemistry and the related sciences developed, fed by regular evening classes and lectures. Among the latter were the Institution's regular series on 'Galvanism', and it was to be as an electrician that he worked from the mid-1880s. He is best known today, however, as a photographer, an occupation he followed for thirty years after 1853. He had a number of partners, but it was with John Burton (1804-80) that he produced his finest and most important work. This was a set of views of Preston and district which was exhibited at the International Exhibition held in the Crystal Palace in 1862. By 1871 the census could describe him as a 'Master Photographer employing two assistants'. His work provided some of the best known images of the town, and his photographs have often been reproduced in recent years, culminating in a Harris Museum exhibition and the publication of many of his prints during the summer of 2004.

J Garlington and E Hesslewood, *Robert Pateson: The Life and Work of an Early Photographer* (2004).

PATTEN HOUSE
The princely Preston seat of the Earls of Derby stood between Derby St and Pole St on the north side of Church St. It was brought into the family through the marriage of Thomas to Elizabeth Patten, and was occupied by the Scots during the battle of Preston in 1715. It stood 'about 30 yards' back from the thoroughfare behind lawns, and was described by Whittle in 1832 as having 'a princely appearance'. By the 1830s an industrial area had grown up around it, and the 'Lord's Factory' had been specifically erected for JOHN

WATSON just over the road. The property was now much less desirable, the upkeep must have been very considerable, and the withdrawal of the Stanleys from Preston duly followed their political rejection at the hands of 'Orator Hunt' in the election of 1830. Preston's greatest house and former headquarters to the DERBY INTEREST was then briefly used as a barracks and a soup kitchen before its demolition in 1835.

P Whittle, *History of Preston* (1837).

'PHOTOGRAPHY' IN PRESTON
Both Fox-Talbot (1800-77) and Daguerre (1787-1851) announced the discovery of their respective processes in January 1839. Just six years later the *Preston Chronicle* announced:

> Daguerrotype Likenesses. Messrs Holt and Eastham, from Paris, are taking likenesses by the above unerring process in 5 seconds at very reasonable charges from 9 till 4 every day at Mr.Caton's Temperance Hotel, 41 Cannon Street, Preston.

Silas Eastham established himself in Preston, and a number of Daguerrotypes from this period preserved in the Harris Museum are attributed to him, including portraits of the Addison family, and the 'View of the Obelisk on the Market Square'. Dated 1846 the latter is perhaps the earliest surviving 'photograph' of Preston. The retouched image shows the view down the entrance of Friargate, the ancient 'Fish Stones', and buildings on the site of the later central post office. On the extreme left the diminutive jeweller's shop in Cheapside appears much as it is today! Charles Wilson, 'tailor and draper', produced a series of views of the town and its buildings in 1852. By this time both amateur and commercial photography were well established, with Preston sporting no less than fifteen 'photographers' in the *Trade Directory* of 1865, among them ROBERT PATESON.

J Garlington and E Hesslewood, *Robert Pateson: The Life and Work of an Early Photographer* (2004).

PILLORY, THE
In 1662 the town's bailiffs were ordered to erect a pillory, but whether as a replacement or an innovation is not clear. Nor is its location clearly stated, but it may have stood alongside the other punishments dispensed in the Town End of Deepdale Road. Rogues, wrongdoers and others could be liberally pelted with rubbish. The last use of the apparatus in earnest took place in 1816 when the 'keeper of a house of illfame' in Back Lane was so punished. The Pillory was abolished for all offences apart from perjury later in the same year. The last person to stand in the pillory at Preston (up to the present time) was the notorious practical joker Mr Ian O'Hagan who was arraigned on the Market Place by special permission of the Borough Council in 1984.

A Hewitson, *History of Preston* (1883).

PILGRIMAGE OF GRACE (1536)

A serious uprising following Henry VIII's dissolution of the monasteries. The Earl of Derby assembled 8,000 men at Preston to suppress local resistance which centred on the abbeys at Whalley and Sawley. In March 1537 their abbots were executed and the REFORMATION was under way in mid-Lancashire.

PLACE NAMES

Most of the settlement geography of the North-West was established in the five centuries between the end of the Roman period and the establishment of the authority of the Saxon kings (*c.*400-930). Many of these communities survive, and their names tell us a great deal about the peoples who established them. In these years three linguistic groups can be identified: the original inhabitants or 'British', Anglo-Saxon speakers entering along the Ribble Valley from Yorkshire (from the sixth century) and Norse speakers migrating from earlier bases in Scotland and Ireland (from the late ninth century). The population was therefore a diverse one, and the process of intermingling may not have been complete for centuries.

The original population is indicated by names such as Inskip (Inscip; 1086 unless otherwise stated), Preese (Pres), Penwortham (Peneuerdant) and Walton ('Waleton'; 'the place of the Welsh'). Saxon names include Fishwick (Fiscuic), Ashton (Eston) and Lea (Lea). Norse names include Amounderness (Aghemundesnes 934; 'the Ness of - the Norseman - Agmundr') and Grimsargh (Grimesarghe), whilst the western Fylde should perhaps be considered Anglo-Norse rather than Anglo-Saxon; Kirkham parish alone contains at least fourteen Norse names. Interestingly some names contain multiple elements: British and Norse at Preesall, Irish and Norse at Goosnargh (Gusansarghe), and Saxon and Norse at Stalmine. Occasionally settlements have composite names, comprising words of different origin, such as 'Eccleston with Larbrick'. Later local government reorganization has added a further stratum of names, such as Lancashire, Central Lancashire and South Ribble.

Though a British settlement may have been associated with a religious community of some sort before 670, the place name evidence for the immediate Preston district is predominantly Anglo-Saxon. 'Prestune' appears in Domesday Book, and 'Preston' in 1094. The name is Anglo-Saxon (Old English) 'Preosta-tun' - the place (tun) of the priests (preosta), and related elements are strongly represented at Lea, Fishwick and Ashton. This is in marked contrast to the predominance of Norse names in the western Fylde, and of British names in the mid-Fylde. The former has led scholars to suggest that Norse communities generally 'filled in' existing gaps in the settlement pattern. Well into medieval times Norse personal names continued to be popular in the Fylde, and Kirkham long had two pronunciations (Saxon

Kirk-Ham, and Norse Kirche-Heim), so that a wide range of accents must have the filled the air at Preston market.

E Ekwall, *Place-Names of Lancashire* (1922). See also the *English Place-Names Society Journal* (1985). A major reanalysis of local place names is currently under way.

PLEASURE GARDENS COMPANY

A privately owned leisure facility established in a former plant nursery on Ribbleton Lane. Miles of walkways were laid out, with an entrance lodge, numerous plant houses and a large conservatory. The gardens opened in 1875 but were not a financial success despite their position on the tram circuit next door to the cemetery (a very popular Sunday venue). The company went into liquidation in 1879, but was reformed in 1882. The horticultural and zoological collections were developed, and a great effort was made to hold attractive events. Flower shows and musical events of all kinds proved very popular, and in 1885 a 'New Dancing Pavilion with hot water, making it a comfortable room at all times', was opened. During the early years of the football craze the Garden's home team - Preston Zingari - seemed likely to emerge as a rival to the North End side. Indeed, had Mr Sudell's outfit failed it is more than probable that the PPG would have emerged as the local League ground, with the team playing their matches alongside Preston's dead, encouraged by the cries of the assembled monkeys, baboons, vultures and other wild animals. At its peak the venture could attract 3,000 patrons each week, with 4,500 during holidays. The Gardens offered an attractive leisure package of events, far ahead of their time, and with something for everyone: exotic plants and fruits, a 'House of Melons', 'Peter the Baboon', 'Bully the Monkey' and their wild animal pals, dancing and drink, music, refreshments of all kinds, football and any other attractions the management could think up. The cost of servicing the mortgage on the estate, however, finally proved too much and this most popular and useful of ventures closed in November 1887.

D Hunt, *A History of Preston North End Football Club: The Power, the Politics and the People* (2000).

PLUG RIOTS

August 1842. See CHARTISM.

POLIO EPIDEMIC (1958-1959)

By the end of April 1959 the scare was easing off and the final local case was reported at Fulwood. In an enormous medical effort 24,013 children and 2,134 adults had received the first course of injections and 7,111 people had had boosters.

Lancashire Evening Post (28 May 1959).

PORT OF PRESTON (1892-1981)

The commercial operation of Preston Dock (the ALBERT EDWARD). The first decade of the municipal dockyard seemed to confirm the predictions of the scheme's critics. In the years up to 1900 the enterprise showed a cash surplus in only three years, and accumulated losses of almost £23,000. Although tonnage quickly increased fivefold to 220,000 tons by 1894, the dock possessed little modern equipment to handle goods and the seaway was still unimproved. Preston's 'infant industry' was thus severely held back by underinvestment. Yet work to straighten and deepen the channel progressed steadily, the training walls reached the 14th mile post in 1910, and the open sea four years later. The Ribble Rate having reached 2s 3d in the late 1890s fell thereafter to reach 1s 6d in 1915, and the port handled 750,000 tons of goods in 1914. The war had a disastrous effect on the dock's trade, and the careful dredging of the river was suspended. By 1919 trade had fallen by 80 per cent and the rate had risen to 3s. The seaway recovered, the first petrol storage tanks had been built in 1915 and the dock returned to profit in 1921. The same year the cotton trade entered a depression from which it would never recover, and the dock was used as a store for redundant shipping. Interestingly, a side effect of the dock scheme now began to make itself apparent, for in 1897 the Dick, Kerr company had established itself on reclaimed land along Strand Road. In time the 'dock estate' would indeed emerge as home to Preston's largest employer, but making aeroplanes!

The inter-war years saw steady progress, particularly in the late 1930s. In 1929, for example, specially heated tanks were built at Ashton to accommodate the cargo of the SS *Ebano* which arrived the following year carrying 2,500 tons of molten bitumen. In 1935 trade exceeded one million tons and with the mortgages now approaching their end the port seemed at last to be cruising into a period of prosperity. In 1938 it handled almost 300,000 tons of coal and coke, 200,000 tons of oil and petrol, almost 200,000 tons of woodpulp, 25,000 tons of china clay, 40,000 Irish cattle and massive quantities of timber for the booming housing market. The scheme provided over 1,000 jobs, and the Ribble Rate was now a minuscule three and five-eighths pence. In April 1939 the 465 foot 8,500-ton tanker *Osthav* delivered Persian oil in safety. To move all these goods the dock railway moved half a million tons of goods on 28 miles of track, with a further 300,000 tons going by road.

The dock had 'an interesting war' under military control, finally serving as a marshalling post for the Normandy landings. Once again the seaway was allowed to deteriorate and the enterprise recorded its greatest ever loss - £88,000 - in 1947. Under Frank Bustard the Roll On, Roll Off system was pioneered at Preston on the run to Northern Ireland using a part of the Mulberry Harbour and a former tank-landing craft, the celebrated *Empire*

A corner of Preston Dock c. 1920. In the early 1920s the dock was used to moth-ball shipping made surplus to requirements by the trade depression, but a period of steady growth began in the early 1930s with improvements to the seaway and the development of petrol import and distribution facilities.

Cedric. From this success the world's first purpose-built car ferries - the *Bardic Ferry* and *Ionic Ferry* were commissioned. The 1950s saw the start of the West Indian service, and by 1968 the port was handling two and a half million tons of trade. Yet by 1976 both imports and exports had halved, the staple coal and china clay trades had been lost, the successful fruit trade moved away, and in 1973 the Larne car ferry had been lost to Cairn Ryan. Successful operations pioneered at Preston outgrew the port, and the cost of maintaining the seaway grew to consume almost half of the income. The port's last commercial visitor, *Hoveringham V* left the Ribble at high tide on 31 October 1981.

J Barron, *History of the Ribble Navigation* (1937). J Dakres, *The Last Tide: A History of the Port of Preston* (1986). See also the Cochraine Collection, and the Preston Borough Council archive in the LRO.

See RIBBLE NAVIGATION COMPANY; RIVER RIBBLE; SLAVE TRADE.

POTTER LANE, SAMLESBURY

Construction of the Samlesbury-Helmshore gas-pipeline in 2001-2 revealed a series of pottery kiln sites over a wide area lying off Cuerdale Lane to the west of Potter Lane. At least two and possibly three groups of kilns seem to be present. They took the form of oval (drainage?) gullies approximately 12m by 8m adjacent to areas of cobbling which probably formed the foundations of the kilns. Their superstructures had long gone and the floors themselves had been disturbed by ploughing. The series of ponds in the vicinity of the sites - previously thought to be related to the flax industry - may have formed from the clay-getters' pits.

Over 9,000 sherds of pottery were found in the gullies and scattered through the adjacent subsoil, comprising 'jars and jugs, smaller numbers of cisterns (large water jars), pipkins (small earthenware pots), and possible tripod and spouted pitchers'. These 'utilitarian' vessels and the low proportion of glazed or decorated wares suggested their use by a rural community. The sherds indicated that the potting complex operated from the thirteenth to the sixteenth centuries, with the majority dating from the fourteenth and fifteenth.

Given the proximity of the rising entrepot of medieval mid-Lancashire it is probable that at least a proportion of these wares made their way to the pottery market in Preston's Cheapside. Analysis of contemporary local pots (such as the water-pitcher found 20 feet down a well off New Hall Lane in 1951) may shed light on wider commercial relationships. Work to date has been essentially 'rescue archaeology', and clearly a great deal of analysis remains to be undertaken on 'Potter Lane' in the years ahead.

Northern Archaeological Associates, *Samlesbury to Helmshore Gas Pipeline: Potter Lane, Samlesbury: Excavation Summary* (Jan. 2005).

POULTON-LE-FYLDE ELK

Perhaps the Harris Museum's most celebrated inhabitant, remains of the elk came to light during the construction of a house on the Great Moss at Poulton. Identified and excavated by local archaeologists Ben Edwards, John Hallam and Brian Barnes, the six-year-old bull elk has been tentatively dated to around 10,000 BC, in a warmer interlude towards the end of the last ice age. Bone barbs associated with the bones indicated that the beast had been pursued and wounded by a party of hunters.

B J N Edwards, *The Poulton-le-Fylde Elk* (1980).

PRESTON DOCK FINDS (c.1884-1887)

Apparently ancient animal bones had been found during the digging of the foundations of the North Union and East Lancashire railway bridges, and the excavation of the Albert Edward dock brought to light great masses of red deer, cattle and horse bones. Many of these came from the great cutting made for the river on the Penwortham shore below the Parish Church where traces of the submerged forest were uncovered. Evidence of human activity comprised a fine bronze spearhead found in the vicinity of the entrance basin, a pair of dug-out canoes, and a good collection of human skulls. None of these finds were adequately reported, and even the general archaeological context of all the material is unknown. Modern archaeologists are generally dismissive of the reported discovery of a pile-built riverside dwelling, though such may well have existed in the area. Many finds were simply thrown away, though the human skulls naturally attracted interest. Recent analysis of this material suggests that it may have found its way naturally down the Ribble system into the tidal pool on the river where it settled. The human and animal bones may thus have come from populations living well beyond the town over a wide area of mid-Lancashire. The Carbon-14 dating of thirteen human skulls supported this interpretation, giving a range of dates from 3820 BC to AD 890; four dates come from the period 3700-3400 BC, but again may only relate to random events. The latest date came from the skull of a young woman whose head wound led to suggestions that she may have been a casualty at a Saxon battle near Whalley in April 798. Speculation, but a clear indication of the archaeological record preserved for posterity by the River Ribble.

D Hunt, *Preston: Centuries of Change* (2003). Harris Museum factsheet. For recent research on the local mosses and related matters see R Middleton, C E Wells and E Huckerby, *The Wetlands of North Lancashire* (1995). R Newman and E Hesslewood, pers. comm.

PRESTON GRAMMAR SCHOOL
See WINCKLEY SQUARE.

PRESTON MARSH
An area of wetland bounded by Watery Lane, Strand Road and the RIBBLE. Before development for housing in the mid-nineteenth century, this flat expanse of about 25 acres was exploited by the burgesses as common grazing, and became the main recreation area for sporting events of all kinds prior to the opening of Moor Park.

D Hunt, *A History of Preston* (1992).

PRESTON MOOR
As the forest to the north of the town was cleared, the unenclosed heath was exploited by the burgesses for rough grazing. Before reclamation after 1830 the Moor lay in a great arc from Ashton to New Hall Lane. It was subdivided into the West Moor (Plungington), the North Moor (mostly present day Moor Park) and the Further Moor (DEEPDALE). Closer in to the centre lay FRIARGATE Moor (along Moor Lane), CHURCHGATE Moor (to the west of Deepdale Road in the vicinity of PRI), and Peel Moor (the CANARY ISLANDS).

D Hunt, *A History of Preston* (1992).

PRESTON NORTH END FOOTBALL CLUB

Effectively the holders of the 'franchise' for professional football in the town since 1883. The club originated among the host of cricket enthusiasts who in the 1860s gathered for the summer game on Preston Marsh - at the extreme *West* End of the town. As the mill-week progressively retreated, the Victorian obsession for sports of all kinds asserted itself among the working classes. With the opening of the Municipal Cricket Ground on Moor Park (1867) players from a number of teams coalesced to form a popular inter-town side called the North End club. Their success owed much to their positive attitude to new ideas, a broad social membership and their willingness to expand into all manner of activities in order to raise money! Under the leadership of William Sudell the DEEPDALE ground was acquired and developed, cricket and rugby gradually lapsed, and an 'Invincible' team of Scottish professional footballers was hired. Though banned from the FA Cup for paying its players, the club became an important and progressive force in the establishment of professional football, and Preston North End were the leading and most innovative side in the world for a decade after 1883.

The emergence of League Football apparently placed the small-town clubs at a disadvantage to their big-city fellows, but the limitation placed on the players' rights (through the 'maximum wage' and restrictive contracts) meant that with very good management such clubs could compete into the 1980s: thereafter a rich uncle would be required! Under William Ord (chairman 1894-1921) Deepdale's facilities were improved and the team narrowly failed to win the Cup in the 1922 Guild year. In the 1920s and 1930s James I Taylor (the 'Joseph Stalin of English Football') and chairman Sir Meyrick Hollins

Preston North End's Finest 1951.

(1921-38) succeeded in restoring a measure of the club's vanished greatness, signing such players as ALEC JAMES, Billy Shankly, Jimmy Dougal and George Mutch. After the Second World War teams built around TOM FINNEY established North End as one of the most attractive club sides in Europe.

Long-term changes in the balance of the game, failure to maintain a sufficient level of investment in the playing squad, combined with Finney's retirement in 1960, began a long (if absorbing) period of absolute decline. Despite the under-achievement of these years the team's appearance at a Wembley play-off final in 1994 strongly indicated that the club's underlying fan-base was remarkably intact, and when the club was taken over a few months later by the Bamber Bridge-based Baxi Partnership the long awaited revival at last got under way.

G Allman and H Berry, *Preston North End Football Club: One Hundred Years at Deepdale* (1982). D Russell, *Preston North End Football Club: 100 Years in the Football League* (1989). M Payne and I Rigby, *Proud Preston: Preston North End's One Hundred Seasons of Football League History* (1999). D Hunt, *A History of Preston North End Football Club: The Power, the Politics and the People* (2000).

PRESTON POLYTECHNIC
See UNIVERSITY OF CENTRAL LANCASHIRE.

PRESTON RACES
Horse races were held on Preston Moor as early as 1695, and became an annual event in 1726. During the years 1786-91 the meeting became absorbed into the town's political rivalries, leading the Whig DERBY INTEREST to organize a separate event on the adjacent Fulwood Moor. The Stanleys were great supporters of the sport, and of course gave their name to the world's greatest flat race. When they withdrew from Preston in 1830 the races came to an end. The meeting was revived for the Guild of 1842, and was held for a few years at Penwortham Holme - the town's third racecourse! Fighting between troops and policemen finally brought the 150-year-old tradition to an end in 1848. Mr Riddell's celebrated horse Doctor Syntax, named after a popular 'cartoon' character, held the Preston Gold Cup, 1815-21.

A Hewitson, *History of Preston* (1883).

PRI
See ROYAL INFIRMARY.

PRESTON SCIENTIFIC SOCIETY
Founded in 1876 the society became a fashionable focus for interest in the natural and physical sciences, though ladies were 'only occasionally admitted at first'. The popular Gilchrist Lectures held in the Guild Hall in 1880 were

specifically aimed at the enormous working-class audience and proved to be a great success. Refounded in 1893 the society had over 700 members within five years, and developed sections (including astro-physics, photography, cinematography and psychology) to explore all areas of science. In 1937 the Record and Survey Society began successfully to record vanishing Preston, and in 1946 one group led by E E Pickering went off to excavate the Roman site at Walton-le-Dale.

This account is based on the society's records. The Record Society's photographs are housed in the Harris Reference Library; for a selection see D Hunt, *Preston: Centuries of Change* (2003).

PRESTON TEMPERANCE SOCIETY (FOUNDED MARCH 1832)

An extremely influential group in the early history of the international Temperance Movement. Preston was changing very rapidly in the 1830s, and though the social cost of unregulated drinking to excess was clear to everyone, there were high hopes for a new order of things. Sober citizens (and voters) would create a rational society and herald a thorough-going moral reformation.

The idea of associating advocates of moderate drinking within specific temperance societies originated in America and spread to Britain in the 1820s. In 1829 a society was formed at Greenock, and in February 1830 one at Bradford. The latter probably came to the attention of JOSEPH LIVESEY through the *Leeds Mercury* of fellow Waltonian Edward Baines. Livesey was a lifelong enthusiast for dietary experiments of all kinds and from January 1831 he began to abstain from alcohol. A Preston society was formed in March 1832 and on 1 September a small and unrepresentative group - the SEVEN MEN OF PRESTON - signed the historic total abstinence pledge which came to be seen as the foundation of the teetotal movement.

Amidst much popular enthusiasm, the sober Prestonians quickly gave the movement its name and manifesto, pioneered the modern treatment of alcoholics and produced a large number of the early leaders. Joseph Livesey's ever growing newspaper interests gave the Preston men and women considerable influence for a short time, and his newspaper - the *Preston Temperance Advocate* - became a model for all the later publications. The movement developed rapidly in the years 1833-5, but fell back thereafter, leading Livesey to bemoan in 1837:

> When we started about four years ago, clothed in tee-total armour... we calculated that by this time our work would be done...we were certainly mistaken...A nation's habits it is proper to observe are not changed in a day.

After 1850 the movement became strongly associated with organized religion and the demand for Prohibition. Since both of these were causes that the libertarian Livesey would have no truck with at all he drifted out of the mainstream of the movement, becoming at times one of its sternest critics.

B Harrison, *Drink and the Victorians* (1971). See D Hunt's paper in I Levitt (ed.), *Joseph Livesey of Preston: Business, Temperance and Moral Reform* (1996).
See MALT LIQUOR LECTURE.

PRINCE'S THEATRE

Preston's second theatre, located on the corner of Crooked Lane and Tithebarn St (theatre 1882-1922, cinema 1922-59). It opened as the 'New Gaiety Palace of Varieties', becoming the 'Prince's Theatre and Opera House', and finally in 1889 just 'The Prince's'. David Hindle has suggested that the Prince's had a great influence on the evolution of the local music hall, and a fire in 1900 was followed by a rebuilding to cater for audiences of 2,000 people. Discipline was strict: 'Seats not guaranteed; No money returned; Police in attendance'! 'WILL ONDA' used the theatre for films after 1913, and in 1922 under his auspices the Prince's became the first of the local theatres to convert to films-only. In 1953 Cinemascope was introduced to try to combat television, but six years later the cinema closed. The building was demolished in 1964 to make way for the Buckingham Bingo Hall and the St Johns Shopping Centre.

J Cotterall, *Preston's Palaces of Pleasure* (1988). D Hindle, (1999) *Twice Nightly: An Illustrated History of Entertainment in Preston* (1999).

PUBLIC HALL

See CORN EXCHANGE.

PUBLIC PARKS

Preston was at the forefront of the movement to provide municipal parks. In 1696 the Corporation decided to purchase 'Mr.Lemon's ground upon Avenham now and heretofore used as a walke planted with trees and (to be) made into a gravel walke'. Subsequent extensions and additions benefited from 'job creation' during the cyclical bouts of unemployment in the cotton trade. In 1844 the walk was extended and in 1847-9 JOSEPH LIVESEY masterminded the improvement of the riverside walk to Penwortham Bridge. In the period 1843-52 virtually the whole of the present-day 26-acre Avenham Park was purchased, and its small farm ('Mr Jackson's cottage') and gardens were landscaped by an army of unemployed mill hands during the Cotton Famine. To the west and beyond the East Lancashire Railway from Avenham Park, the 11-acre Miller Park was given by Thomas Miller in 1864. The park is dominated by a spectacular fountain and the enormous 6-ton statue of the 14th Lord Derby (1799-1869) - surely 'Stanley's Revenge' for his famous defeat at Preston by HENRY HUNT.

The third park to have been developed through public works during the LANCASHIRE COTTON FAMINE was the 100-acre Moor Park. The ancient Preston Moor was enclosed in 1834, a Ladies Walk was laid out (Moor Park

The Midland Hotel from Miller Park c.1910. Writing in the early 1880s Anthony Hewitson was impressed by the town's most fashionable park: 'Very pretty - in many respects quite charming - is Miller Park'.

Avenue), lodges were added in 1836 and the boundary walks and wall were completed in the 1860s, though much of the centre long remained open farmland. The provision of a municipal cricket ground resulted in the formation of the North End club - of which the world has heard much since. Haslam Park (56 acres) was gifted in memory of John Haslam (cotton spinner - Parker St Mills) in 1908 and opened in 1912. The plan was prepared by T H Mawson and required Savick Brook to be dammed to create a large lake. As Colin Stansfield (Preston's architectural authority) has shown, it provided an important element of what became Preston's early twentieth-century garden suburb. Preston's other municipal parks are Ashton Park (86 acres), Grange Park (16 acres), Brookfield Park (17 acres), Ribbleton Park (16 acres) and the Frenchwood Recreational Ground (17 acres). Until comparatively recent times, Moor Park, Haslam Park and Ribbleton Park had open-air swimming pools in the summer, and in 1919 Preston's Open Air School was opened on the north-east side of Moor Park. Malnourished or sickly 6-13 year olds from the borough's schools were admitted for therapeutic stays of around 18 months.

A Hewitson, *History of Preston* (1883). C Stansfield, *Beside the Seaside* (1986). D Hughes (2004) 'Just a Breath of Fresh Air in an Industrial Landscape? The Preston Open Air School in 1926', *Social History of Medicine* 17/3 (2004).

Q

QUEEN'S LANCASHIRE REGIMENT

Headquarters Fulwood Barracks. The regiment traces its roots among eighteen military formations, among them the Loyal North Lancashire Regiment in which the majority of the Prestonians in the army served during the First World War. These units have been the recipients of the VICTORIA CROSS nineteen times, and the regiment still celebrates the anniversaries of a number of the most important actions in which it has participated - Gallipoli Day (15 Feb), Kimberley Day (25 April), Waterloo Day (18 June), SOMME Day (1 July) and Quebec Day (13 Sept).

H C Wylly, *The Loyal North Lancashire Regiment* (1933), vol. 1, *1741-1914*, vol. 2, *1914-19*. C G R Dean, *The Loyal Regiment (North Lancs) 1919-53* (1955). M Langley, *Famous Regiments: The Loyal Regiment (North Lancashire)* (1976).

R

RAILWAYS

In 1820 Britain had no passenger railways; fifty years later it had 13,500 miles of track, rising by 1914 to over 20,000 miles operated by 120 competing companies. Preston had emerged as the principal intermediate stop, at midpoint, on the west coast mainline between London Euston and Glasgow Central. It was also an important railway junction, and no less than eight lines radiated out from the town. The experience of being 'stuck on Preston station waiting for a train' is thus one that an enormous percentage of past and present Britons has endured! The town's first line was operated by the North Union Railway Company and opened in 1838. It linked Preston directly to Wigan and indirectly to the great cities of the south, and from 1840 to 1848 was on the fastest route to Scotland, operating via the Fleetwood-Ardrossan ferry. Although the passengers had to get out and push up the incline at Wigan and called out for faster 'lifts' in donkey carts, Preston duly celebrated the arrival of the first of many trains:

> Loud huzzas greeted our arrival, the bells sent forth their sonorous peals, the Union Jack was unfurled on the parish church, the standard of St.George floated on top of the mayor's mansion, and a band of music played in the gardens.

After their efforts the directors had doubtless earned their 'luxurious viands served up in fine style'.

Preston's rail network developed as follows:

1838. North Union Railway

Linking Preston and Wigan. The station was on the present site.

1840. Preston & Lancaster Railway

The line eventually climbed north to reach Carlisle in 1846 (via Shap Summit), and Edinburgh and Glasgow in 1848 (over Beattock Summit). The terminus on the north side of Fishergate was linked to the Wigan line to the south by a tunnel, but passengers had to pay 6d for the through-service. Many naturally chose to walk between the trains, only to find that the servants of the North Union Co. had omitted to hold their connection south. The carriages had individual names, and were painted a bright yellow.

1840. Preston & Wyre Railway and Harbour Co.

This line operated from a station called 'Maudlands' in Leighton St, and linked Preston and Fleetwood on the rail-ferry run to Scotland. Branch lines from Kirkham to Lytham and Poulton to Blackpool followed in 1846. The Blackpool line - transporting the resort's holiday traffic - became one of the busiest through Preston. Early trains were in the habit of halting near Scorton to enable the driver, and those passengers who wished, to gather mushrooms.

1840. Preston & Longridge Railway Co.

This 6.5 mile branch line serving the local quarries was operated by horses until 1848 and had a terminus in Deepdale St, behind Stephenson Terrace. In 1850 it was linked to the Wyre line by a remarkable 862 yard tunnel passing a few feet to the south of St Peter's church and under Deepdale. The terminus on Deepdale Road was opened in 1856, and the line only acquired access to the central station in 1885 (see discussion of Whittingham Hospital Branch Line).

1846. Preston & Blackburn Railway

After 1849 this was known as the East Lancashire and Liverpool railway. The Blackburn line with its blue and black livery was opened in May 1846: 'The pleasure of the day was much enhanced by the fact that no accident or mischance occurred to cast a gloom over any aspect of the proceedings'. Liverpool trains had to reverse into Preston, so in 1850 a new bridge approached by a 52-arch viaduct was constructed. When the latter proved unstable it was replaced by an embankment.

1846. Ribble Branch Railway

The line originally ran from the station to the bonded warehouse on Victoria Quay, but was extended after 1882 to serve Preston Dock's eventual 28 miles of sidings. Descending steeply from Preston station on a 1 in 29 gradient, the line enters a curved tunnel before crossing Strand Road. Later branches served the west end's heavy industrial works, and the line - which still serves the Tar distributor - is centrepiece of the town's spectacular new transport museum.

1882. West Lancashire Railway

Work began on the 15.75 mile line from Southport in 1871. It was extended through the largely agricultural district as funds allowed and reached Preston in time for the 1882 Guild celebrations. The station, Fishergate Hill, closed in 1900. The line did much to stimulate the local market gardening industry (as did the Ormskirk line at Midge Hall) but failed in 1886. Schemes to link Southport and Blackpool by a bridge across the Ribble at Hesketh Bank came to nothing, and the line fell a natural victim of the Beeching Report, closing in 1964. A short but most interesting length survives to be operated by enthusiasts at Hesketh Bank.

1889. Whittingham Hospital Branch Line

This 2 mile line carried coal and supplies to the County Hospital along a branch which joined the Longridge railway at Grimsargh, where it had a separate station. Essentially a freight line serving the largest hospital of its kind in Europe, passengers were transported free of charge - a service which survived the closing of Longridge line to passengers in 1930. The Hospital line closed in 1957 and the freight line to Longridge in 1967, though the service as far as the Courtaulds factory at Red Scar survived to 1980.

In addition, link lines joined Preston to Bolton (1839), Liverpool (1849, via Ormskirk), and Southport (1855, via Liverpool line). The main north-south line was quadrupled by construction of an adjoining twin bridge over the Ribble in 1880, and a steel bridge was added in 1904. The railways facilitated the town's full integration into the national transport system, and gave a great impetus to its development as the regional centre. They came to dominate an enormous area of the town centre, whilst the outer lines aided the progress of the suburbs, and the hamlet of Lostock Hall emerged as

The proposed line of the railway across Fishergate Hill. Much of this district would be subsumed by the land-hungry central station and the adjacent Butler St goods depot (J J Myres's map of 1836: paper on canvas).

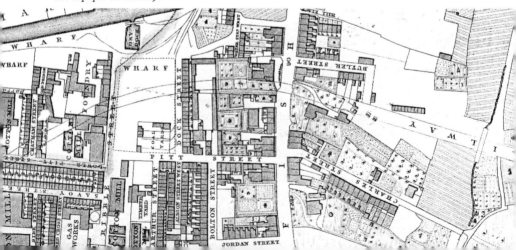

something of a 'Steam Town' of the Lancashire & Yorkshire Railway.
G Biddle, *The Railways around Preston: A Historical Review* (1989). N Parker, *The Preston & Longridge Railway* (1972).

RAILWAY STATIONS
By 1850 the town had five stations serving the jealous and mutually hostile companies. Some were little more than sheds, and two were a good way out of the centre and really quite remote. Gordon Biddle lists them as follows: the North Union's was on the present site, the Bolton line's was at Maxwell House Station just to the north of Fishergate, the Lancaster station was close by, at the end of the short tunnel under Fishergate, the Blackpool station was at Maudlands, whilst that of the Longridge lay far to the east at Deepdale. Later the Southport line had a terminus at the bottom of Fishergate Hill. These services ultimately became concentrated at the central station, which duly became one of the most hated in the kingdom. Before the introduction of footbridges in 1850, railway servants had to herd the travellers at busy times over the rails and between the engines; in quiet times they seem to have been free to roam around at will. When internecine disputes over the station's operation became intractable I K Brunel had to be called in to 'bang heads'. Ultimately the station had to be remodelled, and during the 1922 Guild the station successfully coped with 550,000 passengers and an additional 504 special trains.
G Biddle, *The Railways around Preston: A Historical Review* (1989).

RAZA MOSQUE
St Pauls Road. Preston's first purpose-built mosque, and only the second to be built in Britain, was opened in 1970 at a cost of £35,000. The 12 feet high, 10 feet wide fibre-glass dome was made in Oldham and opened another chapter in Preston's rich architectural history.
D Shepherd and S Harrison, *Islam in Preston* (1979).
    See ISLAM IN PRESTON.

REFORMATION
The series of largely unforeseen events which followed Martin Luther's 'Protest' and the development of the printing press. In England the movement was given impetus by the opening of Henry VIII's dispute with Rome in 1527, and the publication of the English Bible. The rift became institutionalized when the Crown replaced the Pope as head of the church in England (Act of Supremacy 1534), and developed important social consequences with the confiscation of church lands (Smaller Monasteries 1536, Larger Monasteries 1539). Almost 70 per cent of the latter had been sold on by 1547. Penwortham Priory went to John Fleetwood, Thomas

Holcroft took the Friary, and the estate of the old Leper Hospital (the 58 acres of the 'Maudlands') was eventually purchased by Thomas Fleetwood for £300 in 1560.

Acceptance of the theological consequences of these changes, however, was to be a much more tortuous process. At the Parish Church little seems to have changed, and those reforms not to the congregation's liking were - in true Preston fashion - simply ignored. Queen Mary's efforts (1553-8) to restore the old faith met with such success in Preston that one has to wonder just what changes had actually taken place. For example, when urged to restore the statues previously banished from the church the vicar simply dug them up from his garden where they had been hidden for safe keeping! Under Elizabeth the Church Settlement of 1559 produced a liberal and generally acceptable Church of England, and though non-attendance at Anglican services was punishable, fines were low, rarely paid and rarely collected. However, the international crisis with Catholic Spain now gave local events an unwelcome 'political' aspect which the government could not overlook, and affairs in Preston and the Fylde were closely watched from London. Henceforth the steady pressure on local Catholics to conform rose and fell largely in response to external national affairs, and Catholicism continued to be a strong presence and a defining feature in local life throughout the turbulence of the next two hundred years.

Henry VIII proved himself to be just as willing to persecute Protestants on the other extreme of the theological spectrum, and Robert Singleton made vicar of Preston while still a boy in 1516 was executed as a 'heretic' in 1543. In the early years of the seventeenth century the increasingly puritan clergy had a marked impact on everyday life in the town. In 1602 trading on the Sabbath was forbidden, and in 1616 children were forbidden to play in the street. In strongly puritan towns such as the 'Geneva of the North' (Bolton), the game of 'ffoteballe' was outlawed. Under James I and Charles I many Protestants ('non-conformists') now found themselves unable to accept the tenets of the Church of England, in much the same way that the Catholics had a hundred years earlier. Indeed the dispute between the 'high church' Anglicans and the 'low church' Nonconformists was to be perhaps a more important feature of the Civil Wars (1642-8) than differences between Anglicans and Catholics.

With the restoration of Charles II it became the turn of the Preston puritans to find themselves persecuted. Isaac Ambrose (vicar 1640-58) was driven out, despairing of the town's endless disputes, and looking forward to the solace he found walking 'the silent fields and woods' of Garstang. He died 'honoured by God and good men' at his house in St John's St, Preston in 1664. Though sporadic religious persecutions of one kind and another would be a feature of local life for a further century, the ministry of Seth Bushell (vicar 1663-82) marked a more hopeful departure; he deplored the

persecution of anyone, treated all alike, and was 'very courteous to dissenters of all denominations so that none of his parishioners were troubled by him'.
L Warren, *Through Twenty Preston Guilds: The Catholic Congregation of St Wilfrid's, Preston* (1993). D Hunt, *A History of Preston* (1992).

RESTORATION

The end of the republican Commonwealth, the restoration of the monarchy and the formal declaration of Charles II as King. Prestonians gathered in the market place to hear the proclamation and to declare their 'alacrity and loyalty' to the new order. The Corporation underwent something of a purge; Edmund Worden and his compatriots were expelled, Vicar Ambrose was put out of his living at the Parish Church, and those members who had previously been driven out returned. This strongly royalist, high church or 'Tory' line was rewarded with a measure of royal approval in the form of Charles's charter of 1684. By contrast, many of the local gentry families were 'Whigs' - they were Presbyterian and supported the king's rule only at the discretion of Parliament. On the King's death local hopes were high that a large measure of religious toleration would be granted by his successor James II. In 1687 a Catholic missionary baptized over 8,000 people in the Preston district, and the following year Jesuits began to openly celebrate mass in the town for the first time in over a century. But the 'Glorious Revolution' saw the triumph of the Whigs, and pendulum swing back once again. It would be another hundred years before such hopes were realized.
M Mullett, 'To Dwell Together in Unity: The Search for Agreement in Preston Politics 1660-1690', *THSLC* 125 (1974).

RIBBLE

A river which forms the principal drainage basin for a large area of northern, eastern and central Lancashire. Many of the region's principal geographical features still possess variants of their original PLACE NAME and that of the river probably came from the Welsh 'Rhiu Bel', or 'Head River', though a derivation from the 'Belisama Fluvia' - 'Beautiful Stream' - listed by the geographer Ptolemy in the second century is an attractive if less likely alternative. The river rises 600 feet up on Wold Fell behind Ingleborough, and on its 90 mile course to the open sea off St Annes it absorbs the Rivers Hodder, Calder, Darwen and Douglas. Historically these were fine rivers for salmon and sea trout; in June 1760 almost 3,500 salmon were taken in a single day, and the fishermen's jetties or 'cauls' were a common sight on the Ribble through Penwortham and Walton. During the 1860s the annual take of salmon still approached 20,000 but fell away steeply thereafter.

The river delivers plenty of water to Preston, for the 48.3 inches of annual rainfall onto the Ribble Valley (1876-1931 figures) apparently equates to

350,000 million gallons a year, of which the river carries over 500 million gallons a day past the town! A downpour in 1927 was estimated to have produced a surge of 750 million gallons, but drought conditions can reduce this to just five million. However it is the depth of the water passing Preston which is all important in forming the seaway. By Ribchester the bed has fallen over 500 feet to 65 feet above sea level. Downstream of Halfpenny Bridge the river becomes tidal and the 5 feet spring tides would have been enough for Roman shipping to make passage to Walton. At the entrance to the river at Preston Bar (off St Annes) the rise above low water during spring tides is 25 feet 9 inches, rising to 27 feet half an hour later at Preston, and 16 miles upstream. On ordinary tides the rise is about 3 feet lower, and 6 feet lower at neap tides: the tidal range is around 15 feet. In practice typical Baltic steamers drawing about 19 feet had to cross the bar roughly two and a half hours ahead of high tide to enable them to clear the dock sill at high water. Delays could be embarrassing, for low water reveals a desert landscape almost 60 square miles in extent.

Such dry statistics are crucial in determining the size of ships able to approach the town. Had the Ribble been glacially deepened throughout its lower course all would have been well, but such was not the case. In the event the problem only became apparent in the seventeenth century and critical in the nineteenth. Up to this period Preston's seaborne trade rose and fell with the general commercial climate. In 1360 the fishing cauls were blamed for blocking the waterway, and a survey of 1586 recorded eight 'barques' based on the 'Water of Ribble'. Another dispute with the Ribble fishermen in 1691 noted the passage of ships of 40 tons trading in millstones to Ireland and lead to Bristol. Dr Kuerden found that 'a vessall of reasonable burden may arrive from the Western Sea, guided by a knoweing and well skill'd pylot' at 'higher water'. A hundred years later things were little better, for Mr Mackenzie's survey of the coast found the Ribble 'crooked, without buoys, perches and distant landmarks' and visited by only a handful of small ships. In the centuries ahead private and public enterprise would seek to right the vicissitudes of nature and make Preston an ocean-going port.

J Barron, *History of the Ribble Navigation* (1937).

RIBBLE NAVIGATION COMPANY
First Company (1806-1838)
Downstream of Penwortham the river spilled out of its narrow course, effectively impeding access to the potentially deep water wharves at Preston. All three RIBBLE companies had broadly the same aim; to straighten and so deepen the river, and to 'pay' for the works by reclaiming land on either side of it. In 1806 local landowners subscribed for the forty £50 shares in the new company and obtained the first of the Ribble Acts in 1806, since 'from the

uncertain and changeable course of the said river, and the beds of gravel, sand, and other obstructions raised therein it is become very difficult and dangerous'. Stone groynes were built, forcing the river into a single course, buoys and beacons were installed, and large rocks were raised from the river bed. Trade developed steadily from 50 ships in 1805 to 400 in 1820, and in 1825 a new riverside quay was opened. Three years later the first steamship - the *St David* - was seen on the river. In 1830 the corporation acquired an interest in the company, and the next decade saw great progress. In 1834 a shipyard was established at the foot of Fishergate Hill and duly launched the town's first steam vessel. But although the aim of the enterprise was to be able to land cheap foods in bulk directly at Preston, it was still cheaper to ship goods to the town via Glasson Dock and the canal.

In 1833 a committee considered a new idea: the construction of a ship canal to Lytham. This would have cost £105,000, and been a massive 14 feet deep to accommodate ships of 200 tons, with towpaths and docks at each end. An Admiralty survey four years later conveniently demonstrated 'to the satisfaction of the corporation' that improvement of the waterway was a viable proposition. Accordingly, Robert Stevenson & Sons were commissioned to produce yet another survey and report. This found that the 14 feet clearance could be obtained much more cheaply by extending the sea walls and deepening the river at Ashton. To implement the scheme the company was reformed.

See ALBERT EDWARD; PORT OF PRESTON; PRESTON DOCK FINDS.

Preston Dock c.1930.

Second Company (1838-1853)

The new company had share capital of £50,000, about the same as a large cotton mill. A cutting 13 feer deep and 300 yards long was excavated in the red sandstone underlying river bed between Ashton Marsh and Preston, a dredging machine was purchased, and work began to extend the training walls from the quay at the bottom of Marsh Lane to Savick Brook. Stevenson's scheme worked very well since the concentration of the current increased the river's natural scouring and lowered the bed by up to 4 feet. This in turn began to 'bring up' great quantities of very large and ancient trees from the post-glacial gravels at Ashton. On spring tides ships drawing 10 feet could now reach Preston. In 1843 a new quay and warehouse - Victoria Quay - was constructed, and amidst corporation borrowings and further share issues both quays were linked to the railway. Local pride knew no bounds when the town's customs house (removed in 1827) was restored in 1843.

The growth of the customs duty collected reflected the Port of Preston's growth, and rose from £6,309 in 1841 to £19,375 in 1843 and reached £90,000 by 1864. In March 1845 the *Preston Guardian* reported that the New Quay was 'So thronged that the schooners were obliged to lie three deep...We observed 22 vessels at their stations.' The decade was one of opening horizons; the 180-ton schooner *Georgina* brought 'wine direct into Preston from Oporto' (10 May 1844) and the brig *Robert* Baltic timber from Riga (8 September 1844), whilst the *Albion* took coals to Alexandria (16 February 1847). Great hopes were attached to the North American trade, and the 300-ton three-masted schooner *Isabella* was a frequent visitor and a graceful sight on the river. In July 1846 she brought grain and returned with coal on her twenty-two-day run to Quebec and New Brunswick. Her visit in February 1848 caused a sensation and highlighted the Port's growing potential; after a forty-six-day run from New Orleans she landed 400 bales of cotton and 2,200 sacks of wheat.

Third Company (1853-1883)

The company was reformed in 1853 and powers were obtained to extend the reclamation of the 'tide-washed land' along the river. This again proved very successful, transforming the landscape of the Ribble estuary from mud flats, and creating almost 4,000 acres of rich farmland. By 1882 over £35,000 had been raised from land sales, and the model 550-acre farm at Freckleton was worth £1,653 4s 6d per year - almost double the shipping tolls! In the mid-1860s annual trade was approaching 100,000 tons, but this fell away as larger iron ships were introduced and by 1882 it had fallen to under 40,000 tons. In 1865 a new committee was formed to explore the future improvement of the navigation. It commissioned a survey by engineers Messrs Bell and Miller who recommended that the river be initially straightened and deepened to take ships of 500 tons, and deepened thereafter 'as trade required'. But if the scheme was to progress, the construction of a wet dock was felt to be essential.

From this period the question became essentially a political one: the dock would provide welcome economic diversification away from Preston's 'stagnant' cotton trade, but could only be built at colossal expense - to be met by the ratepayers. Opinion in the town was bitterly split, but generally favourable. Drawing on an earlier scheme put forward by the company's engineer Edward Garlick, Sir John Goode's plan of 1882 was adopted. The river was to be diverted onto the Penwortham shore and the dock system built within the former course and Preston Marsh. A 20- or 30-acre main dock would have an entrance basin served by a system of massive lock gates to regulate the water level. It all might be done for £558,150 - surely a bargain in comparison to the scheme envisaged for Manchester. Accordingly (although things would of course turn out rather differently) the Corporation bought out the assets of the third company in February 1883 for £72,500, and the Ribble Navigation passed from private to public ownership.

J Barron, *History of the Ribble Navigation* (1937). See also LRO, DDX 1242/2/10.

See ALBERT EDWARD; PORT OF PRESTON.

RIBCHESTER

Roman settlement in the RIBBLE valley to the east of Preston. Superb, small and friendly museum of ROMAN ARCHAEOLOGY.

RIGBY, EDITH (NEE RAYNER) (1872-1950)

Suffragette, wholefood enthusiast and arsonist. Born at 1 Pole St, Preston, she was educated at Preston High School and Penrhos College, North Wales, before marrying a doctor and settling at 28 Winckley Square. Aware of the poverty surrounding this genteel enclave Edith Rigby joined the Independent Labour Party in 1905, and established a branch of the Women's Labour League in Preston in 1906. The following year she formed a branch of the militant WSPU (Women's Social and Political Union), and was its mainstay in the years up to her arrest in 1913. She attended deputations to London in 1907-8, and Winston Churchill's disrupted meeting at Preston in 1909; following each she was arrested. She was a strong advocate of window breaking, her speciality seeming to be the pub-window brick and black-pudding throwing. In July 1913 her career took a more sinister turn; she planted a bomb in the Liverpool Cotton Exchange (it failed to go off), and three days later set fire to William Lever's splendid timber bungalow at Rivington (it was destroyed, and the wonderful gardens which surrounded it are only today being restored).

Following these events Rigby gave herself up and was imprisoned for nine months. When she went on a hunger strike the authorities implemented the Cat and Mouse Act (whereby a suffragette starved herself, was released and given time to restore her health before being arrested and the process starting over again). She was on her fifth release in the summer of 1914 when she went 'on the run'. On her return she was not rearrested but though the Pankhursts suspended hostilities for the duration of the war she refused to join them and instead founded a Preston branch of the Independent WSPU. With the peace women won the vote, and in 1926 Edith moved to Caernarvonshire. She was a strongly independent but charismatic individual, who would not accept conventional ideas of womanhood, refusing, for example, to wear women's clothes. Her most recent biographer makes the important proviso that her suffrage activities formed only a part of a very full life.

P Hesketh, *My Aunt Edith* (1966). *ODNB.*

RITZ

Cinema, Church St. Opened in March 1937, a short distance from the NEW VICTORIA and the PALLADIUM, the Ritz was hailed as 'one of the most luxurious' in the region. It had a futuristic design without a balcony, reminiscent of the cascading seating at a modern football ground, could accommodate over 1,600 people, and like the New Victoria/Odeon could also be used for live shows. The Ritz closed in 1986 and subsequently became a bingo hall.

J Cotterall, *Preston's Palaces of Pleasure* (1988). D Hindle, *Twice Nightly: An Illustrated History of Entertainment in Preston* (1999).

ROGUE'S WHIPPING POST

This was located at the north-west corner of the Market Place by the junction with Friargate. DR KUERDEN was a firm advocate of 'a slender diet and whipping cheer' to deter Preston's 'vagabonds, rouges, theeves and sturdy beggars'. It seems to have passed out of its original use in the eighteenth century, but the site continued to be used for the flogging of prisoners brought from the House of Correction for this purpose. After receiving their quota of strokes from the cat-o-nine-tails the victim would be 'revived' in a nearby alehouse.

A Hewitson, *Preston Court Leet Records* (1905).

ROMAN ARCHAEOLOGY (80-400)

Occasional discoveries of isolated coins and pottery fragments apart, no evidence has been found to suggest the existence of a 'Roman Preston'. The region's strategic importance is however apparent: the main north-south road on the west coast was crossed in the vicinity of Fulwood by a road linking Ribchester to the outpost at Kirkham, whilst a military supply base on the Ribble at Walton served the Roman forces over a considerable area of northern Britain. The earliest activity may be associated with Agricola's campaigns after 78. At Ribchester a 6-acre stone fort replaced a large turf and timber structure around 105, and a fair-sized settlement (the main Roman military presence in the region) grew up. A visit to the small but superb museum at Ribchester forms a useful prelude to a day's exploration of the remarkable site which still lies under much of the modern village. At Kirkham an Agricolan marching camp, perhaps related to the vanished Portus Setantiorum on the Ribble, was replaced by a small stone fort in the early second century. The Kirkham Hoard of Roman coins (dating from 114-238) was found in 1936.

The finds at Walton indicate a much more complex site. E E Pickering was able to establish that the site was not defensive in nature, but rather some type of supply and storage base, and was occupied throughout the Roman era in the North. Large-scale excavations in 1980-3 and 1997 have clarified the picture. During the second century rows of long timber industrial buildings with hearths and pits developed along the main road. Early in the third century the function seems to have changed, with storage and supply functions now to the fore. The Roman presence in the vicinity of the town was therefore considerable, and lasted (like the British presence in India with which the era is often compared) for around three hundred years. In addition to the usual list of 'What the Romans did for us' must be considered the first airings of Christian belief in the second half of the third century. It is with the settlement of the early clerics in the years after the Roman withdrawal that the story of their Priests-town begins.

B J N Edwards, *The Romans at Ribchester* (2000). D Hunt, *A History of Walton-le-Dale and Bamber Bridge* (1997). D Shotter, *Romans and Britons in NW England* (2004). Publication of the Walton site is forthcoming in P Gibbons, C Howard-Davis, I Miller and D Gardner, *The Roman Site: Walton le-Dale.*

ROYAL INFIRMARY

The progress of health care in Preston has been traced by John Wilkinson. In 1809 a public meeting was held at the suggestion of 'several respectable citizens of this Borough' to explore the establishment of a 'Dispensary for supplying the poor with medicine to their relief in cases of sickness'. In the first six months some 749 patients were seen, and the Preston Dispensary in Fishergate, supplemented by the House of Recovery (1833) and various 'fever sheds' as required, served the town for the next sixty years, during which the population increased seven-fold. In 1870 a new 30-bed hospital was opened at a cost of almost £20,000 on the site of the House of Recovery off Deepdale Road. This hopelessly limited but revolutionary development marked the real start of the medical provision, but as seems to have been the norm with most progressive developments in Preston it was accompanied by much argument.

At the end of its first year the hospital had treated 167 in-patients, 2,626 out-patients, and the staff's wages came to £441 6s 11d. It had been made possible through the benevolence of mill owner John Bairstow (£24,500), and later progress owed much to Sir Charles Brown, the WINKLEY SQUARE local doctor, and W W Galloway of Horrockses, Crewdson & Co. In 1882 a Workpeople's Committee was formed to collect a levy of a halfpence per week from everyone earning over 8s per week. This produced £1,500, rising to over £20,000 in the mid-1920s, and the committee remained an important supporter of the hospital right up to the coming of the NHS in 1948. The Preston and County of Lancaster Royal Infirmary was steadily enlarged, and in 1904 acquired the first equipment to treat cancer. Further expansion followed each of the world wars, as the hospital developed as an important regional health centre. In 1950 the 401-bed capacity accommodated 10,089 patients, and 96,406 people attended as out-patients (Ear, Nose and Throat 19,398; Orthopaedics 13,967; Obstetrics 11,275). The new Royal Preston Hospital in Fulwood came into operation in January 1981, and the final departments of the old PRI closed in 1987.

John Wilkinson, *Preston's Royal Infirmary: A History of Health Care in Preston 1809-1986* (1987).

The Children's Ward, Preston Royal Infirmary c.1905.

RYDING, ANDREW

Gaoled in 1823 for an attack with a 15-inch long meat cleaver on SAMUEL HORROCKS. Following the imprisonment of three Preston spinners for forming a trades union Ryding decided to publicize the injustice of the Combination Laws by attacking the town's largest mill owner Samuel Horrocks MP - 'the cause of the evil'. One Sunday as Horrocks sauntered from church to the home of THOMAS MILLER in Dale St (at the end of Church St) he assaulted him. At Ryding's trial for attempted murder Horrocks described what happened:

> Suddenly I received a blow on the back of my head and thought something had fallen from the house. I received a second blow, again on my head and I perceived it had wounded me.

After a brief struggle Ryding ran off but was apprehended by the startled passers-by. He was in a state of near collapse and greatly agitated, crying out 'Take me, take me!'

At his trial, however, he gave a carefully measured account of his political motives:

> I knew I should be tried for the crime where ... I shall expose the oppression and injustice of these masters ... I took out the cleaver not meaning to kill but to cut ... it was not sharp.

His mother gave evidence that 'From the age of 12 he has had a bad ache and a ringing in his ears and an unsteadiness in his head'. His father Thomas Ryding explained that 'I saw that he was totally unfit for work and would rather maintain him than that he should do any hurt to himself or anybody else'. On the days before the attack he had been very agitated and his parents had been afraid 'of his destroying himself or one of us'. It took the jury just ten minutes to find him 'Not Guilty, on the grounds of insanity'. Ryding was then imprisoned in Lancaster Castle.

Whilst working in Manchester three months before the attack, Ryding had sent an anonymous letter to Horrocks:

> You are the cause of the falling of wages in Preston. Preston spinners are working more than 20 per cent under Manchester ... There are many cotton masters deserve to lose their lives, but you are, it is said, and I believe it is true, the worst of them all; therefore your life must go first.

M Burscough, *The History of Lark Hill, Preston, 1797-1989* (1989); *The Horrockses: Cotton Kings of Preston* (2004). LRO, DDPr 138/32.

See AGITATION.

ST GEORGE'S CHURCH

The church was built in 1724 for the inhabitants of Friargate and the west end of the town, serving as a 'chapel-of-ease' to the Parish Church. The brick building was 'encased in stone' in 1845, and extensively rebuilt in 1885. The rapid growth of industrial Preston was marked by the construction of a large number of new churches, beginning with Holy Trinity (1814-15); St Peter's (1822) and St Paul's (1823-5) were funded from the government's celebrated 'Million Pound Grant' to the Church of England, and along with St George's they all became parishes in their own right in 1844. In recent years St George's has become an interesting venue for artistic and musical events of all kinds and the church's interior is one of the town's great artistic gems. A fine meeting room and a small car park have been provided, though the latter has been at the cost of tarmacking over the grave of our old acquaintance SAMUEL HORROCKS.

T C Smith, *Records of the Parish Church of Preston* (1892).

ST MARY'S, FRIARGATE (1761)
See ST WILFRID'S RC CHURCH.

ST WALBURGE'S CHURCH
At 6 inches less than 300 feet, the church traditionally has the third highest spire in England after Salisbury (400 feet) and Lichfield (353 feet). Built on, or close by, the location of the medieval LEPER HOSPITAL, the site is an ancient one. Work began on the new Catholic church in 1850 to designs in the early English gothic style by J A HANSOM, and although it was opened for

St. Walburge's RC church, St. Marks C of E church and the railway goods depot c.1910. St. Walburge's was built close to the site of a medieval leper hospital which had been sited in the pleasant rolling countryside to the west of the town. Had city status been forthcoming in the 19th century, these churches would have become the town's Roman Catholic and Anglican cathedrals.

ST. WALBURG'S CHURCH, PRESTON

services in August 1854 it was not completed for some years. Time was given for fund-raising and tower settlement before the spire was constructed in 1867, and a new apse was added five years later. The church possesses fine stained glass, particularly in the west window. The cost was initially £50,000, and the 1,300 seats were scarcely sufficient to serve the large Jesuit parish; in the 1880s the church had six Sunday services, with three on weekday mornings, and three or four evening services during the week. The adjacent schools, Hewitson found, had around 2,000 scholars.

A Hewitson, *History of Preston* (1883).

ST WILFRID (634-709)

Bishop of York and Preston's pre-Reformation patron saint. Wilfrid was educated at Lindisfarne, visited Rome in 653 and was a leading figure at the Synod of Whitby (664). One of the great figures of the 'Age of Bede' and the early English church, he was at the centre of the multifarious disputes of the times, defending the faith against heresies, kings and his fellow bishops. In 670 Preston was probably among the 'lands along the Ribble' granted to Wilfrid's abbey at Ripon, and this event has usually been taken to mark the local transition from the old British-Irish to the Roman church. His feast day was an occasion of great celebrations during which (Hewitson assures us) the devout Prestonians of the day heartily 'ate, drank and thanked God for their saint'.

L Warren, *Through Twenty Preston Guilds: The Catholic Congregation of St Wilfrid's, Preston* (1993).

See PLACE NAMES; MINISTER.

ST WILFRID'S RC CHURCH

In 1687 the town's first post-Reformation Catholic chapel was established in a courtyard to the south of Friargate between Edward St and Marsh Lane. In earlier times 'Chapel Yard' had formed part of the track leading down to the Friary and was known as 'Old St. Marie's Gate'. This chapel was damaged by soldiers during the Glorious Revolution in 1689 and replaced in 1761 by St Mary's church 'near the fryergate barrs' at 62 Friargate. The new church had a colourful first few years; it was damaged during the GREAT ELECTION OF 1768, visited by James Boswell nine years later, and set on fire during the Gordon Riots of 1780. Yet St Mary's alone could not cope with the large Catholic congregation and when St Wilfrid's opened in June 1793 it became a chapel-of-ease. Under the impetus of the steady emancipation of Catholics after the First Catholic Relief Act (1778) and the dynamic leadership of DADDY DUNN the congregation expanded enormously and in 1813 St Wilfrid's was claimed to be the largest Catholic church in England: new churches were built (St Ignatius 1835, St Augustine's 1839 and ST WALBURGE'S 1854) and St Wilfrid's itself was extended in 1879. A number

The interior of St Wilfrid's RC Church c.1920.

of schools were established in what almost became Preston's Catholic Quarter - Fox St (1814), Preston Catholic College (1865) and Winckley Square Convent School (1875) - and the 'Institution for the Sick Poor' was established in Mount St in 1878. In spite of great public opposition, St Mary's Friargate was demolished in the 1980s to make way for a car park: it had fair claim to be one of the first post-Reformation Catholic churches to be built in the country.

L Warren, *Through Twenty Preston Guilds: The Catholic Congregation of St Wilfrid's, Preston* (1993). For details of this and the town's other principal churches see A Hewitson, *Our Churches and Chapels* (1869); *History of Preston* (1883).

SALBERG PLAYERS
Spectacularly successful local repertory group of the late 1940s and early 1950s. See HIPPODROME.

SEPTEMBER 1939
The outbreak of the Second World War was marked very differently in Preston to that of 1914. Assured by Ribbentrop that Britain would not go to war in support of her ally, Hitler gave orders for the invasion of Poland at 10.40 p.m. on 31 August 1939, with hostilities to begin at 4.45 a.m. the next day. Britain declared war at 11 a.m. on the morning of Sunday 3 September and France followed suit at 5 p.m. The following day the *Lancashire Daily Post*, having dispensed with its traditional front page advertisements, reported the previous day's events in the town. Many Prestonians had been at church and the great fear was for an immediate air attack:

> There was grim cheerfulness everywhere: public air raid shelters now ready include vaults in the Preston Cold Storage Co in Glover's Court, the tunnel in Woodcock's Court off Fishergate and in the Town Hall basement.

Air raid posts were manned continuously and Saul St Bath was to be used as a decontamination centre in the event of gas attack. A few days later the paper reported that

> There are sandbagged public buildings, now become almost a

commonplace in the familiar landscape and accepted without comment. There are policemen, carrying their steel helmets and their gasmasks: the ARP workers: soldiers much in evidence. E H Booth's appealed to customers not to panic buy ('It is too late to stock up now'), and 200,000 evacuees arrived in the North-West - 65,000 of them en route to Blackpool alone.

The first local casualties came at sea. On 16 September the Fleetwood trawler *Davara* was sunk by submarine, and Able Seaman J Smith was killed when the aircraft carrier HMS *Courageous* was sunk the following day - one week before his 21st birthday. Prestonians were among both the victims and the survivors of the sinking of HMS *Royal Oak* in Scapa Flow on 14 October. Estimates of the total number of war dead are extremely inaccurate and range widely from 35 to 60 million people, plus an unknowable number of wounded and disabled. The British casualties have been estimated as 264,443 dead, 277,077 wounded, 213,919 POWs or 'missing', and 92,673 civilians. In Europe alone 21 million people were made refugees, and 5,700,000 Jews were killed in the Nazi death camps.

Lancashire Daily Post (4, 6 and 20 Sept. 1939).

See Blitz in Preston; War Production (1937-1945); Singapore; Yanks; Vegeltungswaffe; Victory 1945.

SERVICE, ROBERT WILLIAM (1874-1958)

The 'Kipling of the Klondike'. Service was born the eldest of ten children at 4 Christian Road, Preston, and his mother had strong local 'cotton' connections. When he was 4 his father took the family to Scotland and after he left school at 14 Robert worked as a bank clerk whilst educating himself and attending evening English literature classes at Glasgow University. In 1896 he emigrated to British Columbia, and for some years worked on farms up and down the west coast. A rather diffident loner, he developed a keen ear for speech and local doggerel. Having returned to bank work he was moved to the Canadian Bank of Commerce's Whitehorse and Dawson City branches in the Yukon (1904-12) - the epicentre of the Klondike Gold Rush. The publication of his freelance writing and especially his verses written at this time quickly brought him world-wide acclaim, and 'The Shooting of Dan McGrew', published in *Songs of a Sourdough* (1907) made his fortune. Dan became a film, a ballet, appeared on a postage stamp and by the time of Service's death the collection had sold over three million copies.

In 1912 Service was employed as a war reporter covering the Balkan War, and the following year married the heiress of a wealthy Parisian distillery owner. This gave him the means to live in some style, and though he remained a British subject he lived in France for most of the rest of his life. During the war he served with an American ambulance unit and later

Canadian intelligence. After 1918 he travelled extensively throughout the world, from Tahiti to the Soviet Union, and whilst in Hollywood managed to appear on film as himself writing his most famous verse - alongside Marlene Dietrich! His written output was prodigious, though he never claimed to be more than 'A Versifier for Lowbrows'. Between 1949 and his death he produced a further eight books of verses and two volumes of autobiography, *Ploughman of the Moon* (1945) and *Harper of Heaven* (1946). He died at his summer home in Brittany in 1958.

The episodes of his distinguished and colourful life were closely followed in the local press, not least his escape ahead of the German occupation of France during the Second World War. The *Lancashire Daily Post* reported that the non-drinking non-gambler had been staying with his daughter in Monte Carlo where he had developed 'a system' for roulette and was very confident of 'breaking the bank'. Whatever the outcome, this erstwhile Prestonian was able to purchase a villa here after the war!

J Mackay, *Vagabond of Verse* (1995). *ODNB*.

SEVEN MEN OF PRESTON
The signatories of the total abstinence pledge signed at a temperance meeting held on Sunday 1 September 1832. The local temperance group had little problem with the moderate pledge to avoid spirits since Preston was a beer-drinking town! After a discussion with John King in August 1832 JOSEPH LIVESEY drew up a much stricter pledge to abstain from 'all liquors of an intoxicating quality'. This was to become the central tenet of a world-wide teetotal movement but was put to a very poorly attended meeting a few days later and signed up to by just seven members: John Gratrix, Edward Dickinson, John Broadbent, John Smith, Joseph Livesey, David Anderton and John King. Many of the leading members had not attended the meeting and King later claimed that two of the signatories recanted the same night.

B Harrison, *Drink and the Victorians* (1971).

SHAW, BENJAMIN (1772-1841)
Mechanic and working-class autobiographer. Born in Dent, Shaw had no formal education but from the age of 4 attended a 'knitting school'. He worked alongside his father as a 'jobbing mechanic' until the family moved to the mill community at Dolphinholme where he was apprenticed as a mill mechanic. His various autobiographical and family history writings have provided a unique picture of a Preston working man's life and troubles during the Industrial Revolution. These centre around his familial problems and particularly those arising from his arguments with his wife Betty (nee Leeming, ?1773-1828), yet despite their disagreements the couple had eight children. Fortuitously, if perhaps ironically, Shaw had taught himself to read

and write in order to keep in contact with his then girlfriend when she moved to Preston in 1792! The couple married in 1793 and two years later settled in Preston where Shaw worked for JOHN HORROCKS. In 1810 he had a leg amputated and in the five years before his return to work he strove strenuously to educate himself. These efforts came to centre on his 'volumes' of family history and autobiography (1826, 1829-36) which though 'lost' for almost a century and a half after his death, now provide a distinctive and original voice from the past.

A Crosby, *The Family Records of Benjamin Shaw, Mechanic of Dent, Dolphinholme and Preston, 1772-1841* (1991). His papers are preserved in LRO, DDX 1554. *ODNB*.

SHIPMAN, HAROLD FREDERICK (1947-2004)

The trial of Britain's leading mass murderer (and the world's third leading serial killer) took place in the Crown Court, Lancaster Road, Preston, in 1999-2000. The greatly respected Hyde GP was convicted of 15 killings, but the later Shipman Enquiry found evidence for at least a further 200 murders and the final number may have been much higher. His victims were killed by injections of Diamorphine, and were in the age group 47-93. He was arrested in August 1998 following the sudden deaths of a number of elderly women, but continued to protest his innocence until his suicide in Wakefield Prison in January 2004. During his fifty-seven-day trial Preston found itself the centre of a media circus, with daily reports of the proceedings broadcast on national television; rather grotesquely it was to be Preston's greatest media event.

Obituary: *The Times* (Jan. 2004).

SINGAPORE, FALL OF

The greatest military defeat in British history, and harbinger of the end of the British Empire. Following the attack on Pearl Harbour (7 December 1941) Japanese forces rapidly occupied the remaining European territories in the Far East. On 9-10 February 1942 three divisions landed on Singapore Island and on 15 February forced the 90,000-strong British, Indian and Australian garrison to surrender. Around 150 Prestonians, with other local men serving in the 88th Field Regiment, Royal Artillery, (the former West Lancashire Brigade), had been refitted after Dunkirk and sent out in September 1941. As A W Simpson wrote:

> Of the period which followed it is best not to give details. Most of the regiment were sent to work on the notorious Bangkok-Rangoon railway. For those who were there, that is all that need be said; for those that were not, no description would be adequate.

Over 300 men died.

Throughout the war the town was desperate for any news of the men, and it later transpired that the Prestonians were held in camps throughout the Far East. On 5 September 1945 word came from a party of prisoners liberated among the 4,500 held in Singapore Jail itself. The first question the BBC's Far Eastern correspondent was reported to have been asked by a starving survivor was a worried 'How are things in Preston?'

A W Simpson, *288 (2nd West Lancashire) Light Anti Aircraft Regiment, RA, Territorial Army: A History* (1960). *Lancashire Daily Post* (7 Sept. 1945).

SINGLETON, ROBERT (D.1544)

Vicar of Preston (1516-35), 'Heretic', and Lancashire's first Protestant martyr. Appointed vicar as a boy, Singleton had a dispensation for his absence, and worked chiefly in London and the South-East. During his university studies he was converted to Lollardy, becoming variously an agent of Thomas Cromwell and chaplain to Anne Boleyn. In 1543 he was charged with heresy and was executed for 'treason' in 1544.

C Haigh, *Reformation and Resistance in Tudor Lancashire* (1975).

See REFORMATION.

SINISTER AND SADISTIC PUNISHMENTS

Preston's strong suit: see BRIDLING; CUCKSTOOL; GIBBET; PILLORY; ROGUE'S WHIPPING POST; STOCKS.

SLAVE TRADE (c.1745-1765)

An utterly discreditable and fortunately brief interlude in Preston's history. The town's traditional seaborne trade lay with the North European ports, but by the middle of the eighteenth century Kirkham merchants had developed a growing colonial trade with the West Indies. Warehouses for the Barbados trade were built at Skippool on the Wyre (1741) and at Naze Point on the RIBBLE (1761). In 1754 a voyage of the *Clifton* carried local cheeses, shoes and all manner of items to Barbados, and the *Preston* delivered goods to Jamaica. Exports of cloth grew steadily: rum and sugar were a welcome addition to the older maritime staples of hemp, flax and timber, but soon the most profitable commodity of all was attracting the attention of the 'Merchants of Preston'. In 1755 Lloyds List recorded the voyages of three local ships: the *Hothersall* (of Poulton) had landed 150 people at Barbados, the *Betty & Martha* (of Poulton) 65, and the *Blossom* (of Preston) 131 people. Wartime losses and the example of the *Mary of Lancaster* (which was destroyed by escaping 'slaves' off James Fort in the River Gambia in 1761) killed off interest in the ports of the Fylde, and Preston reverted to the traditional Baltic trade. The last local ship to be granted a pass for the West Indies was the *Bella & Betty* of Poulton, sailing from Lancaster in August 1765. Yet Liverpool prospered and the involvement of Kirkham merchants in the Mersey slave trade grew. By the 1780s large cloth exports from the Preston region were passing through the port, providing plentiful work for the hand weavers of Leyland and Walton - they wove 'Osnaburghs', the slaves' heavy linen clothing.

M M Schofield, 'Shoes and Ships and Sealing Wax: Eighteenth Century Lancashire Exports to the Colonies', *THSLC* 135 (1986).

SMOKING

The Prestonians took to this new vice with enthusiasm, but with predictable consequences when the practice of 'Smoaking and taking Tobacco in the streets, back Weends and Lanes' led to buildings being 'unhappily sett on ffire'. In 1702 smoking was banned in shops and houses containing combustible materials, and by workmen 'building, repairing, thatching or slating the same'. Defaulters were to be fined 5s, then a large portion of a labourer's weekly wage. This was a far cry from Kuerden's euphoric endorsement of the practice during the proceedings at the 1682 Guild, where the Mayor's feast had been accompanied by 'All store of Pipes and Spanish Tobacco drenched well with healths in Spanish Wine'.

A Hewitson, *Preston Court Leet Records* (1905).

SOAMES, ENOCH

Poet, and the son, according to his creator Sir Max Beerbohm (1872-1956), of an unsuccessful Preston bookseller. His sad, but alarming, story is told in 'Seven Men and Two Others' (1919). Soames sells his soul to the Devil at 2.10 p.m. on 3 June 1897, in return for being allowed to return to the Reading Room of the British Museum exactly 100 years later to read (as he hopes) all the wonderful things future generations will have written about him. All he discovers is a brief reference in a book called *Inglish Littracher*, said to have been published in 1992 and mentioning 'a stori' by Max Beerbohm about 'an imajinari karraktor' called Enoch Soames - 'a thurd rait poit, hoo beleevz imself a grate jeneus'! On 3 June 1997, exactly at 2.10 p.m., Soames reappeared in the Reading Room, impersonated by the actor Steve Walden.

Mr Soames's entry is provided courtesy of Chris Aspin.

SOMME: FIRST BATTLE (1 JULY-13 NOVEMBER 1916)

One of the most catastrophic battles in the history of the world, and the occasion of the single bloodiest day in the First World War. On the day the British went 'over the top' they alone suffered 57,470 casualties - 20,000 of them killed. The small company of Preston PALS was all but wiped out. They took up positions on the battlefield on 30 June but were held in reserve until 23 July. Their attack failed, 10 officers and 213 men were killed, only about

50 Pals got back to their line, and by August they had virtually ceased to exist as a unit. Torrential rains in October turned the battlefield into a quagmire, and the offensive was called off in November. Over one and a quarter million men had died (625,000 German, 420,000 British, 195,000 French) and the catastrophe was to have an effect on the national psyche which endures to this day.

I Birwistle, 'The Life of the Preston Pals (1914-18)' (1987, unpublished dissertation).

SPINNERS STRIKE OF 1836 (NOVEMBER 1836-FEBRUARY 1837)

In the autumn of 1836 the Preston master spinners, who accounted for just 660 of the 8,500 workers employed in the town's 'spinning side', quickly won an advance of 10 per cent in their wages to bring them up to the level paid in Bolton. The Preston owners insisted, however, that they must give up their right to be members of a trade union. As ever in Preston labour relations the question was one of who was to be the master in the mills. The spinners struck on 7 November, throwing the remainder of the spinning employees - who had no union and no union funds - out of work. By December

The streets began to be crowded with beggars, and the offices of the overseers were besieged with applicants for relief. The inmates of the workhouse began to increase rapidly.

Early in January the masters saw their chance to break the strike and reopened their mills; a slow drift back to work began. A month later the union funds ran out, the strike collapsed and all mills were running normally by the end of the first week in February.

The dispute had been waged at a fearful price to both sides. It was estimated that it had cost the workforce over £57,000 in lost wages, the town's tradesmen had lost business worth £5,000, and the masters had foregone a notional return of £45,000 on their fixed capital. The individual cost was even starker:

Seventy-five persons were brought before the magistrates and convicted of drunkenness and disorderly conduct; twelve were imprisoned or held to bail for assaults and intimidation; about twenty young females became prostitutes, of whom more than one-half are still so, and of whom two have been transported for theft; three persons are believed to have died of starvation; and not less than five thousand must have suffered long and severely from hunger and cold. In almost every family the greater part of the wearing apparel and household furniture was pawned...

The most active strikers 'were replaced by new hands', and about 200 were barred from working in the town's mills ever again. The 'Ten Per Cent' was withdrawn in 1841.

C Hardwick, *History of the Borough of Preston* (1857).

See ANDREW RYDING; LOCKOUT OF 1853-4.

STAGE COACHES

Regular road passenger services, usually along TURNPIKE ROADS. In the boom years before the opening of the North Union Railway (1838) Preston had a considerable traffic centred on the Black Bull, White Horse and Red Lion inns and handled around a hundred coaches a day. One of the early services north to Lancashire left the Axe Inn, Aldermanbury, London, every Monday and Thursday, and took ten days in summer and eleven in winter to reach Warrington, with connections from there to Preston. In 1756 the 'Warrington Flying Coach' could be joined from Preston by horseback en route for the Bull Inn, Wood St, London. The fare was 2 guineas and passengers were allowed just 14lb of baggage at 'check in'. In the early nineteenth century a trip to Blackpool by the new and apparently 'luxurious' mailcart 'on springs' took just six and a half hours and cost 4s 6d - perhaps

Traffic in Church St at the junction with Cheapside, Glovers Court and Fishergate c.1960. In pre-pedestrianization days the policeman (with his elegant hand signals) was a familiar sight at the road junction in front of Booth's town centre store. The final remnants of the Town Hall can be seen on the left.

£100 in modern money. Turnpiking greatly improved the local routes, the southern entrance to the town was improved by the cutting of Preston Brow (bypassing Swillbrook), and the Blackburn New Road was built in 1824. On the eve of the railway age a 'direct' London service left Church St every Monday at 2 p.m., with the return service arriving in Preston on Tuesdays at 9am. The journey time was usually two to three days, but as early as the 1780s the 'London and Liverpool Flying Machine' had cut the trip to 48 hours. The opening of the new central bus station in 1971 (then the largest in Europe) saw Preston re-emerge as a major entrepot on the national coaching system.

C Hardwick, *History of the Borough of Preston* (1857). A Hewitson, *History of Preston* (1883). A Crosby (ed.), *Leading the Way: A History of Lancashire's Roads* (1998).

STANLEY FAMILY
Earls of Derby. Preston's largest landlord. See CIVIL WAR; DERBY IINTEREST; GREAT ELECTION OF 1768; PATTEN HOUSE.

STALIN, JOSEPH (1879-1953)
Real name Iosif Dzhugashvili. Russian tyrant (1928-53) responsible for killing perhaps more people than anyone else in history; enthusiast for Preston-engineered trolleybuses. Experiments with the operation of trolleybuses began in the USSR in 1933, and in 1936 the 'Mayor' of Moscow, Nikita Khrushchev (1894-1971), proposed the trial of British-built AEC vehicles with English Electric drives. A double-decker and single-decker duly arrived, they proved successful, and were then copied by the Russians. Though Khrushchev remained a stout supporter of the wooden-bodied double-deckers, Stalin found time during the Terror he was unleashing (1936-9) to fret about their stability whilst cornering, and no more were built after 1939. The fleet had a blue livery, apart from the two AEC vehicles which sported a white stripe. Amazingly, they carried these distinguished sporting colours from their 'Number One Depot' throughout the Nazi siege of Moscow, survived the war, and were honourably retired in 1948.

B Patton, *Double-Deck Trolleybuses of the World beyond the British Isles* (2004).

STOCKS
The town stocks were located in the parish churchyard. This punishment was reserved for less serious misdemeanours, but was applied with particular ferocity ('a publique example to the terifinge of all others') to malefactors abusing the Mayor, his officials or any of the town officers going about their business. An order of the 1562 Guild laid down incarceration in the stocks for three days on a bread and water diet and a fine of 6s 8d for such offenders. The order was specifically stated 'to apply for ever'.

A Hewitson, *Preston Court Leet Records* (1905).

SUDELL, WILLIAM (1850-1910)

The father of professional football; architect of Preston North End's greatness; convicted embezzler. Scion of an ancient Preston family, Sudell could add three columns of figures in his head simultaneously and after a private education became 'confidential manager' of John Goodair's extensive cotton mill empire. A Free Trade Gladstonian Liberal he had varied sporting interests which he saw as a means of improving the physical stock of the working classes. As a youthful leader of the North End cricketers he pioneered the move to the Old Hey Field and into winter sports. Mindful of the success of the Blackburn clubs he began to assemble a team of Scottish professionals in 1883, with the smuggling over the border of Jack Ross. Sudell did much to promote professional football in England, and the emergence of the world game thus owes him much. His 'Invincible' Preston side swept all before it, famously winning the first League Championship without losing a game and the FA Cup without conceding a goal in 1888/9 - a feat which no club has repeated.

Today he is a largely forgotten figure. Sudell encountered much establishment opposition and after his fall from grace he was effectively airbrushed out of the game's early history. The reason is readily to hand, for in 1893 his employers called in the receivers and two years later, whilst taking a stroll down Waterloo Road, he was arrested. He was charged with having used his firm's funds to subsidize the football team and was summarily sentenced to three years' imprisonment. At the time friends suggested that he had taken the blame 'for another man's misdeed', and this view has recently received support. On release he and his family emigrated to South Africa and his subsequent career as a footballing pioneer and successful sports journalist would tend to lend support to this view. He died suddenly while covering a sports event, and in numerous obituaries former colleagues attested to the extremely high regard in which he was held. Unlike its British counterpart the South African press had no hesitation in recognizing his role as 'the founder of Association Football in England', and of course of the Invincible PRESTON NORTH END Football Club.

D Hunt, *A History of Preston North End Football Club: The Power, the Politics and the People* (2000).

SUNKEN FORESTS

The short periods of relatively higher sea levels experienced along the Lancashire coast in post-glacial times resulted in the inundation - and occasionally the preservation - of the contemporary vegetation. To the south of Southport low tides expose the remains of light woodland at Crosby, and muds revealed by the retreating dunes at Formby preserve the tracks of people and animals exploiting the coastal flats around 6,000 years ago. Much older deposits - the Rossall Beach Peat - can be seen in the foreshore at Cleveleys. At Preston work to deepen the river in the 1840s dredged up large numbers of mature deciduous trees. Many hundreds were recovered for sale in the stretch of the RIBBLE between Savick Brook and the site of the later dock entrance. Specimens ranged up to 63 feet long; one example had a trunk of 30 feet, a girth of 15 feet, and two branches of 32 and 16 feet respectively! Their age is speculative, but the sunken forest at Preston may have been inundated around 4000 BC. Related finds have frequently come to light in the deeper river gravels, most spectacularly during the excavation of the Albert Edward dock: the survival of undisturbed deposits at Penwortham and Ashton is thus strongly indicated, with their tantalizing potential to one day reveal the story of Preston's own lost world.

J Barron, *History of the Ribble Navigation* (1937). D Hunt, *Preston: Centuries of Change* (2003). For recent research on the local vegetation, mosses and peats of the Preston-Fylde region see R Middleton, C E Wells and E.Huckerby, *The Wetlands of North Lancashire* (1995). The volume in this wonderful series covering the South Ribble district is eagerly awaited, see R Middleton, M J Tooley and J Innes, *The Wetlands of South-West Lancashire* (forthcoming).

See PRESTON DOCK FINDS.

SURNAMES OF THE PRESTONIANS

Working from the Preston Guild Rolls, Abrams was able to produce a list of almost 450 surnames of 'the principal families or class seated in Preston'. He took pains, however, to point out that many of them were merely those 'of inferior local families'. The following is thus a list of the families associated with the town in the pre-industrial era:

Abbott, Abraham, Addison, Ainsworth, Alston, Ambrose, Ancram (Earls of), Anderton, Andrews, Arkwright, Armetriding, Arrowsmith, Askew, Assheton, Astley, Atherton, Atkinson, Audland, Aynscough.

Balderston, Balshawe, Bamber, Bancroft, Bankes, Banaster, Barker, Barkley, Barnes, Barton, Bateson, Bayley, Becconsall, Beesley, Benson, Berwick, Bickerstaff, Billesborrowe, Birchall, Birch, Birches, Birley, Birtwistle, Blackburne, Blackhurst, Blackledge, Blacowe, Blundell, Boardman, Bold, Bolton, Bootle, Bostock, Butler, Braddyll, Bradley, Bradshawe, Bragger, Braithwaite, Bramwell, Brandon (Lord), Breeres, Bretergh, Bretherton, Breton, Brewer, Bridgeman, Brockholes, Brograve, Brookes, Browne, Brownelowe, Brownsword, Bullen, Buller, Burscough, Burton, Bury, Bushell.

Cadman, Calderbank, Calvert, Campbell, Cardwell, Carr, Carter, Catterall, Chadwick, Chapman, Chisnall, Chorley, Claughton, Clarkson, Clayton, Clifton, Clitherow, Cockshutt, Cole, Colthurst, Comberall, Cooke, Cooper, Copeland, Cosney, Cossen, Cottam, Cowburne, Cowell, Cowling, Crane, Crichlow, Croft, Crooke, Crosse, Croston, Cuerdall, Cuerden,

Culcheth, Cunliffe, Curtis.

Dalton, Damme, Daniel, Darwen, Davenport, Dawson, Dayntie, Derby (Earls of), Dewhurst, Dicconson, Dickson, Dobson, Dodding, Dolphin, Downes, Drinkwater, Duckworth, Duddell, Dugdale.

Eastham, Eaves, Eccles, Eccleston, Edmondson, Egerton, Ellison, Elston, Elwes, Ergham, Evans.

Farnworth, Farrand, Farrington, Feilden, Fell, Ferman, Ferrars, Fidler, Finch, Fisher, Fishwick, Fitton, Fleetwood, Fletcher, Fogg, Forshaw, France, French, Freres, Fyfe.

Gardner, Garstang, Gellibrand, Gerard, Girlington, Gornall, Gorsuch, Gradwell, Graystock, Greaves, Greene, Greenfield, Greenhalgh, Greenwood, Gregson, Gresham, Grimbald, Grimshaw, Grundy.

Hacking, Haconshaw, Haggerston, Haighton, Hairsnape, Halliwell, Hall, Hallsall, Halstead, Hankinson, Hardman, Harrison, Harrington, Hatch, Hawkeshead, Haworth, Haydock, Hayhurst, Heaton, Helme, Herdson, Hesketh, Heywood, Higham, Hilton, Hindle, Hodgkinson, Hodgson, Hoghton, Holcroft, Holden, Holker, Holand, Hollinghurst, Hollinshead, Holme, Holt, Hoole, Horrocks, Horwich, Hothersall, Howson, Hudson, Hunte, Hynd.

Ingham, Ingolby, Ireland.

Jackson, Jenkinson, Johnson, Jolly, Jones.

Kay, Kellett, Kendall, Kenyon, Kighley, Kilshaw, King, Kippax, Kirkby.

Lambert, Lamplugh, Langton, Lawe, Leach, Leake, Leaver, Leckonby, Leigh, Lemon, Letmore, Lingard, Lister, Livesey, London, Longton, Lorimer, Loxam, Lumas, Lund, Lussell.

Maire, Makin, Markland, Marsden, Marsh, Marshall, Martin, Mason, Mawdesley, May, Meles, Melling, Mercer, Merrie, Midgeall, Midleton, Miller, Mitton, Mollineux, Moore, Morley, Morte, Mosley, Moss, Mountegle (Lord), Musgrave, Myers.

Newsham, Nicholson, Nickson, Norres, Nowell.

Ogle, Ormond (Duke of), Osbaldeston, Ossery (Earl of).

Parke, Parker, Parkinson, Parr, Paslew, Patten, Pearson, Pedder, Pemberton, Pennington, Percivall, Pickering, Pigott, Poole, Presall, Prescott, Preston.

Radcliffe, Rathmell, Rawlinson, Rawstorne, Richardson, Ridley, Rigby, Rigg, Rimmer, Rishton, Rivington, Roades, Robinson, Robson, Rogerson, Rowley, Rydinge, Ryley.

Sallom, Salter, Sanderson, Sandes, Scarisbrick, Sergeant, Shackerley, Shakeshaft, Sharples, Shawe, Shepherd, Sherburne, Shorrocke, Shuttleworth, Sidgreaves, Silcock, Singleton, Skillicorne, Slater, Smith, Southworth, Sowerbutts, Spencer, Standish, Stanley, Starkie, Strickland, Sudell, Sumner.

Talbot, Tarbocke, Tardie, Tasker, Thornborough, Thorneton, Thorpe,

Threlfall, Tipping, Tomlinson, Tompson, Tootell, Townend, Towneley, Travers, Tunstall, Turner, Tyldesley.

Waddington, Walkden, Walker, Wall, Walmesley, Walshman, Walton, Ward, Wareing, Warren, Waterhouse, Watson, Werden, Westby, Whalley, White, Whitehead, Whithalgh, Whittingham, Whittle, Wigan, Wildbore, Wilding, Wilkinson, Williamson, Williams, Wilson, Winckley, Winder, Wingfield, Winstanley, Withington, Wood, Woodburne, Woodcock, Woodhouse, Woodruffe, Woodward, Woolfall, Worthington, Wrench, Wright, Wrightington.

Yates, Yonge, Yorke.

W A Abram, *Memorials of the Preston Guild* (1882). The Preston Guild Rolls may now be viewed in LRO.

Nicholas Grimshaw (1758-1838). Prominent early resident of Winckley Square, friend and one of the financial backers of John Horrocks.

SWILLBROOK

A largely covered but once powerful and clear stream rising in Fishwick and flowing westwards to the south of the line of New Hall Lane, crossing London Road in the vicinity of Barry House, passing through the grounds of Lark Hill to enter the RIBBLE by the Old Tram Bridge. This was the site of the ancient 'Washing Steed' - the town's laundry. 'Swill' comes from the Anglo-Saxon word 'swilian' - to wash. The stream gave its name to the various roads and bridges which crossed it on their rise into the town from the RIBBLE BRIDGE. On the principal of these (sharply to the left of London Road at the foot of Preston Brow) Cromwell narrowly missed death during the battle of 1648.

A Hewitson, *Preston Court Leet Records* (1905).

See SYKE; MOOR BROOK.

SYKE, THE

A streamlet running west, to the south of Church St, which determined the early geography of Preston. Culverted and so hidden from sight for well over a hundred years, the course of the Syke was critical in defining the line of the furthermost extent of the burgage plots along the south side of Church St. In essence the Saxon settlement grew up between the central part of the Church St ridge and the Syke. The stream formed on the Water Willows, a group of fields lying to the east of the present Manchester Road, and may have been fed by a natural spring. The complicated surface relief of this area pushed the stream north and westwards rather than to a shorter and more direct course south to the river. Accordingly the Syke ran as an open watercourse up Manchester Road ('Leeming Street' on the 1847 60″ OS map), swinging

A detail of Bucks 'Prospect of Preston' (1728). Viewed from Hennel Lane, Walton-le-Dale, the Syke forms the southern boundary of the burgage plots. The scene is dominated by the Town Hall and the large houses of the leading families, and most of the pathways (passing through gardens and field strips on their way into the town) survive to this day (from S and R Buck, The South Prospect of Preston in the County Palatine of Lancaster, *1728).*

sharply to the west near the junction with Shepherd St and along Syke Hill. From here the stream follows a course along or slightly to the north of Avenham Lane to follow Syke St, an alley to the north of Cross St. A large iron grid marks its passage here across Cannon St, and during heavy rain the water can be heard flowing beneath it - though watch for passing traffic! The Syke then passes west under the offices of HM Inland Revenue, beneath WINCKLEY SQUARE, along Garden St and under the railway station yards. In the 1850s it emerged to the west of West Cliff running northwards and parallel to it almost as far as Fishergate Hill. Here the Syke took another sharp turn to the west to follow a line just to the south of Fishergate. The stream can be seen flowing into the River Ribble a few metres to the south of the Penwortham bridge at the foot of Fishergate Hill.

A Hewitson, *History of Preston* (1883); *Preston Court Leet Records* (1905).

T

TAYLOR, A J P (1906-1990)
Outstanding British diplomatic historian and bow-tied television celebrity whose formative years were spent in Preston. Ironically, it is the bizarre childhood of Preston's greatest historian rather than his internationally

renowned writings which is of particular local interest here. His father Percy Lees Taylor was then a partner of Taylor Brothers (Bute Mill, Essex St) whose vast income long provided Taylor with an extremely privileged lifestyle, strongly at odds with that enjoyed by nearly all of his fellow Prestonians. Despite this, the only child had a lonely childhood, and in later life he recalled his joy at visits to the local theatre and cinema, and his walks along the canal in 'Haslam Park'. He was a very frequent visitor to the Harris Library from which he borrowed 'practically the whole of English literature', though this necessitated 'a dreary walk through mean streets' from his Ashton home. Yet his was a blinkered view of town life, and on a visit shortly before his death he was shocked to realize that there were whole swathes of Preston he had never visited!

Taylor's parents were ardent Socialists who welcomed the Russian Revolution (1917), supported the General Strike (1926) and were committed members of a then virtually communist Preston Labour Party - despite the fact that Percy Taylor had received around £100,000 as his share of the family business in 1920. AJP's autobiography thus provides an interesting and rare insight into middle-class family life and concerns in Preston during the declining years of the cotton industry. This formidable personality would doubtlessly be less than appreciative of the attentions of this scribbler - who accordingly will swiftly pass on . . .

A J P Taylor, *The Origins of the Second World War* (1961); *A Personal History* (1983). A Sisman, *AJP Taylor* (1994). ODNB.

THEATRE LAND

The concentration of theatres and music halls in the Tithebarn St-Church St area c.1885-1955. Improving terms of employment after the 1850s produced a massively increased demand for leisure pursuits of all kinds. In sporting spheres this phenomenon is clearly associated with the rise of professional football as a mass sport after 1918, but it also produced a remarkable flowering of the theatre and the more popular music hall and variety circuits. Preston quickly emerged as a major provincial centre, with its own distinct theatre land. The town had a long theatrical tradition dating back to the seventeenth century, and the THEATRE ROYAL (1802) had itself been erected on the site of the eighteenth-century Playhouse. After the opening of the Gaiety (PRINCE'S) in 1882 it was estimated that the town had around 9,000 music hall seats, a number greatly expanded by the subsequent opening of the HIPPODROME (1905), the EMPIRE (1911) and the PALACE (1913). It follows that virtually all the music hall stars of the early twentieth century - among them Harry Lauder, Gracie Fields and GEORGE FORMBY - played in the town. Today these traditions live on at the Guild Hall and the Charter Theatre, and at the home of the Preston Drama Club, the Playhouse.

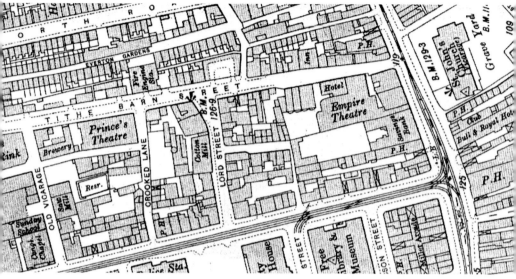

The Tithebarn St district: Preston's 'Theatre land' (detail from the 1909 25" OS map).

D Hindle, *Twice Nightly: An Illustrated History of Entertainment in Preston* (1999).

THEATRE ROYAL
Latterly the ABC Cinema, Fishergate (1806-1955). The Woodcock Court site on the edge of the town, close by the Fishergate Bar, had long been used for public events. Built for the Guild of 1802 the Theatre Royal was the town's principal meeting place prior to the use of the then open-air Public Hall after 1853. Initially a rather severely plain building it played a leading role in the town's cultural and public life. An early programme gives a flavour of the fare popular among the elegant in Preston's age of Jane Austen: it included 'A Loyal Address written and spoken by Mr. Bretherton, in character of a Volunteer of the armed forces'. Paganini, Liszt and Dickens appeared here, along with the leading politicians of the day. Debates would often be carried over a number of evenings; in 1833 Robert Owen gave a series of lectures on his new society, and similar events (with JOSEPH LIVESEY well to the fore among the locals) debated all the current issues of the day - the Reform Act, the New Poor Law and Free Trade. Not all events were so high brow, and it is claimed that Edward Prince of Wales, incognito, attended a 'midnight theatrical performance' during the 1882 festivities.

In 1898 the building was enlarged to accommodate 1,700 people (600 in the pit, 100 in the stalls, 300 in boxes, and 700 in the gallery): 'The new building is a very commodious one, including the most modern

A rare photograph of the Theatre Royal, Fishergate, 1922. For most of the 19th century the Theatre Royal was Preston's principal place of entertainment and many of the great artists of the day - from Paganini to Charles Dickens - performed here.

improvements as to plan of construction, whilst the decorations are superbly handsome.' But the theatre had lost its pre-eminence in Preston with the opening of the new Public Hall (see CORN EXCHANGE) and the PRINCE'S (1882) and later the HIPPODROME (1905). The ubiquitous WILL ONDA was showing films here by 1911, 1916 saw the screening of *Esmerelda* starring Mary Pickford, and the theatre became a cinema in 1926. These efforts having proven successful the building was converted into a cinema proper in 1928. The auditorium was dominated by a huge cinema organ (second in quality only to that at the NEW VICTORIA) which rose out of the floor with its accompanying orchestra.

The cinema closed in 1955, was demolished and replaced in 1959 by the futuristic ABC, 'The most modern cinema of its day!' The 1,400-seater itself closed in September 1982 and was demolished four years later. Today only Theatre St perpetuates the memory of what was for over two hundred years one of the town's most important and fashionable public venues.

J Cotterall, *Preston's Palaces of Pleasure* (1988). D Hindle, *Twice Nightly: An Illustrated History of Entertainment in Preston* (1999). See also J E Adkins, 'A History of Preston Musical Societies 1750-1935' (1947: unpublished manuscript, Harris Reference Library).

THOMPSON, FRANCIS JOSEPH (1859-1907)

Writer and poet. Born at 7 Winckley St, Preston, Thompson wanted to be a priest as a small boy and was educated at St Cuthbert's College, Ushaw. In 1877 he left and began six years of medical studies at Manchester. Thompson's lifelong opium addiction dates from his mother's death at this time - she had been prescribed the drug as a pain killer. Having broken with his family, and living unemployed in London, by 1885 he was reduced to living on the streets. The addict was only saved from suicide two years later by an unknown prostitute who befriended him, and took him back to her room. Here she looked after him and encouraged his poetry. Wilfrid Meynell, the editor of a Catholic journal, recognized his immense talent and organized his recovery and recuperation. The girl, realizing that she now stood in the way of her friend's future advancement, organized her disappearance from the scene. Despite intense efforts Francis Thompson was unable to trace her, but she lives on in his poems.

In February 1888 Thompson recovered from the effects of homelessness and poverty at a priory in Sussex and having managed to 'come off' opium, produced two of his greatest works, 'Ode to the Setting Sun' and 'The Hound of Heaven'. In London he assisted Meynell and his wife's journalistic enterprises, but when he relapsed back onto the drug he moved to a friary at Pantasaph, North Wales. The atmosphere here inspired him to write essays, prose, and reviews, and two collections of his poems were published in 1893 and 1897. His poems frequently centre around the theme of the manifestation of man's supernatural life in human experience, and were not fully appreciated in his own life time. At his death his sparse lodging was found to contain a great mass of his work and notes which, forming the basis of his *Life* published in 1913, brought about his recognition as one of England's finest poets.

Throughout his life Francis Thompson was a keen enthusiast for England's summer game, and lines from his 'At Lords' have become the natural starting point for many a cricketing anthology or history:

And I look through my tears on a soundless-clapping host,
As the run-stealers flicker to and fro,
To and fro: - ,
O my Hornby and my Barlow long ago!

E Meynell, *The Life of Francis Thompson* (1913). B M Beardman, *Between Heaven and Charing Cross: The Life of Francis Thompson* (1988). *ODNB*.

THOMPSON, MARTHA (1731-?)

Early Methodist. Born in Preston, Martha moved to London in 1750 and found employment as a servant. Whilst running an errand at Moorfields she quite accidentally came across a meeting addressed by John Wesley, was impressed and returned the next day. Having warned her to keep away from the Methodists 'for they would drive her mad and ruin her soul', her employer put her into an asylum! Wesley and friends however secured her release and she returned to Preston. Her adventure over, she established a millinery business, married and had four children. In 1759 she began to attend the first local Methodist meetings which were held at Cockshutt House, Duddle Lane, Bamber Bridge.

W Pilkington, *The Makers of Wesleyan Methodism in Preston* (1890).

THORESBY, RALPH

Celebrated diarist who visited Preston in 1702. He described the miles of cloth naturally bleaching under sunlight on the hedges around Bamber Bridge, and was clearly fond of a good walk:

Sept 4th walked...to view the town, wherein are several very good houses...the town chiefly (depends) on the quill, here being kept all the courts relating to the County...We then walked to the fields to an eminency lately purchased by the town, where is a very curious walk and delicate prospects [Ladies Walk, Avenham].

Like many visitors since he found 'much good company here', yet when the Guild Mayor spontaneously offered him the Freedom of Preston, 'we thought ourselves *more free without it*'!

W A Abram, *Memorials of the Preston Guild* (1882).

THOUGHT FOR THE DAY

Inscribed along the top of the Harris Library and Art Gallery in Lancaster Road, 'On earth there is nothing great but man: in man there is nothing great but mind'.

Sir William Hamilton (1788-1856), 'Lectures on Metaphysics'.

TITHEBARN STREET
See THEATRE LAND.

TOP SECRET PRESTON
The town's ancient geographical dominance in the region gave it an important role in air defence preparations during the COLD WAR (1947-91). Estimates of the number of likely British casualties in the event of a nuclear attack varied markedly from 25 to 40 million, and the extent of damage from 25 to 40 per cent, whilst an exercise in 1981 estimated that 75 per cent of the population would be killed immediately. Preston was the Command Group centre for the Western Region of the UK Warning and Monitoring Organization, an area which stretched from southern Scotland to mid-Wales. The UKWMO was established to monitor air attacks, and assist in the administration of the country in their aftermath. Warning of an attack would come from the American Forces, NATO, and the ballistic missile early warning station at RAF Fylingdales (completed in 1963). From the Regional Operations Centre at High Wycombe the 'Attack Warning Red' would be sent out to the regional control centres. Initially the NW control point was located at FULWOOD BARRACKS (the NW military control centre), but it was decided that such sites should be moved away from army bases. Building work on the new command group headquarters began in 1959, and the Preston facility was moved to the former RAF Fighter Command Group HQ in Langley Lane, Goosnargh (1962-91). Here an enormous multi-storeyed, subterranean, concrete bunker with a staff of around 80 and related radar and other facilities would have served the North-West in the event of missile attack. A subsidiary station was located at St Annes and warehouses in Preston, the Fylde and South Ribble contained emergency food supplies. During the CUBAN MISSILE CRISIS, and to a lesser extent the Russian invasions of Czechoslovakia (1967) and Afghanistan (1979) such fears seemed alarmingly real, but the collapse of the Soviet Union in 1991 brought this particular network to an end. Langley Lane went 'non-operational' in 1991 and this remarkable installation - as much a relic of the late twentieth century as the Harris Art Gallery is of the nineteenth - was duly sold off. The Hack Green nuclear bunker near Nantwich, Cheshire, has been developed as a visitor centre.

P S Barnwell (ed.), *Cold War: Building for Nuclear Confrontation 1946-89* (2003). R Poole and S Wright, *Target North West: Civil Defence and Nuclear War in Cumbria, Lancashire, Manchester, Merseyside and Cheshire* (1982).

TOWN COUNCIL
An ancient body, ultimately of Saxon origin, responsible for administering the town's affairs and elected by the BURGESSES. Prior to its reformation

under the Municipal Corporations Act (1835) it was notable only for its nepotism, corruption and the extent of its wine cellar. Well into Tudor times the body had to fight hard to maintain the rights of the burgesses against the arbitrary interference of the local landed magnates. Despite fairly constant protests and disputes the council became in effect a self-perpetuating body, whose members also filled the offices of the COURT LEET and the FOUR AND TWENTY. Queen Elizabeth's hope that the town 'for all future times should be and remain a Borough of peace and tranquillity' was destined to be misplaced. Struggling to keep the management of the town among themselves, the clique of leading families could rarely even agree on the procedures for selecting their Mayor and officers. Accordingly, a furious dispute raged over such appointments in the 1590s, 'to the great greefe and offence of many of the best sorte of people...and much to the discredit of the sturrers uppe of such contencon'.

Efforts were made to conduct council business in as dignified a manner as possible. In 1612 members were ordered to attend church as a body and to wear 'decente and comelie gowns of black cloth' when assembled, and DR KUERDEN provided a welcome account of their apparently orderly if near-byzantine ceremonial seventy years later. The reality of course was rather different; members had to be strictly forbidden from using bad language at meetings ('uncivil or reflecting words'), and from carrying on their conversations when another member was speaking. The formation of parties and 'whisperings privately' were expressly banned, and on the eve of the CIVIL WAR the dangers were real enough. Yet for all its many faults the unreformed council of the Royal Borough of Preston carried the town's progress forward, and upheld local rights for the best part of a thousand years. Its records for the century and a half after 1608 are preserved in the city's celebrated 'White Book'.

H W Clemesha, *History of Preston in Amounderness* (1912).

TOWNFIELDS

The Saxon town was laid out along the narrow ridge which rises to the north of the SYKE stream in the Avenham fields. In the thirteenth century the market place was laid out, and houses were erected along the lane leading onto the Moor. Each of the burgesses' houses along CHURCHGATE, FISHERGATE and FRIARGATE had a narrow strip of garden behind it, and beyond these extended the townfields. These lands were divided into a number of very large open fields which were divided into small strips, and cultivated in a system of six months fallow, six months in crop. The best example is the subdivision of the Great Avenham Field, where the line of very early individual strips was later preserved in the Victorian pattern of

Anthony Hewitson's (1905) composite field plan of Preston in the 17th century (largely based on George Lang's map of 1774, William Shakeshaft's map of 1809, a Preston tithe map of 1824 and J J Myres's map of 1836). Around the urban core lay the burgesses' fields, remnants of the great Saxon and early medieval Townfields (*A Hewitson*, Preston Court Leet Records, 1905).

house building. Well into the eighteenth century burgesses would cultivate their holdings of individual strips in disparate fields around the town. An instance is the small estate purchased by George Addison in 1615: it comprised a burgage in Fishergate and strips in the Great Avenham, Little Avenham, Platford Dales, Hepgreave Meadows and a garden in the water meadows off South Meadow Lane.

In Preston many BURGESSES built barns on the plots behind their house, which in effect became small farmyards in which animals and equipment could be kept. This system was very carefully controlled. Each morning the various herdsmen would call at the houses to collect the burgesses' animals and drive them to the more distant common grazings on the Marsh or Moor. This must have been a picturesque and novel sight in a town largely given over to trade, textiles and the law. The result, of course, was a chaos onto which the town's Court Leet struggled to impose order. The herdsmen (if they turned up at all) did not give the burgesses time to get their animals out, so that the herds were left 'to range up and downe the streets' where they were given to snatching toothsome morsels from the traders' stalls. Accordingly, it ordered in 1655 that

> the bailiffs shall cause the said swinsord to blowe his horn from the church gate bars to the Fishergate bars and along to the Market Place, and then retorne back and take the swyne along.

Notwithstanding these good intentions, when a barrel of beef was abandoned in Friargate in 1658 it soon came to the attention of watchful eyes and 'carried upp and downe the streete by doggs and swine, to ye geat greefe of the neighborringe Inhabitants'. The meat was rescued and given to the town poor.

A Hewitson, *Preston Court Leet Records* (1883). D Hunt, *A History of Preston* (1992).

TOWN HALL

A building designated to serve as a meeting place for the leading townspeople must clearly have existed from the earliest times, but although the burgesses' 'court' is noted in the Customal the first specific reference to a 'certain house . . . vulgarly called the Toll-booth, otherwise the Moot-hall' is not made until 1565 - 500 years after Domesday. This is probably the 'ample, antient, and yet well beautifyed gylde or town hall or toll bothe' described by Kuerden around 1680. The site at the south end of the market square 'in the middle of the Burrough' is therefore an ancient one around which virtually all of Preston's history has revolved. It was beside and actually partially above the town's meat shops (the Shambles), and it seems that butchery commotion and the burning of waste products occasionally interrupted council proceedings.

Ahead of the 1762 celebrations a 'Guild Hall' was added to this building, but twenty years later the Town Hall collapsed, narrowly avoiding

Central Fishergate looking east c.1938. The Kardomah restaurant (left) and Woolworth's (right) are overlooked by the spectacular tower of the Town Hall.

considerable loss of life. A new 'plain, heavy looking brick building with stone facings' was speedily put in place, and served until 1862. Site clearance began with the removal of the timber-framed houses fronting the market place in 1855, and it was decided to erect a spectacular edifice well in keeping with the council's romanticized view of its own past. After much dispute and delay Sir George Gilbert Scott's (1811-78) amazing building was opened with due pomp in September 1867. The central feature was a tower almost 200 feet high; to the east the Guild Hall sat upon an arched arcade which overlooked Fishergate, the cramped west frontage along Cheapside contained the main entrance, whilst the north side had an open theatrical aspect (well suited to ceremonial events) onto the market square.

The interior was even more elaborate, and the decorations went to some length to present an inspired and improved picture of Preston's past. Large letters in the Guild Hall boomed the message: 'Thou Shalt Remember The Lord Thy God, For It Is He That Giveth Thee Power To Get Wealth'. Although the building quickly became too small to run a modern Borough

Council from and the site was cramped and ill-chosen, the Town Hall with its enormous tower and clock face was Preston's most loved building and was the obvious venue for visits by royalty and the FA Cup. A fire in March 1947 extensively damaged the Guild Hall and clock tower, and despite considerable public protest and a heavy insurance windfall (£140,000) the building was never rebuilt, and the last vestiges were removed in 1962. The land was leased to a Canadian property concern (for a hundred years at £36,750 per year) which then proceeded to erect a modern office block - Crystal House - on Preston's most prestigious site. Some years later when Stephen Sartin enquired as to the derivation of this name he was told that it had been that of the mother of the chairman of the Calgary Land Co.!

A Hewitson, *History of Preston* (1883).

TRAM BRIDGE

A wooden bridge originally built to carry the Lancaster CANAL tramway over the River RIBBLE. Rennie's plan was for the canal to descend 222 feet from Clayton Green through 32 locks and onto an embankment and bridge. With the 'North End' to Lancaster completed in 1797, three huge arches of 116 feet were to carry the waterway south, 57 feet above the low water mark, in what would have been one of the great achievements of Britain's industrial

The Tram Bridge seen from the south c.1925. Originally a short-term expedient, the tramway proved a very successful and profitable alternative to the enormous viaduct that Rennie had planned.

age. The expense of the Lune aqueduct and problems at the Whittle Hills Tunnel induced the directors to set aside the £95,000 scheme in favour of a temporary tramway linking the wharves by the CORN EXCHANGE at Preston to the canal terminus at Walton Summit. In the event the scheme was very successful and was retained. A double line of tram plates, each one yard long and costing 5d, was laid over the 5 mile course. The line had three stationary steam engines, a 'Machine House' in Hennel Lane, sidings at Bamber Bridge and rudimentary port facilities at the Summit. When the 'South End' was opened in 1803 it had an immediate effect on the canal's revenues, which quickly trebled, and by 1811 exceeded £15,000 per year. In 1837 the line was taken over by the railway company who continued to work it until 1859. In 1868 the Avenham engine house was demolished, and the plates were taken up north of Bamber Bridge, but the link south from there operated until 1879, bringing Wigan coal to the local mills. The tram bridge has long been an important link in popular walks along the river, and when the wooden structure was at last removed in 1965 it was replaced by a copy in steel and concrete.

S Baritt, *The Old Tram Road* (2000).

TSR-2

Tactical, Strike and Reconnaissance Aircraft. An aeroplane whose abrupt cancellation under foreign pressure precipitated Preston's greatest political and economic crisis of the post-war era, and came to be a symbol in the 1960s of both British engineering excellence and national decline. This revolutionary aircraft was designed to replace the CANBERRA, and much of Britain's aircraft industry (including English Electric) was consolidated into the British Aircraft Corporation in order to build it. Conflict between government departments and the former independents was exacerbated by frequent changes in the Ministry and RAF's specification: important time was lost and costs accelerated. But work started in 1956 and Roland Beamont flew the first prototype (TSR2/XR-219) from Boscombe Down on 27 September 1964. After trials the aircraft flew to Warton on 22 February 1965, giving Prestonians an early glimpse of a plane on which their town's future prosperity was widely believed to depend. Two 30,610lb-thrust Bristol Siddeley Olympus Turbojets gave the TSR-2 a maximum speed of 1,485mph, the plane was 89 feet long, had a wingspan of 37 feet and stood 24 feet high.

The enormous national project was cancelled later in 1965 after pressure (it would seem) from the American government: financial aid was linked to the scrapping of the TSR-2 and the purchase in its place of the Phantom 1-11. Rather bizarrely, it was stipulated that all completed aeroplanes were to be immediately cut up, and the resulting scrap could be seen for some time

The first prototype TSR-2 in its element, 1964 (photo: BAE Systems Heritage Group, Warton).

The second prototype TSR-2 in the final stages of production at Weybridge in October 1964. This aircraft was about to make its maiden flight on the day that the project was cancelled in 1965 and so never flew (photo: BAE Systems Heritage Group, Warton).

stacked up at Samlesbury. Two prototypes did survive, however, XR-220 is at Cosford and XR-222 at Duxford.

R Fairclough and S Ransom, *English Electric Aircraft and their Predecessors* (1987). G Green, *British Aerospace: A Proud Heritage* (1988).

TUMBREL

A form of punishment reserved for female gossips etc. 'of a higher social class than those subject to the bridle or ducking stool'. The lady was fastened into a rough open cart and paraded about the town. A visit to the ducking stool might be an optional extra. Though barbaric it is clear that the victim's utter humiliation was an important psychological element of such punishments. The Preston bailiffs were ordered to provide a 'Tumbrell' in 1662, and after repeated threats were fined when they failed to do so. When the equipment was finally procured the Court Leet was still not satisfied and they were then ordered to 'remove ye Tumbrall to some Convenient place before ye first of May next on pain of XXs'.

A Hewitson, *History of Preston* (1883); *Preston Court Leet Records* (1905).

TURNER, DICKEY

Credited with giving the word 'teetotal' to the English language. An early signatory to the temperance pledge, Richard Turner had a stammer and at a meeting a year later (September 1833) gave the embryonic mass movement its popular name when whilst advocating total abstinence he stuttered that he would 'be reet down out-and-out t-t-total for ever'. It has however been suggested that the word had a very long usage in the northern counties prior to this date. He is buried at St Peter's church close by both the spot where he took the pledge and the bar of the Students Union.

B Harrison, *Drink and the Victorians* (1971). J Pearce, *The Life and Teachings of Joseph Livesey* (1887).

TURNPIKE ROADS

A system under which a company undertakes to maintain a length of road in exchange for collecting tolls from the traffic passing along it. The main road from Wigan to Preston (A49) was turnpiked in 1726, but it was a further quarter of a century before the road north to Lancaster (A6) was improved. The routes to the east followed in 1755 with the turnpiking of the Skipton and Blackburn roads, and an Act of Parliament for the Liverpool road was obtained in 1771. An Act granted a company the right to collect tolls for a given number of years (usually twenty-one) after which it had to be re-enacted. On these occasions efforts were usually made to improve the line of the road, and Garstang Road, for example, was straightened in 1817. The

Blackburn road had a number of very difficult stretches, most notably at Higher Walton and Feniscowles, and an entirely new route via Samlesbury - the Blackburn New Road - was opened in 1824.

Traffic along the turnpikes could be considerable, with long trains of sumpter horses, pack horses and wagons. In the 1770s 'gangs' of thirty to forty pack horses carried heavy loads of coal or lime, and other travellers were warned of their approach by the bell carried by the lead horse. The heavy wagons had enormously wide wheels, giving early prints of this traffic a ludicrous aspect; they were thought to do less damage to the road surface and accordingly were charged at a reduced rate. In 1767 it was decreed that no wagon with wheels less than nine inches broad was to run on the Blackburn road, and accidents were common on the difficult passage up Church Brow at Walton; 'Several injuries haveing been done to people's property especially to Cotton baggs being very much torn'. Though the staff at the turnpike gates were a notoriously dishonest lot, and passers-by did their best to dodge payments by one trick or another, the companies were generally a good safe investment, paying regular dividends. The railways brought about their eventual demise and control of the main roads passed to the new Lancashire County Council. Forgotten for a century, turnpike roads made a surprise come-back in the early years of the new millennium when governments decided that they were the solution to the country's transport problem after all - just as they had appeared to be when local magistrates erected their gates on the Great North Road (A1) in 1663!

A Crosby (ed.), *Leading the Way: A History of Lancashire's Roads* (1998).

See STAGE COACHES.

U

UNIVERSITY OF CENTRAL LANCASHIRE

An institution which has replaced the textile and aircraft industries as Preston's most important employer, and in so doing has transformed large tracts of the town centre. In 1828 John Gilbertson and JOSEPH LIVESEY organized an inaugural meeting to establish an educational reading room for working people. The grandly titled Institution for the Diffusion of Knowledge sought to 'facilitate and promote the diffusion of useful knowledge among the operative mechanics, and others, inhabitants of Preston and neighbourhood'. This was a highly respectable enterprise; the first president was THOMAS BATTY ADDISON and use of the premises in Cannon St was carefully regulated. The library for instance was to contain 'no novels or plays, nor any deistical or atheistical works, nor any on party politics, or polemical divinity shall be admitted'.

In his cellar at Walton Livesey had struggled to educate himself with hardly any educational materials, particularly books, and he hoped that the institution would become a sort of a university for the deprived classes. In this aspiration he may have been influenced by the highly influential Walton Adult School Society which throve in the second decade of the century. Yet he seems to have been disappointed with the longer term level of response, for although the library had over 11,000 volumes by the time of his death and membership had reached a peak of over 700 members in 1857, this was not a high number in a town of around 80,000 people. Furthermore, only a tiny percentage of the members were actually 'mechanics'. The meeting place in Cannon St housed the reading room, a library and educational classes supported by the membership. A building fund was established, land was purchased at the end of Avenham Walk, and a spectacular new building was opened on 24 October 1850.

By the mid-1880s the venture was approaching a crisis point and a familiar

vicious circle had developed: the committee could not run the attractive classes it would have liked due to a lack of money, and funding was based on the income from courses and subscriptions. Apart from these considerations the newly established Free Library was an obvious if welcome 'competitor'. The remarkable will of E R Harris came to the rescue, following the benefactor's death in 1877. The council of the Institution for the Diffusion of Knowledge made successful application to the Harris Trustees, and in 1881 it was announced that the sum of £40,000 was to be made available 'to endow an institute for the promotion of art, science, literature and technical education' to be known as the Harris Institute. The ultimate establishment of a University College was envisaged, day courses of all kinds proliferated and student numbers expanded far beyond anything that could have been anticipated a decade before.

Over the years the Harris Institute's contribution to educational opportunities in the district - particularly crucial in the career profiles of the individual students -

Harris Library and Art Gallery (photo: Preston City Council).

was to be immense. Rising student numbers led to the adoption of teaching spaces across the town, but in 1895 the foundation stone of the Victoria Jubilee Technical School in Corporation St was laid. Two years later the new building opened, and would ultimately become the Preston university's Harris Building. The inter-war years saw an enormous expansion of the provision of technical education, with pride of place given to an actual working cotton mill composed of scaled-down machines. In 1956 the institute was redesignated as the 'Harris College of Further Education', and in its first session could boast 4,437 students. A further stage was reached in 1973 when Preston Polytechnic was formed, and this in turn became the University of Central Lancashire, which today has some 23,000 students.

G Timmins et al., *Preston Polytechnic: The Emergence of an Institution* (1979).

V

VAMPIRE

Pioneering aircraft built at Preston. The prototype of Britain's first jet fighter was flown as early as September 1943 by Geoffrey De Havilland. The following May a production order was placed with English Electric at Preston, and the first of the firm's production run of 1,366 aircraft flew from Samlesbury in April 1945. The Vampire gave English Electric a smooth transit into the modern aircraft industry - much to the consternation of the 'proper' pre-war aircraft companies. It had a maximum speed of 535mph and flew at over 30,000 feet.

R Fairclough and S Ransom, *English Electric Aircraft and their Predecessors* (1987). G Green, *British Aerospace: A Proud Heritage* (1988).

VEGELTUNGSWAFFE OR 'VENGEANCE WEAPONS' (24 DECEMBER 1944)

The raid on the north of England was planned in October 1944, and Manchester was selected as the primary target in early December. In the early hours of Christmas Eve around 50 V1s were launched from aircraft over the North Sea. The terror raid took only an hour and though the missiles generally fell harmlessly over a wide area, 28 people were killed at Oldham. One missile came down to the south of Preston in the fields close to Gregson Lane; no one was seriously hurt but 112 houses were damaged and an enormous number of windows smashed by the blast. As with the 25cwt bomb at Bamber Bridge in 1940, the district had enjoyed a lucky escape.

Lancashire Magazine (Nov.-Dec. 1987). D Hunt, *A History of Walton-le-Dale and Bamber Bridge* (1997).

VICTORIA CROSS

Britain's highest award for gallantry: the Preston district has four recipients, all from actions during the First World War. Private James Towers (Scottish Rifles: 'The Cameronians') survived the war, but Private William Young (East Lancashire Regiment) subsequently died of his wounds and is buried in Preston Cemetery. Private James Miller of Withnell (King's Own Royal Lancaster Regiment) was killed in action, and Corporal John Macnamara of Bamber Bridge (East Surrey Regiment) was killed shortly after winning his VC.

M Arthur, *Symbol of Courage: A History of the Victoria Cross* (2004). H L Kirkby, *William Young* (1985). See also H L Kirkby and R R Walsh, *Seven VCs of Stonyhurst* (1987).

VICTORY 1918

Switching massive forces from their victory on the Eastern Front, Ludendorf smashed through the British lines at the Second Battle of the Somme (21 March-5 April 1918), advancing 40 miles and taking 70,000 prisoners in a desperate effort to 'win the war before the Americans come'. He failed - just! As they were exhausted by the pace of their advance, Haig skilfully counter-attacked. Beaten by the British army in the field, Germany quickly collapsed into revolution and sued for an armistice: North End had just won their fifth game in succession. Like the declaration of war the victory announcement was theatrically managed on the Market Square, where at 10.45 a.m. on Monday 11 November the Mayor was able to announce: 'Glorious news has arrived. The Kaiser has disappeared for ever. The worst enemy that mankind has known has gone from the stage.' At this point the great bell of the town hall clock struck 11 p.m., 'The clock is striking, the last shot has been fired, and the war is over.' Amidst the mill sirens and the air of relief, observers were struck by the extreme seriousness of people's response and church services were hastily organized and were reported to be full *all day*. This was clearly in very marked contrast to the events of August 1914.

H Cartmell, *For Remembrance: An Account of Some Fateful Years* (1919).

VICTORY 1945

The end of the 1939-45 war was greeted with rather muted celebrations in Preston because of the large number of local men still held prisoner in the Far East. On 8 May 1945 it was announced that hostilities in Europe would end at midnight:

> Preston was ablaze with flags and bunting for VE Day. Public buildings and business premises displayed a great variety of patriotic emblems. A striking feature was the colourful show made in the side streets, particularly in Plungington, Ribbleton Lane and New Hall Lane districts.

Two days of public holidays followed. At noon on 15 August the Mayor announced the end of the war in the east, 'With ship's hooters, church bells and railway whistles sounding a welcome to Peace, it did not take Preston people long to get the victory spirit.' In the early hours of the following morning an enormous procession 'headed by a man in a car beating a drum' danced its way around the town: But it was not all fun and frivolity. When they heard the news many Preston women, with relatives still in the far east wept unashamedly. The lone figure of a woman in the front room of a riverside street, holding a handkerchief to her eyes whilst the revellers swept past cheering, symbolises the grief of hundreds of mothers, wives and sweethearts who are still waiting news of a loved one. With the bus men reported to be on strike for 'VJ holiday' payments, Preston began its difficult acclimatization to normality.

Lancashire Daily Post (8 May, 15 August 1945).

Prime Minister Winston Churchill campaigning during the General Election, with Julian Amery MP and Mrs Churchill, Fulwood 27 June 1945 (photo: Heather Halton).

'VISITATION OF ALLMIGHTY GOD'

The Plague of 1631, possibly an epidemic of anthrax. In general the seventeenth-century county magistrates were able to confine outbreaks to specific towns, Wigan in 1603, Manchester in 1605 and Preston in 1630-1. The disease was perhaps brought into Preston in a parcel of cloth, and appeared at the end of October 1630. One of the first deaths was that of James Sudell, 'linen webster'. A 'pest house' was set up, but most infected families were simply boarded up in their homes. Though movement in the county was closely controlled, those that could flee had fled, and the surrounding villages - Penwortham, Walton, Fulwood, Broughton and Kirkham - were quickly affected. Unlike the plague of 1349 this outbreak seems to have been contagious between people; analysis of the Penwortham parish records suggests that there were few isolated deaths, but if a single member became infected (perhaps during a visit to the town) the disease passed through the entire family.

Preston's trade stopped, and by April 1631 almost 1,400 people were receiving charitable relief. Between June and the end of August almost 600 people died. The town's population had fallen from around 3,000 to just 887 - with 253 of the remaining people 'In the Pesthouses and houses shutt upp'. With the passing of the hottest months the epidemic subsided, and by the New Year the outbreak was declared to be over and the markets could reopen. Over 1,000 people had died, perhaps a third of the population. In the Parish Church Christopher Hudson preached to the enfeebled and traumatized survivors what was perhaps the most remarkable sermon ever delivered in that place. His text, which survives in the Lancashire Record Office was, 'Wee had beene as Sodome and beene made unto Gomorrha'.

R S Sharpe-France, 'A History of the Plague in Lancashire', *THSLC* 90 (1938). For the sermon see LRO, DP 353.

WALTON BRIDGE
The lowest bridging point on the River RIBBLE: fought over in 1648. The crossing at Walton was clearly a major factor in the location of the Roman site, but although the fording of the river here is at best a hazardous enterprise no evidence has ever been put forward for the existence of a bridge then - though a wooden one could have been constructed. By medieval times the existence of a stone structure is well attested. This stood a short distance downstream of the present crossing, and on reaching the north side travellers ascended by a series of narrow, steep and sunken lanes to approach the town along the line of Manchester Road as far as the SYKE, from which point a number of ways into the town opened out.

The bridge is mentioned in a deed of 1302 and as the largest non-ecclesiastical public utility in the area its costs were the subject of much dispute. By 1383 the structure had a small chapel with a chaplain who paid 3s 4d per year to collect alms from passers-by; from these he deducted reasonable living expenses and was supposed to use the rest to repair the bridge. In 1403 a new crossing was ordered to be built of stone alongside the ancient one which had been damaged by ice floes. In the 1540s Leland described it as 'the great stone bridge of Rybill having V(5) great arches'. It was fought over in 1648, but sixteen years later was 'in very great decay by reason of the late great inundation of the water'. It was ordered to be repaired and DR KUERDEN could describe it with much local pride as 'One of the statelyest bridges in the North of England'. On more than one occasion severe summer floods cut a new river bed through Walton Cop, rendering the expensive bridge a crossing over dry land and requiring the river to be nudged back along its old course. The present bridge was built in 1781 and the old structure was then demolished, apart from a single pier in the middle of the river which survived to 1867. A second crossing - Penwortham old bridge - replaced the ford and ferry at Broadgate in 1755, and Walton Bridge was widened in the early 1940s.

D Hunt, *A History of Walton-le-Dale and Bamber Bridge* (1997).

WAR PRODUCTION (1914-1918)

The drive towards 'total war' in 1915 had profound consequences for Preston's industrial base, which after 1860 had developed a significant heavy engineering sector. The large foundry firms (Stevensons, Coulthards, Drydens and Fosters) and even the dock workshops were put onto munitions work, and employment grew enormously with women the major beneficiaries. The workforce at DICK, KERR tripled to 6,000, the weekly wage bill rose to £22,000, and a million tons of steel were used to produce in all some three and a quarter million projectiles, 700 machine tools, and everything from miniature trains to huge flying boats. The works played a direct part in the military course of the war, for its 63-inch-long shells were fired at Jutland, whilst the large number of howitzers it refurbished were instrumental in the advance to victory in the late summer of 1918. The company built 100 flying boats and had a further 150 on order when the war ended. Though crude and very much a product of the Dick, Kerr tramshops, enormous progress was made in aircraft technology and manufacture.

Expansion in the wider Preston employment area - notably at the Leyland plants - was equally rapid, absorbed large numbers of women and had similarly important consequences for post-war industry. Leyland Motors produced some 6,000 petrol-driven vehicles, and the rubber industry (notably Wood-Milne and the Leyland & Birmingham Rubber Co.) also expanded enormously. For those not in the forces and able to work these were prosperous times: labour shortages and strikes were endemic, and the munitions workers' wages and the wartime cotton boom kept large amounts of cash in circulation. This was conspicuous in Blackpool at Easter 1916 where workers were reported to be discarding their customary 1s cloth caps in exchange for £1 'velour' hats. But as the submarine siege tightened there was little food to buy, the town's butchers closed three days per week, and in November 1917 it was estimated that food worth 9s 11d in 1914 would now cost a sovereign! The end of the war saw cotton's greatest financial boom but by the end of 1921 it was over, and the industry entered a depression from which it would never recover. The war had brought important changes to Preston's industrial base, women would henceforth play an increasingly important role within it, and new industries were emerging to replace the old nineteenth-century staples.

H Cartmell, *For Remembrance: An Account of Some Fateful Years* (1919). *Lancashire Daily Post.*

WAR PRODUCTION (1937-1945)

The Budget of 1936 was the first to substantially increase military spending, the depression was lifting and the 'long Armistice' was coming to an end. In December 1937 unemployment in the Lancashire towns was still heavy (the figures being Blackburn 14,000, Burnley 8,000 and Preston 6,578), but with its strategic cores at English Electric and Leyland Motors the Preston Employment Area stood to gain very substantially from rearmament. As 1938 progressed a number of important government initiatives began to come on stream, totally revolutionizing the district's industrial base.

The pace quickened after the Munich Agreement in September, and much use was made of the year's grace won by it. By November 1938 almost £12 million had been spent on the Royal Ordnance Factory at Euxton, and the first section of the enormous COURTAULD man-made fibre plant at Red Scar employing 2,000 people opened. The joint Preston-Blackburn Municipal Aerodrome at Samlesbury was taken over by Vickers Armstrong and developed as a Central Aircraft Factory in conjunction with English Electric's Strand Road works. The same month the creation of 5,000 aircraft production jobs was announced at Preston, 3,000 of them at Samlesbury where the first hanger was completed in December 1939 and the first planes delivered to the RAF three months later. The local factories went on to produce 900 Hampden and 2,145 Halifax bombers, and in 1942 another large aircraft factory under development at Warton (to ease production at Blackpool's Squire Gate) was taken over by the USAAF.

Engines being fitted to a Preston-built Handley Page 'Halifax' bomber at Samlesbury, 1944 (photo: BAE Systems Heritage Group, Warton).

As in 1914-18 large amounts of money were pumped into the local economy by war wages, but the problem was to find anything to spend it on. Though occasionally closed by enemy mines, Preston Dock became an important distribution centre, and later a staging post for the Normandy landings. Trade had exceeded one million tons in 1935, with petrol imports accounting for 200,000 tons. Cotton mill production was rationalized and by the first Christmas of the war every mill capable of production was said to be working. Elsewhere, production at the Leyland factories was immense: the workforce at the motor works swelled to 9,000 (3,000 of them women) to assemble 3,000 tanks, 10,000 tank engines, 10,000 other vehicles and sixteen million shells and bombs. In this enormous investment lay the district's post-war future as a major commercial vehicle and plane maker, and the first of the VAMPIRE jet fighters built here flew from Samlesbury as early as April 1945. Despite the catastrophic cost of the war it undeniably revived Preston's languishing industrial base: but why had successive governments been unable to achieve this in peacetime?

F Harrison, 'Industrial Preston through Slump and War' (1994, unpublished).

WATSON, JOHN, & SONS

Pioneers of the factory system in Preston, 1777-1807. Ralph and John Watson, the sons and grandsons of a shoemaker and 'dancing master' respectively, were men of mark in late eighteenth-century Preston. Ralph became a prosperous grocer and was three times Mayor of Preston in the years 1772-84. In 1774 he bought a piece of land in Moor Lane on which William Collinson erected the town's first cotton factory three years later. In this venture the latter was joined by Ralph's brother John, trading as Collinson & Watson. John Watson's career was a remarkable one; he progressed from linen weaver in Brindle, to 'linnen tradesman' in Preston, councilman, and by the 1780s head of the great firm of John Watson & Sons. Through a series of partnerships and family links the business grew to extend across the whole spectrum of the emerging textile industry, from banking and commerce, machine making, to cloth printing and finishing. Confusingly, John Watson was formally succeeded by his sons John and Joseph in 1804, but John Watson junior had really been the dominant influence in the firm for some years.

In the late 1780s the family developed important local interests at Roach Bridge, Samlesbury, and 'Penwortham factory'. Both of these concerns quickly became notorious for their importation and exploitation of orphans from the London workhouses and hospitals. The reformer Joseph Livesey, himself an orphan, found them 'Poor, squalid deformed beings, the most pitiful objects I think I ever beheld'. It was during these years that JOHN HORROCKS of Edgeworth emerged as an important supplier of yarns to the Watsons. Once Horrocks moved to Preston and emerged as a large employer himself, the family found an unlikely ally in the DERBY INTEREST, which feared Horrocks's rising political influence in the Tory cause: cotton masters, it emerged, had the same degree of leverage over the voting intentions of their employees as the old country magnates. To this end the Derby Estate purchased a new mill in Dale St in 1795. Known as the Lord's Factory (and subsequently Starkie's Wireworks) it was purchased by the Watsons for £4,175 in 1803. The Whig Stanleys thus backed the Watson firm in the same way that the Tory bankers supported Horrockses.

The Watson influence was thus at its peak in the last years of the century. In 1799 - a year for which the data are available - the turnover of the Watson and Horrocks enterprises was well balanced at £98,000 and £100,000 respectively. In fact the two firms with their partners and subsidiaries were for all practical purposes the Preston cotton industry; they had given the town a £200,000 per annum industry which had not existed twenty years earlier. The two companies worked much closer together than has usually been supposed, and Watson and Horrocks walking arm in arm cheerfully led the massed ranks of factory workers in the 1802 Guild's Textile Trade procession. Vast profits were made in the early years of the new century, but both enterprises were maintained by a web of credit which was underpinned by a vigorous trade in 'cotton futures' - effectively gambling on the direction of future prices. In 1804 Horrockses made one of only a handful of losses in their history, and three years later the Watson firm failed spectacularly.

The Watson crash was a catastrophe. The failure of the central firm brought down all the related partnerships, though a number of these subsequently recovered. The young workers at Samlesbury were immediately turned out of their apprentice house to fend as best they could, sleeping under hedges and begging along the highways, whilst the partners' homes and personal possessions were sold off to pay their creditors. The enormous sale of John Watson junior's goods included over 10,000 cloth pieces, 10,000lb of yarn, and '400 dozen of very choice old wines, chiefly Port and Madeiras'. This was the town's second great textiles failure, following that of Livesey, Hargreaves & Co. of MOSNEY almost twenty years before. John Watson senior served a term in Lancaster castle and died in 1813, John junior was reported to be working along with other family members on Malta in 1822.

D Hunt, *A History of Preston* (1992).

WAUGH, ANDREW SCOTT (1810-1878)

The man who christened Peak XV whilst Surveyor General of India (1843-62). Commissioned in the Bengal Sappers & Miners (1831) Waugh was appointed to the Trigonometrical Survey of India the following year under George Everest. In 1843 Everest retired and suggested Waugh as his successor. During his subsequent career he was responsible for surveying

over 300,000 square miles, and his work on the NE Himalayan Series of maps fixed the positions of 79 of the highest peaks in Nepal and Sikkim, among them Peak XV which had been 'discovered' by Radhanath Sikdar in 1852, and which Waugh named '*Mont* Everest' in honour of his predecessor. (The local people knew the mountain as Chomalungma – 'Goddess mother of the earth'.) In 1862 he retired, was knighted and in 1870 married Celia Whitehead of Uplands Hall, Walker Lane, Fulwood. He ended his illustrious and much travelled career as a churchwarden at Broughton.
ODNB.

WELLS
Though their town was located high above and some distance away from the river the early inhabitants were able to exploit the hydrographic possibilities of the site's sandy subsoil. To the south of Church St a number of fountains and springs fed the SYKE - the town centre's only watercourse. The 'minspit well' in Mainsprit Weind at the foot of the Church St ridge is close to the line of the Syke, has a good claim to be one of the Preston's earliest wells, and remained one of the principal water sources well into the eighteenth century. The 'Spit' or 'Sprit' element in the name perhaps indicates the original strongly flowing spring or fountain. The site is now covered over, but Kuerden writing in the 1680s describes the picturesque early morning scene as the town's housemaids collected water in what was accordingly referred to as 'Pettycoat Alley'.

Large 'draw wells' were expensive to dig (costing around £20 each in the 1650s) and required constant repairs and cleaning. A minute of the COURT LEET of April 1668 ordered the 'Mainspit Well, Ye Goose Well, and ye foure draw wells within this towne to be repaired and sufficiently clensed'. The Goose Well seems to have been to the south of Church St close by the end of Water St (now broadly Manchester Road), and the four draw wells probably comprised: (1) the Higher Draw Well on the south west side of Friargate near to 'Mellings Yard'; (2) a well at the bottom end of the market place, opened in 1654; (3) a new well on Fishergate between Cannon St and Guildhall St; and, (4) the small well mentioned by KUERDEN in Molyneux Square.

Working from the early town records, Hardwick and Hewitson were able to produce a fuller list of related water sources exploited from time to time. It seems that 'Churchgate', between Cannon St and Water St (a forerunner of Manchester Road) was the best served area. Church St had the Goose Well and Twistleton's, and access to the line of wells along or close-by the Syke - Mainspit Well, Kendall Well (at the bottom of Syke Hill) and a well in Glover St (the southern continuation of Glover's Court). The market place, Back Weend and Molyneux Square had their own wells. In Friargate the wells were strung out from the Higher Draw Well to those between Heatley St and Hill St, and Edward St and Hope St.

To the west of the old town, along the line of Marsh Lane, were the Ladywell (close by the site of the medieval FRIARY) and Marsh Lane Well (popularly called Bugmire Holes). The Maudlands were served by Atherton's Well (at the point where the canal formerly crossed Fylde Road) and Ryding Hey - an ancient well on the north-west side of the Maudlands. Water Lane on the north-east corner of Preston Marsh had two wells: Spa Brow below Wellington St and a well at the north-west corner of St Mark's Road. The former was noted for its 'Strengthening qualities', and water from the latter still fetched a halfpenny a can in the 1830s. The Avenham district was served by a well on the eastern slope of the park below Avenham Colonnade, and another in the south-east corner was famous for its ocular properties. Off New Hall Lane a series of strong mineral springs were noted for their petrifying qualities so that objects left in them were apparently turned to stone. Their survival may be indicated by the iron-streaked stream that enters the Ribble behind the Shawes Arms.

As the town grew, the water supply became an important issue, particularly in the developing areas. In April 1666 one group of residents petitioned the Mayor:

> There are many complaints of ye Inhabitants in the Lower end of the ffryergate for want of water, having none but at a great distance or upon leave, which is burthensome and uncertaine.

They felt that they had missed out on the recent spate of municipal well sinking, 'Hopeinge and prayinge that they may enjoy the privelege'. Needless to say their fellow citizens were often cavalier in their use of the wells

Looking north along Friargate from close by the end of Orchard Street c.1920. The street originated as the way to the moor. Today its late medieval line has been bisected by the inner ring road which cuts through in the middle distance of this view. The property on the left has disappeared beneath the St George's shopping development and the entrance to the 'Hippodrome' complex can be seen on the right.

provided; in 1717 John Threlfall was fined for spoiling the water in one of the Church St wells by steeping his willows for basket making and then letting his ducks swim in it. Respectable townspeople taking their animals to drink at the Syke Trough on Avenham not infrequently found it polluted by the mess left by itinerant carrot-washers, yarn-dyers, and the unimaginably horrible efforts of the pie-sellers to 'wash' their wares!

C Hardwick, *History of the Borough of Preston* (1857). A Hewitson, *History of Preston* (1883); *Preston Court Leet Records* (1905).

WESLEY, JOHN

With his brother Charles, one of the founders of Methodism. The present central chapel in Lune St was opened in 1817 and served a circuit extending 20 miles around Preston. Though Methodists have made a tremendous contribution to the social, political and educational progress of the region, they had a difficult start in the strongly Catholic and Anglican town. Wesley was a friend of MARTHA THOMPSON and a frequent visitor to the villages around Preston, notably Walton-le-Dale. He wrote in May 1781,

I went to Preston, where the old prejudice seems to be quite forgotten ...I preached to a candid audience. Everyone seemed to be considerably affected.

'The little society' had a house in St John's Place, and opened a chapel on Back Lane in 1787, three years before Wesley's final visit in 1790.

W Pilkington, *The Makers of Preston Methodism* (1890). W F Richardson, *Preston Methodism's 200 Fascinating Years* (1973).

WHITESIDE, RICHARD (1878-1923)

China missionary and martyr. Born in Preston, Whiteside's family moved to Leyland where he became a Sunday school teacher at the Parish Church. Whilst working in London he joined the Christian Missionary Society, undertook medical training and was sent to the western diocese of China in 1905. Here he learnt the language and preached at the mission's remote out-stations. He married a fellow missionary but lived in constant danger of assassination by 'Boxer' gangs. After a furlough in Leyland in 1912 he and his family returned to China where he served at Lungan, and was ordained in 1919. The deteriorating internal situation forced his wife to leave China in May 1923, and less than three months later Richard Whiteside was murdered by bandits at Beh-Ko-Shu on 14 August 1923.

W E Waring, pers. comm.

'WILL ONDA' (d. 1949)

Real name Hugh Rain: variously a clown, cinematography pioneer, alderman, director of PRESTON NORTH END, and one of the first Prestonians to own a motor car. Eton-educated and destined by his parents for the church, Rain duly studied to become a music hall clown and was to play a central role in the recreational life of Preston in the first half of the twentieth century. A visit to France in the early 1900s changed his life, for impressed with the progress being made in motion pictures (following Louis Lumiere's demonstration of the medium in Paris in 1895) he brought the first 'Bioscope' to Preston in 1903. The first public demonstration took place at the Public Hall on 19 December that year - Rain's 'Grand Cinematographic Entertainment'. He began to produce locally made one-minute 'shorts' and built up the largest film rental company in the region, based at Kinema House in Corporation St. The problem now arose as to where to show these 'Penny Gaffs', and in June 1908 Preston's first 'cinema' opened in the 800-seater Temperance Hall with the films *Female Highwayman* and *Gamble for a Woman*. For some years Rain showed his films at the local theatres, the HIPPODROME (1907), THEATRE ROYAL (1911) and the PRINCE'S (1913), but in 1917 the 1856 hall was reborn as 'The Picture Palace'. His success was now assured and he was elected to the Town Council in 1920, becoming an alderman in 1935. He became a director at Deepdale and was present at the historic board meeting of 3 December 1931. With his flair for publicity and the intimate understanding of the burgeoning leisure industry Rain proved to be an important member of the club's management throughout the glory years which followed. He died in December 1949.

J Cotterall, *Preston's Palaces of Pleasure* (1988). D Hindle, *Twice Nightly: An Illustrated History of Entertainment in Preston* (1999). D Hunt, *The History of Preston North End Football Club: The Power, the Politics and the People* (2000).

WINCKLEY SQUARE

Preston's fashionable 'Georgian' masterpiece, much beloved of Nicholas Pevsner, and the projected site of a 1960s multi-storey car park. It was the brainchild of William Cross who purchased the Town End Field from his fellow lawyer Thomas Winckley for a superior housing development. Later purchases extended the project to the south, and with Ribblesdale Place Preston acquired an extremely fashionable quarter, standing out in marked contrast to the overcrowded conditions endured along Avenham Lane just a short distance away. In this broad quarter Nigel Morgan has explored the living conditions of both the super-rich (such leading citizens as Nicholas Grimshaw, Richard Newsham, THOMAS MILLER JUNIOR and William Ainsworth) and the extremely poor, but has revealed the existence of a broad band of the interesting 'middling sort' literally sandwiched in between, to the south of Cross St.

Around the square the second generation of residents proclaimed their worldly success in the fashionable architectural style of the day, with Thomas

Miller's restrained italianate villa (NE corner) and a much more flamboyant version on the south corner of Cross St for the rather unlikely figure of William Ainsworth (famous for deploying cannon and muskets on the roof of his mill in Cotton Court to keep the workers out). With their powerful connections the early residents were able to develop a broad range of educational and recreational facilities, producing some of the town's finest

Baines's Map of Preston, 1836 (surveyed 1824). By this date housing development had begun to emasculate the early medieval field pattern, but ironically would preserve the field lines precisely - in the rows of terraced houses which were inserted into them. To the west Winckley Square has been laid out, and the substantial canal terminus and tramway can be seen.

(often now demolished) buildings in the process. The foremost group stood along the east side of the square at the junction with Cross St, and comprised the Winckley Club, the Literary and Philosophical Institution and Preston Grammar School. To erect the 'Club' a fund of £2,000 was raised in £25 shares, it was opened in 1846 and housed a luncheon room, news room and billiard room. It would remain a largely male preserve (industrialists, doctors, bankers, lawyers, military men, etc.) until the 1950s. The adjacent institute was built at the same time and contained similar facilities, housed a museum, and quickly emerged as an important lecture venue. In 1868 the building and contents were sold to Preston Council, becoming Dr Shepherd's Library and Museum, housing Richard Shepherd's bequest of 1761.

Perhaps the most spectacular building of all was the Preston Grammar School: it was built by public subscription to replace the building in Stoneygate, opened in 1841 and was purchased by Preston Council twenty years later. This institution had ancient if rather obscure origins, but the town possessed a 'school' as early as the mid-fourteenth century. Richard Marshall was licensed to teach here in 1399. A second institution can be traced from 1479 when Helen Hoghton established a chantry whose priest was 'to have a fre gramm skole'. Though the abolition of the chantries during the REFORMATION caused problems, the institution survived, and when its funding was gradually improved in the mid-seventeenth century a new school was built (1666), perhaps lower down Stoneygate than its predecessor. In 1728 a house was built close by for the use of the schoolmaster, and it is here that Arkwright did his bit to inaugurate the Industrial Revolution forty years later. The west side of the square came to house the town's Catholic grammar schools. That for boys grew from humble origins in 1865, and the Girls Convent was opened ten years later. By the time of their closure, amalgamation and move to Lark Hill in 1978, the Catholic schools had come to extend almost the whole length of the square as far back as the line of Mount St. For most of the twentieth century, the schools brought life and immense prestige to Winckley Square.

M Roberts, *The Story of Winckley Square* (1988). J R M Heppell, *A History of Preston Grammar School* (1996). M Burscough, *The History of Lark Hill, Preston, 1797-1989* (1989). A Hindle, *A Centenary History of the Catholic College, Preston* (1971).

See SYKE; HOUSING.

WINCKLEY SQUARE RESIDENTS
The 'Haves'
In 1799 William Cross built the first house, at the SE corner of Winckley St, to be followed by Nicholas Grimshaw's adjacent house at the SW corner. Thereafter building continued along the north side of the square in what became known as Winckley Place. Cross's intentions are made clear in a draft

agreement of 1807: the still largely undeveloped square that he had formed was 'to lie forever open and unbuilt upon', houses were to be of a standard type and of good quality, there would be no alehouses, and the proprietors were to meet twice a year to discuss their business. The square soon became the place of residence for Preston's old (legal) and new (cotton manufacturing) elites. Among the former were the long established families of John Addison and Nicholas Grimshaw, and the latter included a veritable 'Who's Who' of the cotton lords (such as John Gorst, William Ainsworth, John Swainson, THOMAS MILLER JUNIOR and John Humber). By the start of the twentieth century a broader range of residents extended to the medical fraternity (notably Sir Charles Brown, one of the pioneers of the ROYAL INFIRMARY), and Dr C S A Rigby whose wife Edith organized the Preston branch of the WSPU from their house at number 28. From here in 1913, having tried to bomb the Cotton Exchange in Liverpool and successfully set fire to Lord Leverhulme's bungalow at Rivington, the elegant lady fled - dressed as a workman, on a bicycle, bound for Ireland!

The 'Have-Nots'
The respectable mansions and villas of Winckley Square overlooking their carefully tended and locked gardens out in the square proper, housed another rather less fortunate population: the large number of servants required to run them. Each servant from the butler down to the under-maids had their own specific duties. Dr Brown recalled that in his parents' house (number 27) the cook had to prepare four meals per day for fourteen people. Enormous quantities of coal were dropped through the pavement grilles into the commodious cellars from which the fuel had to be distributed upstairs throughout the house - an almost continuous process during the cold Victorian winters. There were beds to be made and washing to be done, the latter commencing on a Monday morning at 1 a.m.! It is little wonder that Edith Rigby came to the critical attention of her fashionable neighbours when she began to make careful inquiry into just how they treated and remunerated their servants. The census returns however give a clear picture of the domestic arrangement of the time. In 1851 the house of Thomas Miller had seventeen inhabitants: Miller, wife Henrietta and their five children, Annie Dickson their governess, and nine servants headed by Peter Walmesly (butler) and Elizabeth Mathews (cook). The immensely wealthy Richard Newsham and his wife Agnes, by contrast, got by with the help of just a cook and a pair of maids. On his death he left his valuable collection of art - the Newsham Bequest - to the Harris Museum where it can be enjoyed by all today.

M Roberts, *The Story of Winckley Square* (1988). C Brown, *Sixty-Four Years a Doctor* (1922). 1851 Census.

The home of the Winckley Club on the east side of Winckley Square, c.1905. Another of the town's lost but remarkable buildings. Thomas Miller's italianate villa stands at the top of the square, and the Syke runs below the road in the vicinity of the Hansom Cab. Opened in 1846 this was 'purely a social club of the upper class kind'.

WIRELESS BROADCASTING (1900)

In January 1900 members of the PRESTON SCIENTIFIC SOCIETY attended a demonstration of the new medium in the TOWN HALL: 'Mr Cuming spoke of Marconi's marvellous experiment made last year' when he had succeeded in transmitting a wireless message from a steamship to a receiving station at the Needles 45 miles away. After the lecture he 'caused a wireless message to be sent through the space' from one end of the Guild Hall to the other, which carried the New Year's message - 'Hope for better Luck in South Africa'.

Preston Scientific Society records.

WISE, AUDREY (NEE BROWN) (1932-2000)

Trade unionist, politician and MP for Preston (1987-2000). Born in Newcastle the daughter of a sugar-boiler and labour councillor, she was a Labour Party member at the age of 15. In 1951 she married John Wise, and throughout the 1960s the couple were tireless campaigners for peace,

Some of the 10,000 Americans based at Warton gather around a B-24 Liberator bomber, 1944 (photo: BAE Systems Heritage Group, Warton).

especially in South America and Vietnam. Illness delayed the development of her political career, but she represented Coventry SW (1974-9) and supported Tony Benn's challenge to Neil Kinnock for the Labour leadership. She failed to win election at Woolwich in 1983, but was successful at Preston in 1987 - a seat she held until her death. A colourful if controversial character, she supported progressive causes of all kinds and was a keen walker and gardener. Her son once found a note on the kitchen table: 'Revolution in Portugal, gone to see it. Here's £5 - buy some food'! *ODNB*.

WSPU
Women's Social and Political Union. See ELEANOR BEATRICE HIGGINSON; EDITH RIGBY.

YANKS (1942-1945)

Squires Gate airport at Blackpool was developed as a major aircraft factory producing Wellington bombers, and a satellite factory was planned for Warton. In October 1941 (two months *before* Pearl Harbour) American officials asked for use of the site 'once they had entered the war'. The first USAAF staff arrived in March 1942 and within two years 10,000 men were employed here servicing and repairing aircraft. In what was claimed to be the 'World's Greatest Air Depot' over 10,000 planes were processed, with 800 during the month of 'D-Day' alone, and over 45,000 aircraft movements were logged. Many leading personalities entertained the troops here, including Glenn Miller, Louis Armstrong and Bing Crosby. Warton was deactivated on 3 September 1945 and by mid-February 1946 the Americans, who had become such a feature of life in the town and surrounding area, had left as rapidly as they had arrived.

Harry Holmes, *The World's Greatest Air Depot: The US 8th Air Force at Warton 1942-45* (1998).

See DICK, KERR; FRECKLTON AIR DISASTER.

YARD WORKS

Stanley St. One of the most famous industrial sites in the world; now a supermarket. See JOHN HORROCKS.

Z

ZINGARI

Football team. North End's rivals for footballing supremacy in Preston in the early 1880s. See PLEASURE GARDENS; WILLIAM SUDELL.

ZOO

See PLEASURE GARDENS.

The Final Word from a Prestonian . . .
'The clock is always slow: it's later than you think!'
(Robert Service).